EXCEPTIONAL MOUNTAINS

EXCEPTIONAL
MOUNTAINS

A Cultural History of the Pacific Northwest Volcanoes

O. ALAN WELTZIEN

University of Nebraska Press | Lincoln & London

Library of Congress Cataloging-in-Publication Data

Names: Weltzien, O. Alan (Oliver Alan)
Title: Exceptional mountains: a cultural history of the
Pacific Northwest volcanoes / O. Alan Weltzien.
Description: Lincoln: University of Nebraska Press, 2016.
Includes bibliographical references and index.
Identifiers: LCCN 2015047730
ISBN 9780803265479 (hardback: alkaline paper)
ISBN 9780803290402 (epub)
ISBN 9780803290419 (mobi)
ISBN 9780803290426 (pdf)
Subjects: LCSH: Northwest, Pacific—Geography.
Northwest, Pacific—Environmental conditions.
Volcanoes—Social aspects—Northwest, Pacific—History.
Mountains—Social aspects—Northwest, Pacific—History.
Regionalism—Northwest, Pacific—History. | Outdoor
recreation—Environmental aspects—Northwest, Pacific—
History. | Mountaineering—Environmental aspects—
Northwest, Pacific—History. | Consumers—Northwest,
Pacific—Psychology—History. | Nature—Effect of human
beings on—Northwest, Pacific—History. | Environmental
policy—Northwest, Pacific—History. | BISAC: HISTORY /
United States / State & Local / Pacific Northwest (OR WA).
NATURE / Ecosystems & Habitats / Mountains.
SPORTS & RECREATION / Mountaineering.
Classification: LCC F852.3 .W39 2016 | DDC 917.95—dc23
LC record available at http://lccn.loc.gov/2015047730

Set in Minion Pro by Rachel Gould.

To Two Bills
William L. Lang, extraordinary editor
  and
William E. Neighbor Jr., lifelong friend
at many altitudes

The Snowpeaks

"Long stately procession,"
snow pearls rise
north-south pendant, tiny
arc in the girdling
Pacific rim fire.
Though some point
like Mt. Hood and
Jefferson, more bulge,
domes curve
above serrated peaks.
Tahoma and Shasta
spread gigantic glacial skirts
far above forested ridges
above us.

Snyder says, "West coast
snowpeaks are too
[fucking] much!"
They defy knowledge,
spurn our yearning for
contact, lure us with
boots crampons ropes,
cameras brushes and pen.
Braided by glaciers, they
mask fiery throats,
steam below snow,
their sleep temporary:
St. Helens blowing
her head off one May
morning, 1980.

Volcanoes awaken our
desire as we trace
their curves,
stretch our gaze
of ourselves.

Shining horizon anchors often
cloaked behind thick grey
curtains, they exist apart—
we so want
to be
part of them.

—O. Alan Weltzien, from *The Snowpeaks*

CONTENTS

List of Illustrations   xi

Acknowledgments   xiii

Introduction   1

1. The Legacy of Exceptionalism   9
2. Standard Routes, Standard Highways   39
3. Cities and Their Volcanoes   72
4. Green Consumerism and the Volcanoes   97
5. Wilderness and Volcanoes   130
6. Volcanoes and Crowds   173

Epilogue   205
Notes   215
Bibliography   225
Index   235

ILLUSTRATIONS

1. View south from Camp Muir on
   Mount Rainier   11

2. *Mount Hood*, by William
   Samuel Parrott   34

3. Mazamas inaugural climb on
   Mount Hood   43

4. Parking area at Paradise,
   Mount Rainier National Park   59

5. A Washington State ferry in the
   San Juan Islands with Mount Baker   74

6. Mazamas expedition approaches the
   crater and summit of Mount Baker   102

7. A Mazamas encampment near
   Mount Rainier   102

8. An early Mazamas hiking trip
   on Mount Rainier   104

9. Iconic view of Glacier Peak
   from Image Lake   157

10. Mount Hood's south climb route
    with Crater Rock and Steel Cliffs   199

ACKNOWLEDGMENTS

This book grew slowly and, at times, painfully. It originated decades ago when I lived in Puget Sound and hiked, whenever possible, in the Cascades, my first mountain range. I studied Mount Baker during Camano Island summers and Mount Rainier, the other seasons. Later I came to know Washington's Glacier Peak, Mount St. Helens, and Mount Adams, several among Oregon's multitude, and California's Lassen Peak and Mount Shasta.

My climbs precipitated other, more sustained inquiries into the Northwest's volcanoes. I wanted to know everything about them, particularly as the human footprint on and around them accelerated. I began reading the remarkable Weyerhaeuser environmental history series published by the University of Washington Press. Later I pitched this book idea to William L. Lang, a distinguished Northwest historian, for a small series he edited. Though the series has languished, Lang proved an able mentor, editor, and friend, and the dedication reflects, at least in part, my gratitude.

This book would never have blossomed without interlibrary loan, and in that capacity I want to thank Denise Rust, of the University of Montana Western's Lucy Carson Library, for her reliable help. Among my Montana Western colleagues I particularly thank Steve Mock, gifted mountaineer and teacher who taught me rock climbing and who, in June 1993 led two friends and me up the Emmons-Winthrop route on Mount Rainier. That climb yielded a personal essay, "On Tahoma" (*The Climbing Art*, 1995), and it and other volcano climbs led eventually to this book.

Friends too many to name in my three primary professional organizations—the Western Literature Association (WLA), the Association for the Study of Literature and Environment (ASLE), and the Pacific Northwest American Studies Association (PNASA)—have expressed steady interest and support over the years. They have tolerated my obsession with the Northwest volcanoes. I would single out Paul Lindholdt, of Eastern Washington University, who introduced me into PNASA and who more than matches my interests in Pacific Northwest Studies, ecocriticism, and bioregionalism.

I would also thank the anonymous readers at more than one university press, each of whom challenged me to clarify my lines or argument and ranges of reference. I particularly thank Bridget Barry, of the UNP, for believing in this book and signing me to Nebraska, where I join many WLA and ASLE friends as authors.

Finally, I thank my late mother, Lorraine B. Weltzien, who for decades sent me a steady stream of news clippings about Rainier and other mountains, and who accepted my obsession, though she never understood it. I also thank my two friends from early childhood, Galen P. Stark and Bill Neighbor, with whom I climbed Mount Baker more than twenty years ago. Bill's role in my life is reflected, in part, in the dedication. Galen, retired career NPS employee who worked in both Mount Rainier National Park and North Cascades National Park, loves the Cascades, particularly Rainier, at least as much as I do. For many years we have hiked together, scrambling above tree line.

In addition I thank my family—stepdaughter Melinda, and sons Alec and Joel—for their support and especially my wife, Lynn M. Weltzien. Like my late mother, she does not enjoy hiking in the mountains. But she has let me indulge myself every summer, and has proven a sturdy sounding board and advocate as this book unfolded. Her support of my writing is unwavering.

Any errors in fact or interpretation remain my own.

EXCEPTIONAL MOUNTAINS

INTRODUCTION

On a sunny day in late June 1994, I stood atop Mount Baker's summit hill, Grant Peak. Preceding parties, one with a black Lab, had retreated, and two friends and I had the summit to ourselves for more than ten minutes as though it were our turn, in a steady queue, at some panorama viewpoint. The image of that dog replays itself in my memory. Its presence made Baker's summit a commonplace urban scene rather than any sort of wilderness experience as promised by policies and management practices in the past half century. The portrait with dog suggests the "different world" of the volcanoes resembles a familiar urban or suburban one, and that's a dangerous illusion, one with baleful spiritual and practical consequences. That illusion derives from the prominent position the volcanoes occupy in the minds and hearts of a sizable segment of the population.

In the Pacific Northwest, the volcanoes form, for many, one strand of regional identity. Because of that strand, admirers and users need to adopt new habits and influence agency personnel to modify wilderness mandates while rebalancing the fraught tension between access and resource preservation (e.g., "wilderness experience"). The increasing scale of skiing, hiking, and mountaineering has changed the face of the volcanoes, especially at the convergence points (e.g., standard routes), where they've taken a beating. In too many places, usage conflicts with policy. Visitors particularly need to modify their practices in some cases and, however indirectly, influence agency personnel to modify their wilderness-driven mandates while strengthening resource *preservation* in the face of unchecked *access*: those abiding mandates and oft-contrary agendas. Increased accessibility and too much love for the wilderness result from a robust population increase.

Many Puget Sounders, myself among them, grow up watching the volcanoes—especially Mount Rainier—trying to catch their seasonal and daily moods, to understand their mass and place. It's hard to stop looking. Approaching Mount Rainier by car or foot, knowing where it will be if it is "out," visitors strain their eyes, willing its appearance before it actually appears. Walking to junior high in a Bellevue just before skyscrapers, I aimed directly for its broad dome looming above Somerset, dwarfing everything in sight. Some residents lean on Rainier sightlines all their lives. My family, like other northwesterners, used to picnic at Paradise or Sunset, primary destinations within Mount Rainier National Park (MRNP), and I ate too much as my eyes tried to consume the overwhelming curved mountain just above. On one picnic my family escorted my grandmother and a friend of hers from Bethesda, Maryland, who was making her first trip to the Northwest. A familiar pattern, wherein natives display their best goods to visitors. Rainier, after all, remains the Evergreen State's number one tourist attraction. No state contains anything remotely like our biggest volcano.

Yet Oregon claims far more volcanoes than Washington's five. How far must one travel to find a string of volcanoes comparable to Oregon's?

In my youth I closed the distance between my home and Mount Rainier as frequently as I could, hiking western and northern sections of the Wonderland Trail, sizing up the mountain from Plummer Peak or Gobblers Knob or Burroughs Mountain. For the past two decades my family has returned to my first geography from our home in southwestern Montana, and as I-90 tops out at Ryegrass Summit after a twelve-mile pull up from the Columbia River, if there is high pressure and high cloud cover (or none),

Rainier's upper half bulges just south of west, beckoning. It's just too big, too much, and some of us spend our lives trying to absorb it, or at least understand our relationship to it.

Mount Rainier is not my only sacred mountain, though it remains the primary one.

Mount Baker has been my summer volcano since early childhood, when my folks bought waterfront property on Camano Island's east side. Many in northern Puget Sound and southwestern British Columbia count on Mount Baker morning, noon, and night during the year's longest days when its perennial snow cover lights the summer sky. Some among them imagine closing the distance with both Rainier and Baker; though a chubby kid, I wanted these volcanoes close up, under boot, and eventually I climbed.

Mount Baker dominates British Columbia's lower Fraser River valley, where most of the province's population lives. John Keeble's novel *Yellowfish* defines Baker in a way that captures its place in the lives of thousands on both sides of the border. Keeble's portrait of Baker defines the domineering presence of volcanoes in the regional imagination: "Its size and light were utterly dominating. Without it the elements of the landscape—the lesser mountains, the river, the bottom land, and increasingly now, the rock outcroppings—would be changed. . . . The mountain cast its net, its white, colorless shadow, over everything in sight."[1]

This virtuosic rhetoric with its animist metaphors defines the volcanoes' place in the Northwest's self-portraiture. Keeble's sentences mimetically strain to evoke and approximate a geographical domination that is a fact of life and wellspring of privilege. His Mount Baker poses only one among myriad artistic examples in modern history that have endeavored to size up and salute this geography.

Of course, watching the Northwest's volcanoes requires steady patience, at least from the west side, as seasonal cloud cover drops like a thick gray rug down to a thousand or two thousand feet, and days or weeks pass before a new weather system and rising air pressure lifts it. Residents speak familiarly about whether a particular volcano is out, but when it is "in," hiding behind thick swaths of clouds, residents think sober thoughts knowing that sooner or later their volcano will be restored to its rightful place, and their souls recharged. Puget Sounders used to grow up believing low cloud cover was the norm for nine or ten months of the year. When "the mountain"—take your pick—is out, they shake their heads in wonder and feel sorry for residents of not only Kansas but Massachusetts or Georgia or even Colorado or California.

These exceptional mountains form a geographic core of Pacific Northwest identity both past and present.

The volcanoes distill the regional imaginary as no other feature except the Columbia River, the Northwest's primary river and powerful symbol of its heritage. They symbolize a Northwest privilege. In modern history the region's most exceptional mountains have always played a central role in the formation and refinement of regional identity. They function as a complex set of mirrors in which some of us indulgently size ourselves up. Through this sustained gaze, we look real good: As mirrors, they reflect generations of regional history during which the Northwest has tilted from wet (or dry) boondocks to mecca. The accelerating in-migration in the twentieth century's second half confirms the region's status as arrived and attractive. The mountains pose as a special optic through which to assess changing attitudes and behavior near and on themselves. Many kinds of people lay all kinds of claims upon the volcanoes, a species of vertical tabula rasa upon which we write our stories. Now that hiking and mountaineering have become mass sports, some of those claims have created problems at the volcanoes' most popular locations.

In the twentieth century's second half people come to the volcanoes in far greater numbers, engaging in more diverse activities than ever before, and at some sites our love affair with them creates practical, visible problems. That love affair sometimes obscures, to our peril, the fundamental differences between these arctic islands, as they've often been described, and the primary topographies of our lives. We must see beyond them as inevitably distorting mirrors even as we figuratively hold them in our embrace. To read the volcanoes is to read ourselves, and we need a fresh look.

The volcanoes inspire testimony of many sorts. There is little doubt about their visual benefits. Those describing them cannot resist using words like "float" or "majestic" (or adding "gorgeous" in the next paragraph). A common Puget Sound mantra, one that pinpoints a spiritual and emotional dependency, goes "Have you seen the mountain today?" The asking and answering that question—whether it's Rainier or another volcano—confers a sense of solidarity and privilege. Seeing "the mountain" gives the viewer a lift. We rely on volcano sightlines to confirm facets of our identity and status: without them, we'd be far less than we are. It's an old and unavoidable gesture, taking our measure, since their height and shape ground us.

California claims Mount Lassen and gorgeous Mount Shasta, second-highest volcano in the range and beacon in the northern third of that state. But excepting those two peaks, the lower forty-eight states' volcanoes cluster in Oregon and Washington. Volcanoes appeal to the imagination of childhood and remain centers of delight and potential terror (the latter tincturing the former). It's no accident that Oregon's Willamette Valley, terminus of the Oregon Trail, was frequently described in paradisal terms, and that almost 75 percent of Oregon's population lives there. The valley's beauty is framed by the forested coastal range to the west and the Cascades to the east, capped by at least a dozen volcanoes or volcanic fragments (depending on the count).

The valley's identity, and central Oregon's, derives in part from that bead of volcanoes. For the nineteenth-century westering America, this Garden of Eden was bordered on one side by virtually unique, potentially fiery mountains. While other states or regions also boast mountains close by, none except Hawaii lay claim to volcanoes that crown both the range and, arguably, the regional ego. Outside Alaska, Hawaii, and northern California, only Washington and Oregon divide their territory by a line of volcanoes. Some inhabitants of both the green west and brown east stand taller because of the volcanoes that divide yet unite them.

Jokes about Puget Sound's and Willamette Valley's endless rainfall dissipate once the skies clear and residents lift their heads to the Cascades, which prove a special case beyond the Rockies. According to one scholar of American tourism, the U.S. western landscapes have long claimed precedence on the world stage, since "the myth of exceptionalism has a life of its own as the Rockies rise in front of westward-bound travelers."[2] The language given Rainier and the other volcanoes, puffed up yet inevitably falling short of the thing itself, explains a great deal about human behavior, particularly in groups, around or on the snowpeaks. Certainly it reflects the region's vaunting pride in its crowning natural endowment and helps explain its steady rise in status over the twentieth century.

In my youth, when the mountains came back out I sensed I lived in the best possible place. This brand of local chauvinism is as common as it is potent, and American notions of optimal landscape, descended from the European credo of the sublime, confirm the Northwest brand. In Gary Snyder's "The Climb," he speaks for all who have fallen under the spell of Northwest volcanoes: "West coast snowpeaks are too much! They are too far above the surrounding lands. They are in a different world."[3]

That "different world" continually impinges upon the human world—particularly, it could be argued, for natives and long-time inhabitants. Or climbers. Climbers enter that "different world" en masse, trying to close the eternal gap between it and their own variable everyday worlds. Both towering fact and symbol, the volcanoes record a rich and changing cultural history as increasing numbers come close for similar and sometimes novel reasons. The most popular, Mounts Hood and Rainier, have been subject to a disarming array of uses over the past century and a half, from lightshows to cemeteries. These provide one measure of a matured regional identity and reveal a series of contentious pressure points as contrary values—preservation and access—clash.

Accustomed to seeing few people in mountainous southwest Montana, and feeling both a native and a visitor in the Cascades, the crowd scenes on these standard routes disturb me. I take our Aussie shepherd dog with me on easy day climbs in the nearby Rockies, but not to volcanoes. Access remains a cherished value, but a black Lab suggests not only a certain human density but also a set of assumptions and practices that are out of balance on volcanoes. Skiing or hiking or climbing a volcano does not resemble a vigorous stroll in the park, of course, and this study analyzes those assumptions and practices that document the differences as well as the ostensible similarities between those two domains.

I realized I began skiing and hiking in the Cascades of the 1960s, at precisely the moment legions of baby boomers took to the mountains. Thousands grew up planning daytrips and backpack trips based on the Mountaineers' 100 Hikes series. Those books changed the game and changed the regional mountainscapes forever.

Many pushed higher, and the scale of the sport changed. Like most new or amateur climbers, I (a mediocre technical climber) was destined for the standard routes. But as the sport grew, those with high natural talent or skillsets took on all possible routes, particularly those posing the greatest technical challenges or dangers, in far greater numbers.

In the Cascades, the volcanoes have always been the biggest tourist magnets. In addition, regional population has escalated sharply since the 1960s, Washington's having more than doubled, and many more folks referenced the snowpeaks in their lives. Ever greater numbers wanted to draw close, even quit their cars and don a backpack or strap on a climbing harness and crampons. This study takes the pulse of the snowpeaks in the early twenty-first century, assesses what is old and what is new as people gather, in increasing numbers, near and on them. The country's most exceptional mountains provide a unique lens through which to study the region's accelerating development over the past century and a half. Through that lens, the place of the volcanoes in the regional psyche grows as apparent as the need to revise some of our policies and practices on them.

1 | THE LEGACY OF EXCEPTIONALISM

> In various travels and expeditions in the territory, I had viewed
> the snow-peaks of this range from all points of the compass, and
> since that time . . . I assert that Washington Territory contains
> mountain scenery in quantity and quality sufficient to make half
> a dozen Switzerlands, while there is on the continent none more
> grand and imposing than is presented in the Cascade Range north
> of the Columbia River.
>
> —Lieut. A. V. Kautz, *Overland Monthly*

The towering position of the volcanoes in the Northwest ethos
is foregrounded in regional literature and historical writing. Exceptionalism—the notion that we're something special, given our
landscapes—provides the preferred rhetoric, a chauvinistic master
trope, in the fond story many northwesterners tell of themselves.
To understand that story, we must define that sensibility then trace
its evolution. The Northwest's special endowment depends in part
on what I will call the sociology of the snowpeaks. At the top of
the region's remarkable topographies float the volcanoes, as virtually every contemporary Northwest literary history or general
history claims, and above them all floats Mount Rainier—Tacoma,
or Tahoma in the Yakama language—undisputed crown of the
lower forty-eight states' upper left corner. Like Pacific salmon,
Rainier, in its myriad views, poses as the quintessential Northwest
icon. As such it has served as a commonplace market brand and

television backdrop, even appearing on commemorative postage stamps. Its image endorses a range of products and, since 1987, it has graced Washington State license plates. Rainier is ubiquitous.

Rainier figures centrally in Washingtonians' mental map. The Evergreen State's topographies write its psychological landscape, and at its imaginative center rises Mount Rainier, the state's biggest mountain and epitome of the acute lure of the West Coast's volcanoes. Only four peaks outside Alaska and Hawaii—California's Mount Whitney and three in Colorado—edge slightly higher, but Rainier's mass and isolation dwarf them. Rainier looms almost three miles above Puget Sound, Washington's inland sea, only forty-five miles or so west of it. Certainly since white settlers began crowding the old Oregon territory north of the Columbia River, some have been trying to take its measure and absorb it in sundry ways.[1] Coming to grips with Rainier pinpoints but one story of regional identity formation as its potential meanings inform northwestern self-representations.

The challenge of language and self-referentiality was captured by novelist Thomas Wolfe on July 2, 1938, at the tail end of his whirlwind tour, *The Great Parks Trip*, when the North Carolinian writer confronted Rainier in Saturday morning sunlight: "We stood trying to get its scale, and this [is] impossible because there was nothing but Mountain—a universe of mountain, a continent of mountain—and nothing else but mountain itself to compare mountain to."[2] The challenge of Rainier or the other volcanoes consists in part of articulating exactly what they mean, given their unique stature and size. The difficulty—or for Wolfe, impossibility—of understanding in no way lessens the chronic effort to do so: a rich history of affinity and interpretation, particularly as these compose one idealized self-portrait.

Defining the volcanoes means defining ourselves. More recently, journalist Jon Bell writes in *On Mount Hood: A Biography of Oregon's Perilous Peak* that the first sight of Hood "brands your perception, marks your memory, nearly sends you careening off

FIG. 1. View south from Camp Muir (10,000 feet), on Mount Rainier's most popular climbing route. The panorama features (*from left*) Goat Rocks (volcanic remnants), Mount Adams, Mount Hood (faintly in center), and Mount St. Helens. National Park Service, U.S. Department of the Interior.

the road."[3] Many—whether natives or newcomers—struggle to understand their own stature in relation to these tallest of all mirrors. They try to absorb their endless astonishment into quotidian lives, which proves an endless frustration and pleasure. Journalists, climbers, and legions of residents and visitors assign widely variable interpretations to the Northwest volcanoes.

The volcanoes' meanings spread far beyond the scientific and factual and across the gamut of subjective human experience. When people gaze upon the volcanoes, they unwittingly study one palimpsest upon which Northwest psychology has written itself. One strain runs through the evolving gaze: some conclude that these peaks are special and we must not be far off the mark, ourselves. Along the way such settlers old and new have come to regard themselves as unique, like the Northwest volcanoes themselves, the latter constituting the outer sign of election and inner grace. This theme of good fortune threads through contemporary regional history, journalism, and literature. That story of self-regard seemed firmly established well before the twentieth century's end, the volcanoes proving a signal instance of what two scholars have recently called "ecotopian exceptionalism."[4]

Rainier and the others dominate the literature just as they dominate the skyline. The special claim of regional literature derives from the population's obsession with our remarkable landscapes.[5] In Northwest literature, landscape has always been foregrounded as its storytellers and writers, like good Emersonian transcendentalists, have probed a spiritual connection between self and physical environments. In the regional psyche, the Cascades divide west slope green from the brown beyond the mountains' east slopes, and the volcanoes crown the range, lending it superior beauty, shape, and excitement.

Late Northwest composer Alan Hovhaness voiced an ancient and abiding view when he defined mountains as "symbolic meeting places between the mundane and spiritual world" (Notes to *Mysterious Mountain*, 1955). Volcanoes with their visible-invisible connections to earth's interior pose a special case, and when Northwest writing turns to the volcanoes, it strains to capture spiritual experience. West slope urbanites, especially after a Northwest winter, typically recharge their batteries when freshly spying a nearby volcano. When those long seasonal carpets of stratus clouds lift and the jagged line of Cascades, highlighted by the line of volcanoes, becomes visible again, a large segment of the population feels newly grounded and privileged.

Writers repeatedly describe the Big One as "almost godlike," "the physical presence of God," and such deification seems unavoidable. In *Greater Portland*, historian Carl Abbott states, "Mount Hood hovers over Portland like a watchful god."[6] The presumption of deity is common among the snowpeaks. If Rainier and Hood are godlike, at least when visible, what does that make those who lived or live within their sight? How does their fond gaze circle back and enlarge themselves? Rainier inspires the development of a robust if not inflated regional ego. The reverential language of the past 150 years rebounds onto its users, and manifestations of this tendency can be plotted as increasing legions of admirers have come to the volcanoes.

The volcanoes exert a magnetic attraction over nearby urbanites, Northwest poet Tim McNulty, for example, proclaiming Rainier as "recreational Mecca and spiritual retreat."[7] "Recreational Mecca" and "spiritual retreat" tug against one another as they recommend different behaviors. For example, how active or passive should our bodies be near this place? Yet both beckon people closer, as pilgrims enacting a spiritual discipline. The summons leads to both a healthy—or unhealthy—self-esteem and to a range of unintended effects. The influence of mountains upon identity formation, a commonplace in the literature of mountaineering, gains fresh force in the history of Euro-American testimony about Rainier, particularly from those who most literally close the gap between selfhood and divinity: climbers.

I am treating Mount Rainier as the epitome of the Northwest's volcanoes, as its height, size, and reputation both old and new proclaim its dominance over the regional imagination. Of course, some portions of the population ignore the volcanoes just as many depend upon them in various ways.

Shifting landscape priorities and styles of tourism meet in the Pacific Northwest. This "national drama of self-affirmation," one could claim, manifests itself with particular vigor in the "new" Northwest: a region that has been variously interpreted, like California, as "West of the West."[8] The myth and its accompanying drama of self-affirmation gain particular potency in the Northwest, for in its "sacred ground" casual tourists and natives alike raise their glances and confront a mountainscape unique in the lower forty-eight states, one from which they continually draw sustenance in negotiating and confirming their identities. In the national imaginary the region shines as an ultimate American West, a last best place, a culmination of our westering yearnings. From the nineteenth century through the early and mid-twentieth century, styles of tourism shifted from primarily a spectator mode to increasingly participatory roles as more tourists actively used their bodies within their chosen landscapes. In the Northwest the stage was thus set for hikers, climbers, and skiers to turn to the volcanoes for their status.

This deepening cultural embrace of the volcanoes tells an important regional story, and a key strand of Northwest identity can be plotted through writing devoted to them. To trace the evolution of that strand means to analyze and critique the sense of special regional endowment. Reviewing that literature shows regional identity transitioning from hinterlands to hot spot, from being a shy, gawky kid in the back of the class to a preening, self-impressed star. Nineteenth-century accounts of the mountain, particularly Theodore Winthrop's (1863) and those pioneering climber-writers collected by Paul Schullery (1987), reflect the growth of exceptionalism. A series of twentieth-century texts, culminating in the representative figure, in the early twenty-first century, of poet and mountaineer, Gary Snyder, document its legacy and durability.

The evidence addresses two fundamental issues: How do visitors or artists voice a volcano and give it language, and how do they speak of themselves after encounters both distant and close up? To write a volcano is to bring it into human reference and impose some human scale: to bring it down to the size of words even as those words insistently point above and beyond themselves. To write Rainier assumes as well that such endeavor uniquely fits and belongs to this giant volcano, not the lower volcanoes—let alone any old jagged peak. The survey yields a story of dramatically changing regional self-definition, one that tilts from periphery to center. Along the way, a spiritual and emotional reliance upon this huge icon has grown exponentially. Increasingly, many mark themselves as distinct and privileged according to their relationships with it.

Of course, the region's white history poses only the most recent episode in the ancient drama of human contact with volcanoes. A short span of historical time, one defined by white migration and settlement, has resulted in a dramatic paradigm shift. For Native peoples such as the Nisqually and the Yakama, the values attached to what whites call Mount Rainier accrue from untold centuries of living nearby. For Native peoples, veneration proscribes visitation: Tahoma stayed off-limits because of its sharply divided meanings. Ta-co-bet, meaning "nourishing breasts" or "the place where waters begin," is home to "Sagale Tyee, the Creator, the Great One" as well as angry "spirits of the mountain."[9] The story of Nisqually origins and migration explains their anxiety and caution about the latter. Sluiskin and Indian Henry, Klickitat and Yakama guides, respectively, of the first (1870) and subsequent (1884) Mount Rainier ascents, did not step onto snowfields or glaciers due to longstanding tribal taboos. Most Native guides remained below snowline though some individuals climbed, perhaps on vision quests.

If local tribes almost entirely worshipped the volcanoes from a distance, believing them the domain of demonic spirits expressed in occasional eruptions (e.g., the nearly annual eruptions of Mount St. Helens, from 1831 to 1857, known to the Cowlitz tribe and stray white traders or settlers), white visitors enacted contrary impulses. Modern attitudes toward the sacred volcanoes precisely reverse Native attitudes: many are discontent with distant "holy land," and want them close up and personal, in the foreground.

Nineteenth-century writing about Rainier illustrates the origins of that tribal-white reversal. Initially the volcano stayed in the background. On May 7, 1792, the expedition led by George Vancouver, at anchor in what they named Discovery Bay, first sighted the mountain Vancouver named for an officer friend. An expedition artist made a sketch of the view and Vancouver interpreted the volcano as a promising sign for British settlement of the region. The sketch, or at least a London artist's engraving of it, as the original no longer exists, bears little resemblance to Rainier's sprawling dome; rather, it suggests an auspicious symbol, but nothing spectacular in its own right. For Vancouver and his practical British colleagues, agents of Empire, Rainier formed a scenic backdrop for agricultural settlement, a new colony; the volcano per se held less interest except, perhaps, as a source of rivers. What mattered were the forested and watered landscapes below it, and their potential uses. Forty-one years later an adventurous Scots physician, William Fraser Tolmie, trekked from Fort Nisqually into what is now Mount Rainier National Park (MRNP), botanizing for herbal plants. Tolmie, after whom a peak is named in the park's northwest quadrant, is the first recorded Euro-American to directly approach the volcano.

Subsequent generations of American visitors, disciples of philosopher Edmund Burke's gospel of the sublime and the picturesque, seized upon the volcano itself. Like the initial influx of European mountaineers, they pursued and described sublimity in romantic terms, and the volcanoes drew them like flames. They had absorbed the crucial paradigm shift from "mountain gloom" to "mountain glory": instead of ugly excrescences best avoided, mountainscapes became, by the nineteenth century, a key topography of the human psyche.[10] The Theodore Winthrops had been nurtured on William Wordsworth and the other romantic poets, for whom mountaintops presaged states of eternity to which the imagination continually strives.

Winthrop, Rainier's single most important nineteenth-century advocate, left an ambivalent legacy in the cultural embrace of volcanoes. For Winthrop, Rainier comprises his north star, as he structures his travel narrative, *The Canoe and the Saddle*, around the mountain. Winthrop emphasizes Rainier's transformative potential and the "spiritual benefits of both the mountain and the region as a whole."[11] Those "spiritual benefits" became a watershed of regional self-regard. *The Canoe and the Saddle*, widely reprinted in the two decades following Winthrop's death in 1861 at only the age of thirty-two, extravagantly promoted the far-flung region and its premiere mountain. An outsider, Winthrop worshipped Rainier as eagerly as he ignored his native guides, their tribes, and signs of white subjugation increasingly evident around him. The tendency toward adoration and private communion not only feeds self-esteem but can remove celebrants from responsible participation in history—in those processes, malign or otherwise, that characterize their own time. Carried far enough, the worshipful pose becomes solipsistic and blinds one to surrounding ground realities including the fundamental differences between self and the object of worship. More than anything else, climbing into an ostensibly metaphysical realm expands the inflatable boundaries of selfhood: that is the guarantee of mountain glory that spread rapidly by the late nineteenth century. But personal mountain glory often fostered gendered nationalist and imperialist agendas common in much mountaineering rhetoric of the twentieth century—political fallout from the romantic gospel of sublimity.

Winthrop's literary responses to Mount Rainier set a pattern that continued through pioneering accounts of climbs and across the twentieth century. It's an old story of seduction and addiction, of participating in the "aesthetics of the infinite"; or it's an old story of pilgrimage. In this pattern, imaginative or physical exposure to Rainier resembles a love affair, an enchantment transitory or sustained, in which the visitor loses herself in the beloved. Near or on this magic mountain, the pilgrim is temporarily transported out of clock time as she surrenders to it. Since indigenous peoples around the world construe particular mountains as animate beings, and many religions venerate particular summits as sites for revelation, climbing a volcano recapitulates an archetypal journey with an archetypal plot (approach, difficulties overcome, summit climax, descent denouement). Climbing a volcano—"alive" in a way other mountains are not—only adds frisson to the journey.

To apply Winthrop's sermon and ascend Rainier means to encounter a timeless ideal and to open oneself to epiphany—and the lingering effects of its enchantment, the possibility of permanent change, of personal transformation. This mountain fever, the promise of the climber's high, teases crowds, in our time, onto snowfields and glaciers.

Mountain fever derives from a special kind of concentration, an almost trance state of heightened awareness dependent upon the rhythm of legs and lungs. Extreme focus and exertion prompt extreme perception and meditation in this restatement of the archetypal journey. This zone proves an addiction for masses.

Yet enchantment carries risks, particularly if the climber pays less attention to his physical environment and more to his self-esteem. Egos wax and wane in the mountains according to individual personalities and immediate experience. Mountain time variably balances pride and humility, self-aggrandizement and self-effacement. As much as anything, this mix marks criticisms of the romantic sublime, the gospel of mountain glory. Contemplating or climbing a volcano transports us out of ourselves, removes us temporarily from our mortality and chronology. That does not mean climbers shed any expressions of stewardship. On the contrary, a reverential mind-set more typically leads to an assumption of responsibility, however slender its expression. Ideally volcano experience results in increased caretaking, not carelessness, because it forcibly reminds its participants of their tiny place on them and within other landscapes. The lesson in humility often inspires an ethic of stewardship.

In its structure *The Canoe and the Saddle*—gold standard among nineteenth-century Northwest travel narratives—imitates a volcano climb and attests to the symbiosis between remarkable mountains and remarkable selves. The narrative's shape—approach, proximity, withdrawal, like a bell curve, a climb—forges the archetypal model for volcano visits. With Winthrop we ride south-southeast down Puget Sound from Port Townsend, a guest in Winthrop's canoe and, like Winthrop, leaving the paddling to his Klallam guides, as though approaching Rainier directly. Before it, Winthrop praises in inflated romantic style as though a priest at the high altar. The central chapter of Winthrop's memoir, titled "Tacoma" (in deference to the Native name), includes a long, interpolated tale, "Hamitchou's Legend," set on Rainier and told to Winthrop by "a frowzy ancient of the Squallyamish" at Fort Nisqually (92). The narrative chronicles his passage along Rainier's northern then eastern perimeters, the mountain receding as he reaches The Dalles on the Columbia River, his journey's end. The whole design approaches then recedes from the Beloved: a slower, longer version of the plot followed by tens of thousands of visitors, whether climbers or not, ever since.

Years before John Muir sang the mountain gospel of California's Sierra Nevada, Winthrop defined "volcano fever" in the Northwest, and the heightened terms of engagement have changed little since then. His charged language sets the mold. His first image of Rainier takes the form of a perfect reflection on the sound's surface (29), and the reader graduates from inverse image to ideal Platonic form, the thing in itself. Winthrop glosses his sermon—"only mountains, and chiefest the giants of snow, can teach whatever lessons there may be in vaster distances" (30)—before and after his slow north-south survey of the volcanoes. Hard to grasp those "lessons" in "palpable ether," as though the prophet speaks in tongues. Nonetheless, for many Rainier poses as a tangible connection with infinity and as a result affords endless homilies to the witness, however close or distant.

In his infatuation with Rainier, Winthrop endorses the romantic view of mountains as symbols of divinity. Given this credo of affinity, it logically follows that increasing numbers would close the gap and literally interpret the metaphorical challenge of mountain glory. This is the clarion call to the mountains, which eventually engenders mass mountaineering on Northwest volcanoes. Many, myself included, accept the call. That sensibility runs through the supposedly more secular present, as every cliché about mystical experience or spiritual epiphany or uplift alters but does not negate it. The New Englander poses as advocate and translator of mountains' spiritual benefits, and his effusions helped shift the paradigm from background to foreground.

A watershed figure like Winthrop proposes volcanoes as the region's most "sacred ground," as they provide "spiritual benefits" otherwise unavailable. He never specifies what these are. His privileging of Rainier is as influential as his claims are ethereal, and both strains affect subsequent interpretations and behavior on the snowpeaks. For such a prophet, Northwest volcanoes provide scaffolding for regional chauvinism since their "grand and stirring influences" (198) will inspire a better breed of Americans. An Edenic setting nurtures a superior people. In Winthrop's triumphant vision, sustained contemplation somehow creates better lives. This booster's logic proves elusive, the grand prediction characteristically omitting the details: "These Oregon people, carrying to a new and grander New England of the West a fuller growth of the American Idea . . . will elaborate new systems of thought and life. It is unphilosophic to suppose that a strong race, developing under the best, largest, and calmest conditions of nature, will not achieve a destiny" (90–91). In Winthrop's roseate view, the "grander New England of the West" derives from the exceptional peaks.

For the Winthrops, the American Adam—to borrow an old cliché from American literary history defining New World American identity, usually white male—will newly reemerge in the region and birth a "strong race." This visionary gospel forms, as always, wishful thinking.[12] Such a self-proclaimed promoter as Winthrop claims a consensus about our national essence that is both enduring and laughable. This proper noun ("American Idea") presumes a reductive common vision naïvely embraced and endlessly critiqued. Yet *The Canoe and the Saddle* predicted a regional ethos that manifested itself more than a century later, one in which the volcanoes serve as a primary symbol. That ethos enabled the late nineteenth-century and early twentieth-century settler Northwest to gradually shake off its inferiority complex.

More recently, regional chauvinism has restored Winthrop's book to the status it enjoyed in the late nineteenth century.

Climbers' narratives printed between 1876 and 1902 (and collected in Paul Schullery's *Island in the Sky*) provided variations on Winthrop's theme and together fostered the growth of regional exceptionalism. These accounts further link the volcanoes, especially Rainier, to regional identity: their testimony grounds Winthrop's transcendental rhetoric.

If Rainier looms as symbol for a Winthrop, subsequent writers such as John Muir, having closed the distance, also treat Rainier as fact. They created one publicity stream whose momentum helped pressure the creation of Mount Rainier National Park in 1899. Published in both local presses and national magazines (e.g., *Overland Quarterly, Atlantic Monthly*), these samples of late nineteenth-century travel writing, of variable quality, generated national interest in the Northwest's dominant volcano analogous to Muir's and Clarence King's literary accolades for California's Sierra Nevada range. Soon enough, for example, railroads (e.g., Northern Pacific) retained writers who contributed to this interest and thus boosted tourist revenues. In the first generation of transcontinental railroads, when Rocky Mountain and Pacific coast tourism became big business, owners quickly grabbed onto that and created profitable new markets. The Northern Pacific assumed variable advertising roles for monumental landscapes such as the Northwest volcanoes.

Early climber August V. Kautz's paean (see epigraph) not only extolled a particular American mountainscape over all others, but called readers to it. Kautz nearly summited (July 10, 1857) four summers after Winthrop threaded his way eastward across Naches Pass. Declining weather conditions and the late hour of the day forced Kautz to turn back before reaching Columbia Crest, just a few hundred feet below Rainier's highpoint.[13] He waited nineteen years to write his account, which was published immediately before the nation's Centennial summer and thirteen years before Washington statehood. His hyperbolic invitation links the Cascades, and particularly the snowpeaks, to national identity. His centennial boast applied the Emersonian gospel to make the United States new, not some old-world makeover: in belittling Europe's Alps, Kautz used Washington's mountainscape to proclaim the American Adam, a fresh home-grown humanity defined apart from European precedents. His essay, a prideful act of ownership, placed Northwest mountains in the gallery of outstanding Western landscapes that nineteenth-century America championed as part of its world-class heritage and identity. The volcanoes became objects to variably admire, contemplate, climb, and brag about over many generations, as tourist paradigms shifted. Writers such as Kautz led Americans to believe that nothing in Europe can match the American West, let alone the Northwest corner.

Pioneering climber-writers threw down the gauntlet, beckoning readers to reach Rainier and infuse the extraordinary—and extraordinarily difficult—into their mundane lives. Half a year after Kautz's account, Hazard Stevens, son of territorial Governor Isaac Stevens, published a more polished story in the *Atlantic Monthly* of what Rainier historians agree was the first successful climb, completed by Stevens and Philemon B. van Trump on August 17–18, 1870. Stevens's brag (e.g., "this colossus among mountains") matches Kautz's. Another early climber, George Bayley, echoed Kautz's fervid celebration of the mountainous Northwest.[14] For such, Rainier summit's "field of vision" surveyed the new Promised Land, a rhetoric that caught on slowly but flourished by the late twentieth century.

From the beginning, travel journalism sustained and elaborated Winthrop's rhapsody, ultimately drawing crowds to the peak. Early climbing accounts paint pictures similar to Winthrop's, as each climber-writer, through the approach-climb-return plot, endeavors to define Rainier's "fine lesson" and personal transformation, extolling volcano climbing as a desirable agent of change. Such testimony leads, ultimately, to industrial-scale tourism near and on volcanoes.

Some tried their hand at landscape composition: for example, a minister from Snohomish, Washington brushed a broad canvas, from sea level gradually upward, his set description conjuring this "ideal mountain" and climaxing with its broad dome.[15] These verbal labors were more than matched by those oil painters, descendants of the Hudson Valley School (i.e., the luminists), who captured Rainier or other snowpeaks on canvas. The most famous writer among these pioneering climbers, John Muir, bestowed his blessing, saluting Rainier as "noblest" among the West Coast's "fire mountains." He trotted out the same metaphors and championed the same summit panoramas but reserved his greatest praise for the alpine parks on Rainier's south-central flank—"the richest subalpine garden I ever found, a perfect floral elysium"—which quickly became known as Paradise: an irresistible brand that explains, as much as anything, the twentieth-century story of MRNP and crowds.[16]

The predictable cheerleading increased its lure by posing a fundamental ambivalence about volcano climbing. Attraction and alienation provide an energizing tension in mountaineering, and Muir gave voice to it. While some writers predictably detailed physical exhaustion followed by endless summit views—the clichéd ascent plot—he remarked the risks inherent in that personal transformation. Muir, an inveterate summiteer, proposed that "more pleasure is to be found at the foot of the mountains"—say, the Paradise alpine parks—than "on their frozen tops."[17] Winthrop's distant communion with Rainier proved less easy and assured when atop it. Physical exhaustion and alienation provide the complications in the archetypal journey. Such a psychic distancing as suggested by Muir underlines the twinned danger and lure commonplace in ascents, particularly on such a dominant volcano. Certainly it defines the challenge of Rainier.[18]

The cautionary note represents not only a further teaser, but a theme sustained by many subsequent visitors. The tops of arctic islands prove a risky setting for transformation because they resist habitation: though increasing numbers would regard the mountains as "home," Muir defined Rainier's crater as far from home, and more generally volcanoes and especially summits remain *other* than a home. Mass mountaineering grew out of the contradiction that people belong (temporarily, at least) on summits, yet never belong in such precincts. To court the beloved or to complete the pilgrimage carries risks.

The creation of Paradise as a central MRNP village and destination by Muir and other publicists enacts Winthrop's boosterism and the subsequent story of tourist concentration in the volcano's vicinity. It's another developers' cliché: build Paradise from an alpine park and they will come. Ever the rhapsodist, Muir also labeled those parks "lower gardens of Eden." By the time the well-known author and founder of the Sierra Club republished his "Ascent of Mount Rainier" three years after MRNP's founding, its lavish, superlative rhetoric—stock answer to how one writes a Rainier—sealed Paradise's reputation, an area the Nisqually and Yakama had called Saghalie Illah, "Land of Peace."[19] Roughly half a century later the brand was sustained by an early caretaker who titled his account of wintering over (1919–20) with his bride *A Year in Paradise* (1959). As Paradise Found, the precinct quickly become primary visitation site, and remains the launching point for the most popular climbing route (via Disappointment Cleaver), pioneered by most of the earliest summiteers including Muir. In this Paradise, visitors most have the chance to absorb the mountain's "lessons," so the sentiment goes.

The accounts of these early ardent supporters try to capture Rainier's size, dominance, and life-changing health values. They express a rhetoric of religious conversion that applies and specifies Winthrop's symbolic Rainier. They write Rainier and their new selves out of a tradition of special revelation, intimating the ineffable—and irresistible. Of Winthrop's prophetic party, they testified as religious witnesses, recommending a transformation that outlasts their temporary exhilaration. The first woman to climb Rainier, Fay

Fuller (1890), spoke for not only the earliest climbers but future crowds: "All who have the opportunity, and who live in sight of this lofty pinnacle we almost reverence, who have never climbed the mountains, and want to begin life anew might profitably spend a few weeks next summer on its hillside, if they want to fall in love with the world again."[20] This language of conversion epitomizes the salubrious, happy "contagion of mountain-climbing," in one pioneer climber's phrase.[21] Volcano fever fuels the addiction of accomplishment: that potential conversion promises a lot. If time on Rainier's glaciers and craters means renewal, even rebirth, climbers return as different people.

The biggest mountain yields potentially the biggest climb and change. The attraction of Rainier and accompanying testimonials illustrate a vigorous turn in Winthrop's "American Idea," as late nineteenth- and early twentieth-century recreational tourists took to the mountains to test their mettle and set new contours of personal identity. In this milieu of masculine virility and nationalist aspiration, Theodore Roosevelt became the role model and Northwest volcanoes and other mountains, ideal proving grounds of selfhood. Philemon B. Van Trump, the individual who climbed Rainier more than anyone else before 1900, published a spirited defense of "the contagion of mountain-climbing" in the first *Sierra Club Bulletin* (1894). A local Roosevelt, he emphasized the volcano's heroic challenge whereby the climber can transcend physical pain to accomplish the worthy goal of summiting. In this period that goal was heavily tinctured with gendered and imperialist agendas, which influenced local and national mountaineering for generations.

The language of religious transformation proved exportable, removed in time and space from the volcanoes. The railroads targeted a broader audience through their promotional materials. For example, in 1895 a Northern Pacific copywriter published a florid Rainier account in its *Wonderland* travel guides. He let out all the stops in his thoroughly corny invocation and "homage," his effusions superficially echoing those of Winthrop. A canny pitchman, he wrote copy to increase traffic and profits. His lengthy narrative decried the challenge if not impossibility of translating Mount Rainier, of chronicling the ineffable. Like many before and after him, he used a well-worn rhetorical strategy, protesting his failure yet summoning the mountain after the fact, from great distance.

The strategy of word painting (or something similar) underlines the vividness of the evocations and proves that language, like photographic images and other artistic responses, becomes indefinitely reproducible away from the thing itself. Rainier and all the others are both familiar and unfamiliar in their endless reproductions (e.g., coffee table photography books or online images). Language inherently falls short yet is subject to limitless imitation and copy. And facsimiles take on a long life of their own, in the marketplace and elsewhere. But no matter the brand familiarity, the de-mystification never completes itself: the volcano remains more than our language about it.

The *Sierra Club Bulletins* and those *Wonderland* guides served contrary audiences and agendas, which competed for a long time at Rainier and the other volcanoes. Though both promoted the volcano, the Sierra Club and its Northwest offshoots stressed preservation, not development, from the beginning. These diverse expressions of that lofty "American Idea"—volcanoes as sites for personal change or for tourist business—continue to compete for dominance through the present.

The latter nineteenth century, then, revealed a rhetoric of superlatives and quasi-religious conversion about the biggest volcano: a linguistic approximation of the region's gifted mountainscape. This rhetoric compensated for Washington Territory's, and young Washington State's, boondocks image, so far from the country's population and cultural centers. In more recent guises such rhetoric honors the biggest and expresses the ultimately inexpressible. The linguistic challenge of Rainier grows in direct relation to proximity:

the closer one comes to or on Rainier, the greater its power and transformative potential.

The second fundamental issue, how we speak or write about ourselves after time with the volcanoes, also includes, in its answer, some expectation of recognition: a social confirmation of personal transformation. Those who stray well beyond Paradise's or Sunrise's meadows represent a species of secular pilgrims who all seek personal renewal. One MRNP historian describes a Tacoma street scene after an 1894 climb: "[Major Edward] Ingraham's party of thirteen men and women paraded down the street . . . attired in alpine clothing and with alpenstocks in hand, looking 'like a band of warriors,' chanting: 'We are here! / We are here! / Right from the top / Of Mount Rainier!'"[22] The long-ago scene suggests a ritual requirement of dramatic display and public acknowledgment asked by climbers, who presume some acknowledgment of that transformation that inflates and alters the self.

For many the social confirmation guarantees the personal transformation as though the latter entirely depends upon the former. The recognition expected by Rainier summiteers has not disappeared. One version of Northwest chauvinism consists of climbing the volcanoes and broadcasting that achievement. It is also reflected in late twentieth-century mass mountaineering and regional histories of the sport, some (e.g., REI: *Fifty Years of Climbing Together*, 1988) even claiming the Northwest as the birthplace of American mountaineering in the decades framing World War II. Other communities—New England, Colorado, Yosemite—shrug off this claim.

One strand of Northwest sensibility, then, depends upon people's unfolding cultural uses of the volcanoes. In the preferred narrative we belong to them in some respects just as, in others, they belong to us. Many northwesterners embrace this fiction of entitlement. For them, whether nearby or at a distance, Rainier signifies not only an emblem of divinity or the otherworldly, but a convex mirror reflecting back some portion of their gaze and faint intimations of its superlative status. They take pride in Rainier and the lower volcanoes as though maintaining a proprietary relation to them. When such folks watch Rainier, they watch themselves in some physical and spiritual relationship to it, like tiny human figures in the right foreground of a sprawling Albert Bierstadt mountain canvas. The perceiver always figures in the perceived panorama. In somehow taking its measure, they inevitably take or include their own and in the process, come out looking good.

That visual connection enlarges them and confirms their happy choice in living, temporarily or permanently, within its sight-lines. The gleaming images of the volcanoes confirm northwest-erners' healthy—or too healthy—self-regard. Many, though by no means all, bask in their glow. Contemporary evidence suggests northwesterners have taken Winthrop's claim about the "fuller growth of the American Idea" as gospel. Certainly many published testimonies exist confirming the region as one special place, an ultimate West. The substantial in-migration of the past two generations demonstrates that many have sought out the Northwest. The state of Washington, for example, numbered below three million inhabitants in 1960; in a little over half a century, the population has climbed above seven million. Longtime inhabitants and newer arrivals preen themselves in part because of the spectacular topographies, particularly the show-off snowpeaks. Twentieth-century texts show the earlier rhetoric about Rainier subject to further specification and, in some cases, qualification. As the habits of imaginative appropriation increase in number and kind, dependency upon the volcanoes as one constituent of regional identity deepens.

As every Northwest history avers, if Northwest pioneer descendants or new arrivals felt peripheral to other U.S. regions in the welter of popular or promotional images more than a century ago, Rainier and the other volcanoes inspired a contrary view, one that took precedence by the mid-twentieth century. The Cascades as rich endowment compensated the region for its remoteness.

Northwesterners are a long way from New York or that other Washington but the volcanoes symbolize their inheritance, in the region's self-flattering story: a view that extended the Rainier rhetoric of superlatives to all the snowpeaks. For example, North Cascades conservationist Grant McConnell's midcentury essay, "The Cascade Range," singled out the volcanoes for tribute:

> In the neighborhood of any one of the volcanic peaks, that one dominates everything within sight . . . the personality of the nearby peak obliterates the sense that other mountains can exist. Thus each of the big volcanoes has its tributary region. . . .
>
> There is nothing in the nation remotely resembling any one of them, let alone their long stately procession. (*The Cascades: Mountains of the Pacific Northwest*, 77, 79)

Our metaphorical appropriation of volcanoes measures one pattern of human use of them. McConnell's "long stately procession" defines the height of the Northwest's geographical status and unifies the volcanoes above the surrounding Cascades. Anyone who has spent much time in the Cascades high country attests to the accuracy of McConnell's claim. Even in the extraordinary North Cascades, the Alps of the lower forty-eight states, Mount Baker and Glacier Peak always dominate the west-northwest and southern vistas, respectively. Once high enough anywhere in the range or from a plane, under clear skies one discovers the volcanoes' rising in a loose, north-south line. Mountaineers and others grouped them just as ancient peoples clustered stars into constellations. Those familiar with Washington's five volcanoes accept, without qualification, the notion that each Northwest volcano bears a distinct personality—compare composer Alan Hovhaness's symphonies to/about Mount St. Helens and Glacier Peak—and each visually dominates neighboring, lower mountains. The same animist energy holds true among Oregon's far more numerous volcanoes.

With the snowpeaks, writers' and artists' habits of figuration seem inevitable, given Rainier's history of rhapsodic language.

These habits mark human dependency and appropriation. Consider the subtitles in Stephen L. Harris's *Fire and Ice: The Cascade Volcanoes* (1976), a "volcanic and glacial history": "Oregon's Volcanic Playground" (The Three Sisters), "Guardian of the Wilderness" (Mount Jefferson), "The Forgotten Giant of Washington" (Mount Adams), "The 'Fujiyama of America'" (Mount St. Helens—before 1980), "White Goddess of the North Cascades" (Glacier Peak), and "The 'Great White Watcher'" (Mount Baker). Harris's familiar terms, like earlier Nisqually or Yakama or Lummi or other tribal epithets, tag particular volcanoes in relation to the others; they also bridge our understanding of their geology. McConnell's regal metaphor also animates and ennobles the region's most exceptional mountains, and his boastful credo underlines every writer's panoramic survey since Winthrop's symbolizing Rainier.

Because of diverse Rainier meanings—Rainier as tourist business and as site for potential transformation—both regional inhabitants and visitors increasingly have wanted the Cascades, above all the crowning volcanoes, close at hand. Given the publicity streams, the draw is unavoidable. Like gleaming white magnets, volcanoes pull crowds who seek connection onto their slopes. Many seek this locus of the sacred under their boots and crampons. The "challenge of Rainier" distills and climaxes the national brag about the Washington Cascades voiced in 1876 (see epigraph). The grip of Rainier or others on the regional psyche and self-portrait adheres, if anything, more strongly now than in the nineteenth and twentieth centuries.

Part of its power derives from the peculiar lure of volcanoes, which become a palpable connection between one's body and the earth's molten interior, between pulsing microcosm and macrocosm, and an emblem of human transience. However long their dormancy, people speak about volcanoes being "alive" as other mountains are not. Volcanoes remind us of a felt connection, however slight, between our transitory selves and the changing face of the planet. That sense of impermanence affords, for some, a measure of consolation. With some vulcanology under our belts, and knowledge of particular volcanoes' particular threats, we employ volcanoes as a frame of reference for our own potential or actual disturbances, and our mortality. That sensibility, antithetical to the Neoplatonism of Winthrop and his successors, is shared by contemporary visitors or residents, many of whom know, particularly since Mount St. Helens' 1980 explosion, something about risks from volcanoes.

Volcanoes pose as symbols of permanence or impermanence, depending upon generation and temperament, and thus solicit a wide range of artistic and scholarly response from the early twentieth century through the present. Those habits of figuration measure varying degrees of imagined or desired connection. The responses rewrite more than they dispute the earlier style of rhapsodic rhetoric. In the case of Rainier, two poets unsurprisingly engender a different volcano from vastly different perspectives. Marianne Moore's big poem "An Octopus" (1924) ranges all over the place, likening Mount Rainier to a giant "Octopus / of ice," labeling it "Big Snow Mountain" and "Mount Tacoma," and quoting from then-current government pamphlets on our national parks. This poem's roving, restless eye suggests the peak as a series of ecosystems and portrays the whole as nothing if not dynamic—and scary in the popular imagination (cf. title metaphor). In her triptych, "Three Ways of Looking at a Mountain" (1992), Denise Levertov proposed a distant, anti-romantic view that ironically recalls Winthrop's symbol of eternity. She concludes her first poem, "Settling," asserting Rainier's huge presence even when invisible. If the mountain is not "there" it's there, and settling in means accustoming oneself to a presence that is often absent.

With the volcanoes, imagined connection does not always depend upon physical proximity. The sociology of the snowpeaks encompasses populations at lesser and greater remove, but typically within their sightlines. Many Seattle residents like Levertov (in her final years) prefer Rainier at a distance which, given infrastructural limits, is a good thing. She proposes, in her second poem, "Against Intrusion," distance superior to closeness in this homily: "How clearly it speaks! *Respect, perspective, / privacy,* it teaches. *Indulgence / of curiosity increases / ignorance of the essential*" (italics hers). In voicing Rainier, Levertov interprets its meaning both differently and similarly to Winthrop's extended definition. Levertov articulates a minority opinion, as privacy has become rare for most tourists or climbers. In this paradoxical view, knowledge decreases with intimacy. The lesson of detached perspective affords a holistic, composed understanding reminiscent of that held by the Yakama and Nisqually, one unavailable close up. Awe demands distance and mass visitation, even if it occasions personal transformation, precludes full knowledge. Detachment enables understanding, and Levertov's poems privilege the vantage of urbanites or those who remain at the far end of their precious vistas.

"Ways of Looking" implies ways of knowing, and in the late twentieth century most residents or visitors favor intrusion (vs. Levertov's second poem) in one mode or other, as access grounds familiarity. Many have rejected her "essential" meaning of Rainier (an "Open Secret," Levertov's third poem) since they increasingly demand an array of contacts. They want it more than remote: "This mountain's power / lies in the open secret of its remote / apparition, silvery low-relief / coming and going moonlike at the horizon, / always loftier, lonelier, than I ever remember." The rhetoric of superlatives remains, as does the tradition of Neoplatonic image, the "moonlike" "apparition" (see Winthrop's initial Puget Sound reflection). But if Rainier is "lonelier, than I ever remember" ("Open Secret"), the personification downplays if not denies the thickening pattern of human connection of the past 150 years. The loneliness Levertov ascribes to it suggests its lack of referentiality for those who live within sight of it. She defines The Big One through two paradoxes: the "open secret" of its abiding remote image, and its "loftier" yet "lonelier" reality. The volcano's otherworldliness has no bearing on human affairs, it's no altar; or, more commonly, it feeds regional self-esteem, its height somehow improving citizens' own bearing. Many want to be there.

That yearning remains secure in the twenty-first century, Levertov's dissenting voice notwithstanding. According to this chronic desire, one source of our greatness remains clear. As many commentators have noted, the region has long outstripped its original white stigma as hinterlands and backwater. Patterns of self-representation, the favored local/regional story, always make participants look good, particularly to the extent Northwest self-representations are infused with "invocations of nature spirituality."[23]

The preferred Northwest narrative concerns this "sacred landscape," the tendency to spiritualize our topographies since these constitute, in historian William G. Robbins's words, "the centerpiece of our regional iconography."[24] If our iconography constitutes our essence, the outer sign of our collective inner grace, then the volcanoes form a center. Robbins's scholarly anthology, *The Great Northwest: The Search for a Regional Identity* (2001), works between potential tensions in its title's two halves: between myriad signs of ongoing identity "search" and a consensus of "greatness." Arguably, the search has slowed in the early twenty-first century because most inhabitants, if questioned, construe it as over. Great mountains, particularly the snowpeaks, form part of the core of "great Northwest" on anyone's list. The consensus is inevitably self-congratulating and insufficiently self-critical.

"Nature's Northwest" climaxes other Northwests that together constitute the region. Instead of being defined by outsiders, many northwesterners proactively gild their region, taking their cue from coastlines, salt water, rivers, mountains, and literally above all, volcanoes. The case is perfectly made by the cover chosen for Robbins's anthology: "Detail from *Mt. Hood*," by William Samuel Parrott (Portland Art Museum). A late nineteenth-century painting, product of the American romantic landscape school, reasserts the volcanoes' dominance in the contemporary regional imaginary.

This detail confirms the volcanoes' contiguity. No miniscule

FIG. 2. *Mount Hood* (1885), William Samuel Parrott (1843–1915), Portland Art Museum. Parrott, whose studio was based in Portland, painted Mount Hood and other Northwest volcanoes many times. The influence of the luminists shines in his work. Wikimedia Commons.

figures in the left or right foreground relieve the focus upon Parrott's Mount Hood; only a couple of drift logs balanced on some lakeshore boulders momentarily pull our eye from the far shore of the still lake (presumably Lost Lake), and that distant line, along with the foothills behind, insistently draw our eyes upward to the top third of the cover. The painter has foreshortened the mountain as though with a powerful telephoto lens, and his oils have simplified its lines and rendered it snowier than usual. The viewer gazes upon an idealized Mount Hood on whose western façade two enormous ribs, or spurs, separate several glaciers. Parrott's *Mt. Hood* towers over the lake to an extent that it does not over Portland, but the imaginative claim feels contemporary, not only nineteenth-century. Parrott's romanticized *Mt. Hood* underlines its domination over the Oregonian imagination and sustains the regional tradition of superlative rhetoric. Like his *The Three Sisters from Clear Lake,* and Sanford Gifford's and Albert Bierstadt's paintings of Mount Rainier from southeast Vashon Island, *Mt. Hood* visually captures that tradition of magnificent awe, of language straining at its own borders to signify the grandeur of volcanoes initiated by Winthrop and imitated ever since.

Other contemporary evidence including scholarly histories and poetry links the volcanoes' dominance with the issue of regional identity in ways that show the latter sustained, in part, by the former. There is no getting around the volcanoes or the increasing human play on or below them. The cover of *The Pacific Northwest: Growth of a Regional Identity* (2010), for example, follows suit from the Robbins cover, again featuring Mount Hood from Lost Lake— likely the most popular perspective except Portland's. Over and over, Mount Hood and the others provide a regional brand and striking visual and psychic benchmark.

The Rainier rhetoric of superlatives and testimony, a capstone feature of "nature's Northwest," continues unabated through the present, sometimes turning in countercultural directions. Such turns only increase the volcanoes' cultural value for new population segments. That reconfirmed cultural value sanctions increasing uses close up—contrary to the recommended detachment of Marianne Moore or the distance of Denise Levertov. The value grants renewed license to mountaineers as pilgrims. Immortalized as hip mountaineer Japhy Ryder in Jack Kerouac's *The Dharma Bums* (1958), poet Gary Snyder, native northwesterner, brings a new-old spiritual cachet to the Northwest volcanoes. In the 1940s Snyder climbed all of them, and he shows himself a descendent of the Winthrop tradition who lends the volcanoes a Zen Buddhist aura in his "Mt. St. Helens" sequence (*Danger on Peaks,* 2004). Through Snyder, an Eastern aesthetic with ever-widening appeal is imposed on the volcanoes such that they become, for reasons similar to the first generation of Rainier climber-writers, a highly sought mode of self-realization.

Once again the volcanoes loom as both fact and symbol, as emblems of permanence and impermanence. Snyder spiritualizes "the snowpeaks" with new nuance, mountain climbing serving as a form of prayer, an extension of the Buddhist tradition of walking meditation. In "The Climb," Snyder's invocation recognizes and endorses the contemporary paradigm of the volcanoes as site for personal growth, itself only the newest version of the old theme: "the big snowpeaks pierce the realm of clouds and cranes, rest in the zone of five-colored banners and writhing crackling dragons in veils of ragged mist and frost-crystals, into a pure transparency of blue."[25] His Himalayan credo sounds an essential clarion call for baby boomers who read Hermann Hesse's *Siddhartha* in the 1960s and 1970s. The credo became one of the primary attractions to Northwest climbing, at least standard route ascents, by the twentieth century's end. It is cool to climb, like practicing a zazen, and the Eastern flavor lends further mystique and status to the aspirant. In this recent variation on the theme of volcanoes affording self-transcendence, too often the subsequent boast eclipses the transcendence.

Ultimately, those two issues—giving voice to a volcano (apart from geology) and voicing one's relation to it—overlap more than not, as my survey has proven. People can't really speak about them apart from their experience, imaginative or otherwise, of them. The two issues presume an essentialist view of language and that which it defines. For example, Snyder's definition of the volcanoes, like the Rainier rhetoric since the late nineteenth century, seemingly derives from the mountains themselves. That is the governing illusion— Snyder borrows images from Tibetan Buddhism, after all. Ditto the illusory notion that the definition is not exportable to other volcanoes and regions. Rather, the language about the snowpeaks presumes their uniqueness. Those who write Rainier or any of its sisters do so in the conviction that their words, however imperfect, belong only to it. The assumption is that a singular relation exists between it and the language it attracts. Writers' incomplete or approximate language, however frequently imitated or copied, about them exists only in relation to them, not any other mountainscape. Northwesterners posit an essentialist view of their relationship to this highest landscape. The volcanoes provide a rich and diverse legacy, a prominent inheritance, and our language, whatever scholarly or journalistic or artistic mode, marks our dependency.

Within the past century a paradigm shift has occurred involving the outcomes of recreational tourism. The volcanoes have acquired new forms of prestige on a massive scale as people seem, in many guises, to rely on them more. This shifting sociology derives from the rise of status tourism, which can be defined as packaged experiences of faux-authenticity dependent upon commodification and perceived status.[26] It's all about buying your way into cool places, perhaps at some personal effort. When mountaineering trips serve as a vehicle to increase social status, the results have been dramatic on the volcanoes. Recreation and self-fulfillment have been core values there for a long time. Only in the past few generations have they grown indistinguishable from status, as though bragging rights exceed the older value of personal transformation on Rainier and its sisters.

Northwest volcanoes not only represent primary sites that enhance status. They make people feel better, and better about themselves. Their linguistic legacy feeds local identity wherein well-being easily and inevitably becomes privilege. After all, as many have remarked, more than a few Puget Sound residents claim a special affinity with their five volcanoes just as Willamette Valley residents do with their more numerous ones, deriving from their views both a personal relationship and a subsequent sense of entitlement. Those sightlines, from all compass points, account for the aura of smugness that has grown steadily recently, along with the population. Whether on I-5 or I-90, or flying in or out of SeaTac or Portland airports: to write Rainier is to write themselves, so regional thinking goes, and its legacy of superlative rhetoric spills over into self-definition. Taking the measure of the mountain means taking their own in some regards. In the process, more than a slight residue of complacency has accreted in local imagery and publications, promotional and otherwise. This complacency in turn beckons more masses to Rainier and the other volcanoes, and in some cases those masses leave a dirty imprint.

2 STANDARD ROUTES, STANDARD HIGHWAYS

> It is our Shangri-La. But it is also very much a landscape at risk
> from overuse, urban pollution and, in a way, from itself, given its
> fundamental volcanic activity.
>
> —David Nicandri, *Sunrise to Paradise:*
>   *The Story of Mount Rainier National Park*

The funnel illustrates the modern history of people at Northwest
volcanoes—themselves inverted funnels, with the throat inside
rather than extruding. In the past century, when most approach
or climb a volcano, they willingly gather at a few points, like a
narrow throat. This transportation pattern demands constriction,
not diaspora. Downhill skiing on Mount Hood or at Bachelor
Butte, as it's developed since World War II, poses the extreme case
of constriction: after all, skiers fan out from and converge upon
central lodges and parking lots. But visitor centers and standard
routes similarly exhibit the perils of pre-planned concentration.

   In the Northwest, national parks depend upon exceptional
mountains. The fifth and sixth national parks, Mount Rainier
(MRNP) and Crater Lake (CLNP), have demonstrated since their
founding the seminal role of volcanoes in regional identity. MRNP,
the final park created in the nineteenth century, was the first dedicated to a volcano. Its 1899 genesis confirmed Rainier's leading
role in the region's mental map. Washington's two subsequent national parks, each epitomizing differing generations and philoso-

phies of preservation, tourism, and management, exist because of mountains.

Oregon's only national park, Crater Lake, created three years after M R N P, commemorates the Northwest's largest volcano 7,700 years after its eruption and collapse. Geologists estimate Mount Mazama's explosion as forty-two times more powerful than Mount St. Helens' 1980 eruption, and approximately four times as much of Mount Mazama vaporized as St. Helens. When visitors sight Crater Lake's diameter from myriad vantages, and the rim of peaks enfolding it, they picture a volcano that dwarfs Rainier. A giant round glass atop Oregon's Cascades, a shocking shade of blue, Crater Lake overwhelms visitors with its size and depth. Whether walking or driving along the rim, imaginatively just inside its surface, visitors can reconstruct, in their mind's eye, the impossibly giant dome of Mount Mazama and its inconceivable blast.

The Northwest's first two national parks highlight the prominent role of our most exceptional mountains in the nation's visual iconography. The national affirmation of Northwest volcanoes at the turn of the twentieth century capped, in some respects, nineteenth-century United States' veneration of monumental landscapes in the American West: a tendency explained by an increasingly popular aesthetic of "big" landscape composition and rapidly accelerating (and shifting) habits of tourism.

With far more people living near, and playing on, Northwest volcanoes, potential eruptions obviously pose considerable human danger. Regional residents and visitors live with the knowledge of the fifty-seven dead from the 1980 Mount St. Helens explosion. Mount Rainier is officially rated as one of the country's most dangerous mountains since, according to hydrologist Carolyn Tiegen, over one hundred thousand people live on ground that reveals lahar (volcanic debris or mud flow) deposits.[1] Wy'East, Mount Hood's older, native name, implies, among other things, a resting spirit. Oregon's quintessential mountain icon, Mount Hood has the dubious distinction of being the second most climbed volcano on earth, the numbers approaching typical conditions on Japan's Fujisan in high season. More ski on it than climb it, and more again live in the path of historic debris flows to the west and north. Dormancy presumes its opposite, when geologic events and human chronologies meet. While risks can be minimized (e.g., far more stringent zoning ordinances and enforcement), ultimately humans have no control over geology; we stand a better chance of mitigating other problems stemming from accessibility and overuse.

Both Mounts Rainier and Hood represent bellwethers of change, particularly in the ongoing problem of crowd control—too many in the funnel's throat on select summer weekends, for instance. Visitors and residents alike are inevitably drawn to the volcanoes, causing a painful dilemma that captures the primary challenge of agencies such as the National Park Service and the Forest Service in the twenty-first century. Too many leave their imprint with a vehicle or boots—or trash. The span of the past century reveals changing patterns of degradation where they step. Historic and contemporary commitments to accessibility and increasing convenience explain the challenges of overuse as seen through the overlapping stories of auto travel, skiing, and climbing. How we get there, how we play there, and how we reach a summit all manifest that bourgeoning desire for contact and connection. These stories variously illustrate the baleful consequences of industrial-scale tourism.

Even such marketing decisions as book covers acknowledge the Northwest obsession with outdoor recreation: activities that descend from an earlier paradigm of activist (i.e., recreational) tourism. Books about the Northwest, particularly travel books, regularly feature a volcano on their cover as though it signifies the region. This sense of entitlement, of "*ownership* of nature's endowment," creates a series of problems, for example at particular sites on particular volcanoes.[2] Personal "mountain glory" becomes an issue when many seek it at the same time and place.

As nearby mirrors or blank slates where some regard them-selves and express their affinity, the volcanoes unsurprisingly reflect streams of organized publicity and promotional materials. At Mount Rainier, where thousands climb per season, almost all climb in the summer on the two standard routes: the vast majority on the Disappointment Cleaver-Ingraham Glacier route on the south side, and the rest, the Emmons-Winthrop Glacier on the northeast side. Yet other, more demanding routes (e.g., Liberty Ridge on the northwest side) have also seen far more parties in the past generation. Mount Hood has been represented as a volcano for the masses since July 19, 1894, when a crowd gathered on its summit with the express purpose of founding the Mazamas.[3]

On Hood, an average summer season sees ten thousand climbers, the vast majority chunking up the southern route above Crater Rock. But even the Cooper Spur route on the northeast side and the demanding west side routes see more traffic than a few decades ago. These volcanoes, like the others, reveal both a dispersal and concentration of climbers, the latter—standard routes—far exceeding the former.

These standard routes have come to resemble Mount Rainier's Longmire–Paradise or White River–Sunrise roads in their congestion. Like standard routes on other volcanoes, they imitate the congestion of Interstate 5 between Everett and Olympia, Washington, between Vancouver, Washington, and Tigard, Oregon, and above all, within Seattle and Portland city limits. By the late twentieth century, standard routes resembled not only their approach highways but also prized urban neighborhoods. They presented miniature versions of crowded metro scenes—and metro problems. There is a new thickness here that is even stranger because of glaciers and rock ridges.

Congestion in various guises partly explains the threat to Northwest volcanoes posed by urban pollution (see epigraph). Urban proximity means not only bad air but also new conceptual categories. The Everett-Olympia megalopolis adversely impacts Rainier, which rises just east of I-5 and the linked cities. Mount Hood is defined by juxtaposition to urban sprawl as approximately

FIG. 3. The famed photo of the Mazamas inaugural climb on Mount Hood via the Coopers Spur (northeast) route, July 19, 1894. The photo, unintentionally comic, reveals the traditional style of a group climb, with a single rope and plenty of alpenstocks. Inset photo is of W. G. Steel, first president of the Mazamas. Wikimedia Commons.

two million Oregonians, more than half the state's population, live within seventy-five miles to the west. Mount Hood National Forest's (MHNF) western boundary lies only twenty miles from Portland's eastern city limit, and in the early twenty-first century, it defines itself as an "urban national forest"—a recent designation in U.S. Forest Service history. "Urban national forest" poses an oxymoronic challenge and inevitably means, among many implications, auto congestion and pollution—a baleful legacy of city proximity. An "urban national forest" defines itself according to a nearby city or cities: a high population density living next door. Cities creep to the woods. Clearly this changes the historical identity of national forests—originally conceived as domains distinctly apart and away from population centers (e.g., Gila National Forest, New Mexico)—and demands new lenses and a different set of management protocols.

Because they reference us in so many ways, people want to arrive near volcanoes quickly. In Washington, private vehicles have carried increasing thousands to Mount Rainier for a century or more. Compared to Mount Adams and Mount Baker, Rainier is far more roaded, at least two highways crossing its southern and eastern skirts. Only Mount St. Helens, since its national monument status, also draws visitors to the west, south, and northeast via paved roads. From its beginnings, Mount Rainier National Park was designed with cars in mind, as several studies have documented. It's all about getting to the mountain, and the quicker, the better. Visitors expected a quick trip then and still do today.[4] Sometimes, though, the quick trip has slowed due to congestion on two-lane mountain highways.

With Mount Hood, traffic flow has always been part of the modern white story below its southern flanks, and the Barlow Road Historic District (within Mount Hood National Forest) preserves the extant, westernmost pieces of the old Oregon Trail. Zigzag, a hamlet west of Barlow Pass and a ranger district within MHNF, commemorates a particularly steep section of the trail: it connotes industrial-scale transportation, not a Native path. Portions of U.S. 26 and Oregon State Highway 35 were built along the trail route. Oregon's best-known volcano, beacon of the Columbia River Gorge, dramatically ushered in the final miles of the Oregon Trail, and had thus been a palpable part of the United States' great western migration more than a century and a half ago. Only Mount Hood's north side (i.e., upper Hood River drainage) lacks a highway; Oregon's many other volcanoes are less roaded, though several highway passes (Santiam, McKenzie, and Willamette, as well as the pass just south of Mount McLoughlin) exponentially increased their accessibility.

The published narratives of pioneering climbers in *Atlantic Monthly* and *Overland Quarterly* sold Mount Rainier to national audiences who, a generation later, would crowd to it. John Muir's climb included the first photographer, Arthur C. Warner, whose camera, plates, and tripod weighed over fifty pounds and whose images complemented the rhapsodies of Muir (*Pacific Monthly*) and his fellow proselytizers. Similar narratives were published extolling Mount Hood. Come to Paradise, Timberline, or beyond! With both volcanoes, the majority of early climbs championed a central, southern route that, for reasons of weather and ease, became the standard routes. Road development tied into these routes so that most visitors (whether climbers on not) were funneled to a pair of locations. Different sections of the funnel reinforced one another. By the twentieth century's first decade, large, expeditionary climbs sponsored by the Mazamas or Mountaineers required elaborate infrastructure including transportation, as their histories document.[5] Gone were the days of long rides on horseback, negotiating forest and river canyons.

Particularly since the 1950s mountaineering on both volcanoes dispersed itself over a variety of routes of increasing technical difficulty. But most climbers converged on these standard routes—that narrow throat—because they afforded, and still afford, the best chance of summiting. Standard routes match novices with the easiest way up. It's simple addition. The match-up enhances the likelihood of bragging rights, and from the beginning the achievement of summiting proved a significant lure and rationale. It remains one of the most potent versions of status tourism: there's nothing like pointing to a distant Northwest snowpeak, or gazing upon its online images, and telling others, "I've climbed it." Altitude feeds attitude, in the Northwest and elsewhere.

Yet the early work of public relations revealed contrary agendas. With Rainier the boosterism eclipsed cautionary notes or alarms about landscape degradation. Almost all early climbers and promoters represented unabashed, full-throttle developers whose volcano gospel solicited mass visitation. That 1876 essay boasting Washington's mountains (see epigraph, Chapter 1) closes by predicting Rainier as a place for resort development: "When the locomotive is heard in that region someday, when American enterprise has established an ice-cream saloon at the foot of the glacier, and sherry-cobblers may be had at twenty-five cents half-way up to the top of the mountain, attempts to ascend that magnificent snowpeak will be quite frequent."[6]

From the beginning access engendered amenities. The dessert fantasy illustrates standard, late nineteenth-century American travel expectations reflected in the Northern Pacific Railroad *Wonderland* guide series, which targeted leisure visitors, not necessarily more active recreationists. That 1876 booster-climber was right about the railroads but wrong about sweet amenities being an inducement for climbers. His prediction signifies a narrow recreational, commercial reduction ("American enterprise") of Winthrop's "American Idea." In this reduction, coming to the volcano requires desirable goods and services, not necessarily new experiences. About sixty years passed after August Kautz's 1857 summit attempt before the Longmire–Paradise road became a reality and lured autotourists. Ironically, for a brief period an ice cream stand squatted at the base of Nisqually Glacier: ice upon ice. Build a stand and they will buy and slurp. But big groups already traveled to Rainier, Baker, Hood, and other volcanoes, thanks to the pioneering mountaineering clubs, the Mazamas and the Mountaineers.

Subsequent trailblazers also made prescient claims about development at Rainier. The first woman to climb Rainier linked contrary values: its private transformative potential and tourist potential for the new state of Washington. The latter—her painterly sketch with conifers as frame—would become a Northwest visual icon, an aesthetic amenity. Her particular advocacy remains as valid now as when first published: "It is a beautiful ride through the wilderness, alone with nature and her wonders, with scarcely a sound to break the silence. Great tall trees line the winding trail, so tall you can not look up to the tops, so straight they seem like pillars of an ancient building, and this trail the aisle through which one passes to admire. It is then one can realize the resources of this state and dream of its future preeminence."[7] This Chamber of Commerce copy, Northwest boilerplate that fueled regional chauvinism, links visionary potential (e.g., Winthrop) with tourism broadside. The tensions between those agendas foreshadow common dilemmas observable on standard routes and elsewhere. The promised rebirth preached by early climbers turns problematic in the presence of crowds.

The quiet solitude of this sketch could only be imagined by visitors a generation after 1890, the crowds already descending on the volcano. But the description of west slope forest, old growth or not, quickly became a fundamental aesthetic criterion governing Northwest road design and management, one that has changed little since. The metaphor of the forest cathedral, a nineteenth-century romantic cliché, retains much currency in the popular imagination—and among many road designers. Celebrated in painting and poetry (e.g., William Cullen Bryant's "Thanatopsis," 1816) for generations, the cathedral as track or roadbed arched with conifers became a west slope commonplace, almost a birthright. Riding towards the volcanoes or the ocean, I remember so many conifer arches casting damp shade, a thin slice of sky overhead.

The green curtain illusion retains great power, as though motorists straddle winding Native American paths through undisturbed ranks of forest, far removed from their usual domains. By the twentieth century's third decade, most visitors experienced the tree tunnel from car seats. The tree tunnel remains arguably the primary design and outcome on many secondary highways—no matter the clear-cuts one hundred yards or less behind the screen, particularly near the coast: a deliberate visual deception. Motorists crave the temporary shelter and sanctity of a wooded tunnel. As the century wore on, in many locales these tunnels comforted motorists even as they hid logged tracts just beyond sight.

In the late nineteenth and early twentieth centuries, the gospel of development held sway, as volcano publicists drew virtually no distinctions between the notion of set-aside land or park and full-service resort. It's all about amenities, however modest or "inadequate." The prevalent mind-set favored access and infrastructure as though these arctic islands resembled coastlines or lake (or river) shores. Another booster-climber preached the same gospel for Rainier: "Some day in the near future, when a good road has been made in Paradise valley, it will become one of the greatest summer resorts on the coast. All the natural resources for such a resort are there now, and it would not require any great amount of capital to develop them."[8]

Part of the drama of MRNP management in its first decades centered on a changing and increasingly restricted definition of the word "resort." All Paradise needed was "capital," and capital arrived seventeen years after MRNP's founding with the formation in 1916 of the Rainier National Park Company (RNPC), the park's central concessionaire. That same year, which also saw the creation of the National Park Service (NPS), work on the first Paradise Inn began, and the inn opened for business the following year. John Muir's "lower gardens of Eden" quickly filled with people pursuing a variety of activities—some ridiculously inappropriate by twenty-first century standards and some, trashing the place: for a few years in the early Depression, golfers teed off at Paradise; a generation earlier, campers hacked away at live shrubs and trees for their campfire wood.[9]

In this era, the market for national parks would be sustained through corporate backing controlled by the NPS. The legendary first director of the NPS, Stephen T. Mather, brilliantly sold both the current parks and an expanded NPS to an increasingly mobile public. Handsome, wealthy, generous, and unstable, Mather was a marketing genius who genuinely believed conservation and endless promotion go hand in hand. Mather brought the masses, increasingly in hired or personal "motors," to the parks, and he envisioned the growth of the parks occurring through careful collaboration with private enterprise. His collaboration with his young assistant, Horace Albright, anchored the NPS in its initial decades and manifested itself through their frequent motor tours of current or potential western national parks, including the Northwest.

Development of Mount Rainier National Park and the rapid growth of Rainier National Park Company go hand-in-hand as though the Park is a priori linked with a range of accommodations. Most could not imagine the park apart from amenities and services. They brought clear expectations of convenience if not comfort (and ice cream) with them. Accommodations depended on increasingly quick and easy access. Once the volcano became the center of a national park, an elaborate infrastructure insured endless employment for a host of civil engineers. The same story played out at the collapsed volcano and deep lake in Oregon.

From the beginning, mass transit—railroads, then roads— developed according to access to Paradise and the climb beyond it, and again, this example served as prototype of most volcano trailheads and standard routes. The first Paradise tent camp, the poetically named Camp of the Clouds (1896), a gritty tent city surrounded by stumps, belied its airy, even angelic promise. Soon enough it gave way to increasing creature comforts, as visitors inevitably wanted more than old canvas tent walls. From the mid-

1880s, the Northern Pacific Railroad offered excursions to Wilkeson on its branch line, then horseback travel to what became MRNP's northwest corner (Carbon Glacier and nearby alpine parks like Spray Park). After 1904, the Tacoma Eastern Railroad, a local line merged into the Milwaukee system in 1918, hauled thousands of visitors to Ashford, only six miles from MRNP's main (Nisqually) entrance.[10]

The latter route proved more popular than the Northern Pacific's Wilkeson run because of Paradise's draw and climbing route. The Mountaineers and interested others took the Tacoma Eastern (the "National Park Limited"). And by the 1920s, the heyday of the Tacoma Eastern, auto tourism eclipsed railroads as the preferred mode of tourism. Visitors like my grandparents wanted to reach Rainier's base according to their own schedule and whim, and the sooner, the better. Tourism shifted from railroad to private schedules.

Road traffic and MRNP share a long history, one that links the quotidian with the exotic. Significantly, cars entered MRNP in 1907–8, before any other national park. By 1908 motorists chugging up the Longmire–Paradise road (not completed until 1915) reached, with a short walk, the terminus of Nisqually Glacier. Rainier's twenty-six glaciers proved a primary attraction in MRNP's initial decades.[11] The fact that it is the most glaciated mountain in the country outside Alaska only whetted the appetite to *see* some "rivers of ice": a monumental novelty, further proof of the United States' landscape heritage. Nowhere else could motorists drive to a glacier's terminus. That fact captures, in miniature, a primary paradox in western American travel and further illustrates this parable of constriction: one can reach the spectacular—a frozen arm of poet Marianne Moore's icy octopus—from sea level passively, with little or no physical effort.

Auto tourism grew up alongside the National Park Service, as private vehicles remain the central mode and reference of most visitors' experience. Auto tourism reenacts the late nineteenth-century mode of heritage or reverential tourism—with a difference. The paradox of auto tourism brings the natural world close up but it remains, figuratively if not literally, beyond the windshield: closer but still removed, beyond the footlights.[12] This rich paradox presumes that windows bring the outside world, particularly as framed by landscape aesthetics, into our eyes and imaginations rather than create a permeable barrier which seals off and distances the outside. The illusion deludes motorists given the inescapable fact that we often remain seated, passive, and virtual: spectators at least one remove from sensory participation in the mountain scenery. The outside is magnified yet we remain within a theater of glass walls, bodily detached. We love to sit, especially behind or above an engine. The paradox notwithstanding, for a century private vehicles have dictated the meaning and shape of access within both national parks and national forests.

Windshield volcanoes foreground themselves because of road design, wherein approach highways figure as part of their drama. Within MRNP's early history, the design and construction of Eugene Ricksecker's Longmire–Paradise highway rendered it a model "scenic narrative." Ricksecker, the Tacoma-based assistant engineer, mapped the roadbed as though it were a natural feature, part of the ridges and canyons southwest of the alpine parks of Paradise, a dark glacier with hairpin turns. Such road designers, here and on other volcanoes, regarded their designs as part and parcel of the volcano's symbolic heritage.[13] This design philosophy extended even as it distorted the nineteenth-century gospel of mountain sublime, as though paved roads and vehicles represented transitory appendages of a volcano's rich meanings. This core tenet of NPS road aesthetics enhanced the illusion of car approaches being extensions of Rainier itself, like its radiating glaciers and ridges. Seated and stationary, motorists bring some diminished version of the mountain's meanings inside their windshields.

If mountain roads are storied, part of the story presumably passes from the mountainscape to those who approach or recede.

By the summer of 1915, motorists could not only drive to Rainier's south side, but to Yellowstone geysers and over Tioga Pass in Yosemite National Park. Approach roads carry some of the meaning of spectacular national parks and peaks. Washington Highway 504, the main (westside) approach to Mount St. Helens, was designed, particularly in its remodel after the 1980 eruption, very much as a scenic narrative which climaxes with Coldwater Ridge and Johnston Ridge just beyond. As motorists approach these ridges, the horseshoe-shaped volcano with the opening to the north progressively discloses itself like a stage curtain slowly widening.

For a few, roads weren't necessary. In a stunt symbolic of the twentieth-century love affair with tires—a new claim to possession—a motorcyclist in 1925 followed the preferred climbers' track to the 9500-foot level on Mount Hood.[14] Why not ride to the top, as motorists would later do on Colorado's Mount Evans and Pikes Peak? Let the motor do the work, according to this clamorous mind-set.

While volcanoes don't lend themselves to amenities development, some locations at their bases do, and cars bested trains for access. In the early twentieth century, Mounts Baker, St. Helens, and Hood had become destination resorts, as had the Cascades Lakes south of South Sister, Diamond Lake below Mount Thielsen, and Crater Lake. Road access to Mount Hood had developed earlier than any other volcano; for west slope folks, visiting it meant retracing in reverse direction the final miles of the Oregon Trail, the nation's most famous nineteenth-century westward migration route. Tiny communities around Mount Hood had seen extensive commercial developments before the Cascade Forest Preserve was dedicated in 1907, absorbed into the Oregon National Forest in 1908, and renamed Mount Hood National Forest in 1924. At least three lodges were built along Mount St. Helens' Spirit Lake in the two decades after 1913.[15] Crater Lake Lodge opened in 1915 (and the improved CLNP company hotel, in 1928), and the rim drive—another scenic narrative displaying its sundry facets as a continuous story—was finished in 1918.[16] The most famous mountain lodge in the region, Mount Hood's Timberline Lodge—built by U.S. Forest Service, Works Progress Administration (wpa), and Civilian Conservation Corps (ccc) crews—opened in 1937, long after the roadbed of U.S. 26 had been regraded. Timberline, at the base of Mount Hood's standard, south climb route, reveals the same concentration of climbers because of similar chances of summit success as at Paradise.

During initial surges in development many local constituencies, desiring both national recognition and amenities infrastructure, tried but failed to persuade the nascent National Park Service to elevate "their" volcano into a national park. The failure of the nps to name other volcano national parks in the 1910s through 1930s illustrates the role of chance as well as the prior claims of various commercial interests. In retrospect it looks like a crapshoot, one in which most of the snowpeaks lost. After the precedents of Rainier and Crater Lake, local lobbies bombarded the nps and the competition, along with initial lodges or villages or ski hills, doomed the cause. For example, local interests lobbied hard for a national park centering on Mount Hood after 1911.

During their busy summer in 1915 nps director Stephen Mather and second-in-command Horace Albright were besieged by Northwest promoters. Albright, a bright young Berkeley lawyer recruited by Mather and like him a vigorous outdoors enthusiast, participated in many "field studies" trips by train, car, horseback, and foot. The Mather-Albright pair grew extremely close, an uncle-nephew relationship confirmed on these trips. As Albright chronicled in old age, "*Many people from Seattle to Portland were urging us to make national parks out of every volcanic mountain from Mount Baker to the California border. Mather and I agreed we couldn't make every peak a park and didn't have time to inspect them. We already had Mount Lassen, which had been erupting and was quite the sensation. It had been a national monument and in 1916 was upgraded to a national park.*"[17] The chronic eruption of Mount

Lassen (southernmost of the Cascade volcanoes) in 1915 coincided with the initial proliferation of the NPS, which ensured its preservation. The "accidental" publicity of eruption placed Lassen in the company of Mounts Mazama and Rainier.

By contrast, the other Cascades volcanoes, dormant, failed to make the grade because of supposed aesthetic inadequacy, commercial (e.g., mining) claims, cost, or, for Mather, redundancy. Recalling the summer of 1918 and an onslaught of lobbying, Horace Albright stated, "We declined to consider . . . Mount Hood, Mount Baker, Mount Shasta . . . and many other beautiful areas because they did not measure up to what we regarded as national park standards or had too much commercial development or too many inholdings, or because the cost was prohibitive considering what the Congress would give us."[18] According to Northwest mountains historian Harvey Manning, the biggest volcano and biggest crater were enough for Mather and Albright in 1923 and subsequently.[19]

Therefore if the NPS included two Northwest volcanoes it had enough. Given subsequent NPS growth, those early verdicts are lamentable. If park status meant preservation, the other volcanoes lost out in the short term. Commercial developments and inholdings precluded Mount Hood, for example, as several lodges dotted its flanks by the 1910s. Though the powerful preservationist Harold Ickes, Franklin Roosevelt's secretary of the interior, promoted park status for Mount Hood in the 1930s as well as an "Ice Peaks National Park" proposal centered on several Northwest volcanoes, World War II fiscal priorities killed the effort.[20] The USFS attempted some other modes of preservation at the snowpeaks, but their efforts couldn't match a national park designation.

Whether in a national park or not, volcanoes lured motorists, and that meant convergence at the end of steep, curving roads. As at Mount Hood, the first generation of CLNP history illustrates the validity, if not a priori necessity, of the funnel design at Crater Lake. In its initial decades few visited for a variety of reasons, including rutted roads and primitive accommodations. According to

Horace M. Albright, CLNP "was in terrible shape, and something drastic had to be done,"[21] and in that same summer of 1915, the underfunded CLNP was on his and Mather's itinerary. The approach from Klamath Falls proved as primitive a road as these two had bumped over, and they'd traversed a lot of country. Mather and Albright, with CLNP Supervisor William G. Steel and two others, spent two August days traveling Crater Lake's perimeter, planning in detail the rim drive as a scenic narrative with the usual tourist infrastructure: pullouts, trails, accommodations. The rim drive (today's Route 7), which would take the entire Depression decade to build, concentrated visitors on and along the road tracing the circumference of the Northwest's largest volcano. When the Mather and Albright party departed Crater Lake, the longer road from the lake to Medford proved worse than the Klamath Falls road. Mather, known for his verbosity, found the road too much of a challenge to conversation: "He just held onto his hat with one hand and a handkerchief over his face to ward off the dust with the other."[22] Subsequent publicity sped up the rebuilding of Oregon State Highway 62, among other routes. Visitors were funneled to the lake via two access roads and the "village" near its southwest shore, and then followed its rim drive.

Roads both satisfy and inflame demand for quick access. The auto demand on Paradise—almost 250,000 vehicles per year by the late 1920s—spelled the end of the railroad by the early 1930s, and visitors to the park have never looked back.[23] The White River–Sunrise road, finished in 1931, and the Stevens Canyon Road, finished in 1952, extended the park's commitment to democratic access through further scenic narratives, though they failed to relieve the crowd pressure on Paradise. One state highway accesses Mount Baker, rising from northwest to northeast; St. Helens (before 1980) was accessible via one paved highway along the Toutle River, on the west side. Because of its straightforward standard climbing route (one considerably easier than Rainier's), Mount Adams also became subject to mass climbs in the early twentieth century. The

USFS built a dirt-gravel road and large parking lot and trailhead for those accessing its standard climbing route. Glacier Peak, like Oregon's Mount Jefferson a so-called "wilderness volcano," has always required a long trail approach. Visitors, including climbers, didn't want long approaches.

The blend of big landscape composition and mountain auto tourism—with the latter's reliance upon the funnel design and scenic narratives—is perfectly evidenced in novelist Thomas Wolfe's *Western Journal: A Daily Log of the Great Parks Trip* (1938; 1951), the final, hasty production of his short life. His journey began with CLNP on June 20, 1938 and ended with MRNP on July 2, 1938, with Wolfe sprawling his tall frame across the back seat of the capacious coupe and his two companions (newspapermen) doing all the driving. The two Northwest volcano Parks thus frame this archetypal, fast journey by car of monumental western landscapes.

The bond between the volcanoes and paradisal imagery of Oregon—part of the national imaginary since the mid-nineteenth century, if not earlier—does not change over time. Claiming "unapproachable the great line of the Cascades with their snow-spired sentinels Hood, Adams, Jefferson, 3 sisters, etc.," Wolfe rhapsodizes, approaching Crater Lake, "the virgin land of Canaan all again—the far-off ranges—infinite—Oregon and the Promised Land."[24] For a visitor in the late 1930s, paved roads were part of scenic grandeur, "the great line" and its conventionally biblical idealized application. Such motorists approached quickly but passively.

In the transportation story, access raises the bar and boosts expectations. Access changed the scale of visitation and provided the infrastructure for industrial tourism at the snowpeaks.

Particularly since the World War II period, speed and convenience became the touchstone. After all, the baby boomers famously took to the roads and the western parks en masse with their parents, and didn't mind being jostled too much as long as they reached the mountains according to plan. When added to the core value of volcanoes—conversion, self-realization, status—quick access drives the changing human footprint on and around them. Contrary to earlier indigenous attitudes, recent visitors assume access to be an inalienable right. And we want it quick.

In the postwar boom period, the National Park Service's Mission 66 program formalized the typical visitor's brief experience as a day trip with quick planned stops marked by pullovers, signage, a visitor center, and other amenities. The auto-based plan codified, in some respects, Mount Rainier's meanings for visitors from mid-century through the present. For the baby boomer generation, overlook plaques and informational kiosks providing a little history, geography, or geology with visuals became the tangible signs of Rainier's story. Pullouts with chosen vistas packaged and conflated educational and aesthetic occasions, and proved the durability of nineteenth-century "heritage" tourism. What tourists behold forms part of national if not personal identity.

Even more baby boomers took to the hills in station wagons rather than with boots. Visitors drove when and as they wished, their numbers increasing in proportion to the regional in-migration of the twentieth century's closing decades. By the 1960s in MRNP, parking was a serious problem at both Paradise and Sunrise, and planning efforts to disperse traffic to lower elevations met with little success. Folks wanted to get higher, reach the end of the road, and a 1960 photograph of Sunrise shows a jammed parking loop, station wagons positioned at various angles. In 1967, 479,525 vehicles entered MRNP carrying 1,805,863 visitors. The cumulative result made Paradise, or Mount Hood's Government Camp, sometimes resemble a suburban mall. Traffic issues have only grown worse in succeeding decades. A scant generation later, with thousands on Mount Adams's standard, South Climb route, Gifford Pinchot National Forest Roads 8040 and 500 winding past Morrison Creek and Cold Springs campgrounds to the trailhead resembled a long thin parking lot, vehicles snaked at odd angles off the mountain road. The congestion imitated an urban intersection with traffic backed up for blocks, clear passage proving a challenge.

Of course, it's not just auto traffic that's paved Paradise and created a series of problems including parking. Concentration and carelessness have beaten up the scenery. Early twentieth-century damage from loosely regulated camping at Paradise grew, by the century's final decade, to include battered meadows showing shortcuts and ruts, and scars elsewhere from other past uses. The damage illustrates a story of unchecked access, insufficient preservation, and perhaps incompatible uses. A welter of mitigation and restoration activities has been underway there for a generation or more.

This array of impacts occurred once the hikers, campers, skiers, day-trippers, and climbers reached the volcanoes in vehicles. A long *Seattle Times* story titled "Anything But Lonely At The Top," (August 7, 1994) scrutinized the cumulative impact of cars in MRNP, a legacy of the midcentury driving tour paradigm. The title unwittingly describes the wide summit scene as well: both road's end and climb's end reveal crowds. The byline and inside title don't mince words: "We're Wearing Out Our Welcome at Mount Rainier" and "Backup on the Road to Paradise." In the 1980s alone the number of cars increased drastically, with fewer in each car and those folks less likely to leave their vehicles for any length. The pattern continues in the Mount Hood National Forest in the early twenty-first century, as its Strategic Stewardship Plan (2006) reveals a tendency toward day use by urban visitors: "The average length of stay measured in 2003 was 6.7 hours."[25] MHNF wilderness areas are used similarly to urban or state parks in the three-county, metro-Portland region.

This disturbing trend of quick thick visitation exacerbated an attitude present since the late nineteenth century: the tendency to treat these notable peaks as extensions of urban space. The data also suggest an increased embrace of cars' enforced passivity as well as the changed meaning of a visit. Both imply a greater disconnect from sustained, palpable outdoor experience, though the legions of hikers, backpackers, and climbers attest to the contrary. It's not just that people get there fast, but most look around and depart

FIG. 4. Part of the parking area at Paradise—"paved Paradise." Mount Rainier National Park's most crowded location. National Park Service, U.S. Department of the Interior.

soon. Two end-of-century realities at MRNP include increasing entrance fees and full parking lots, notably on summer weekends. But raising entrance fees every year or three contradicts the NPS commitment to open access. Crowd containment costs money, and personnel costs to keep the roads and facilities open and clean grow, though budgets do not.

In the past generation the notion of "carrying capacity" has received increasing scrutiny as a management tool, and national park researchers have extensively studied its validity for plant and animal systems as well as human visitors. But carrying capacity is problematic, in part because it's a shifting target. Given the crowds at places like Paradise or Timberline, some argue for a return to public transportation systems, claiming considerable public sentiment in favor. Such systems are popular in Glacier and Rocky Mountain National Parks, for example, though they garner some criticism at the latter according to research surveys. Any calculation of optimal vehicle loads and distributions within MRNP or MHNF with its ski hills is extremely difficult because of the number of variables, and because "optimal" might be a sliding scale over decades. While the idea of fixed limits, in cars or on trails, seems the best solution, it flies in the face of the American commitment to unrestricted access. Recreationists resist rationing.

The old Tacoma Eastern Railroad track has been extolled as "an heirloom," "a dedicated corridor with its own perspectives on Rainier and its own rich history."[26] This track forms another example of what the NPS calls "cultural history," an earlier mode of mountain tourism worthy of preservation as another resource. A master scenic narrative, it runs from Tacoma to Ashford, the town closest to the MRNP's primary, southwestern entrance. Some would like this railroad to run again after almost a century of silence since Tacoma Eastern veterans have testified that "it is *the* best way to approach the Mountain."[27] Enthusiasts advocate its gradual, unfolding approach that depends upon the slow time of a century ago. Whatever its attractions (above and beyond nostalgia), it seems a hard sell in a world marked by instant and immediate. Also, MRNP planners must devise and implement comparable mass transit for visitors inside the Park, perhaps something comparable to Glacier National Park's famous fleet of open-top "Red Jammer" buses, according to park websites "the oldest touring fleet of vehicles in the world." The thirty-three 1936–'39 vintage Red Jammers haul sixty thousand tourists per season. This new-old Tacoma Eastern Railroad proposal faces challenges, though, including overcoming the modern paradigm of personal convenience, which has reconfigured the meaning of access.

While Northwest volcanoes remain highly sought destinations, with notable exceptions their status as destination resorts has diminished by the late twentieth century. Mount Rainier National Park is a test case in contrary agendas, and review of its twentieth-century management philosophy discloses an initial expansion and subsequent contraction of that tourist definition.

Asahel Curtis, famed Northwest photographer, embodied as much as anyone the development credo, to the point where he eventually parted ways with several organizations he had played central roles in (e.g., the Mountaineers) because they did not advocate his full-speed-ahead infrastructure agenda. Younger brother of the nationally known photographer, Edward Curtis (from whom he was estranged), Curtis wanted paved roads in all four of MRNP's quadrants, for instance, and in retrospect his simultaneous preservationism and expansionism appear untenable. He wanted Rainier for personal transcendence and Rainier for big tourism, and saw no contradiction between these. Emergent MRNP philosophy, defining the volcano and park as an "artifact of culture" or treasure (like the Tacoma Eastern Railroad, more recently), increasingly checked the commercial view (e.g., Rainier National Park Company) of the Park as a commodity bank.[28] Descendants of these contrary views define contemporary tensions and behaviors at other volcanoes. Though the former paradigm prevails for the most part, new versions of commodification have emerged.

Sometimes desires conflict in the convergence zones. Mount Rainier remains largely a day-use park, one conducive to one-stop visitor centers, picnics, and quick nature walks. One segment of the public demands more amenities; another demands more wilderness and traffic control. The fact that these segments are often the same only reveals a governing paradox in MRNP management history. As though we're descendants of Curtis, we want "virginal" nature and creature comforts, untrampled alpine meadows and lattes and, always, quick access—like convenience stores. In the bottleneck we naïvely want it both ways.

Mount Rainier National Park also exemplifies changing modes of recreational tourism at Northwest volcanoes, since they're primary sites for sustained physical exercise in varying forms. The earlier leisure resort paradigm sponsored some activities and infrastructure plans incompatible with volcanoes. Dog sledding proved a short-lived novelty in the 1920s, as did a nine-hole golf course a few years later; in the early Depression years, not enough affluent golfers drove to Paradise with their clubs. Plans for a tramway were rolled out in the 1920s and again in the late 1940s but none was built. Nor any chairlift, though in the years before and after World

War II, public interest pressured park officials to build one above Paradise. NPS officials also faced considerable political pressure from Washington State business interests and Senators Warren Magnuson and Henry Jackson to construct a high-rise hotel in the early 1960s, but they held firm against it.[29] But concessionaire business was so good at Paradise that park management failed to disperse tourists elsewhere. Folks wanted the end of the road, the higher elevations.

Clearly, some of those activities or plans typify cities rather than volcanoes, and in retrospect they appear stunningly naïve, not unlike Asahel Curtis's plan for a highway across the northern tier of the park, from the Carbon River Road to what became the Sunrise Highway above the White River canyon.

How we reach the volcanoes influences how we play near or on them, and hardtop roads and mass-produced autos exponentially increased the possibilities and the illusion that volcanoes extend urban or town recreational space. The chairlift controversy at MRNP's Paradise in the 1940s evidenced the surging popularity of downhill skiing, a new sport that concentrated people far more than hiking or climbing. By the 1930s at least three volcanoes attracted new masses equipped with long boards and poles. "Being on the slopes" came to mean something distinct and prized. Mount Rainier became, along with Mounts Baker and Hood, the birthplace of Northwest downhill skiing.

Local businesses unsurprisingly capitalized on the new sport: the activity, product lines, and advertising unfolded symbiotically. In MRNP's first three decades, visitors had snowshoed and cross-country skied into the park in increasing numbers, and the first ski jumping tournament took place in 1917. Outing clubs (e.g., the Mountaineers or Seattle's Rainier enthusiasts known as SOYPs or "Socks Outside Your Pants" in the 1920s) promoted skiing, as did Seattle-area businesses like Eddie Bauer, K2 Skis, and Frederick & Nelson, which made and sold ski clothing and equipment.[30] Once Americans took to downhill skiing, Paradise, Timberline and the other Hood hills, and Mount Baker quickly turned into winter meccas. Seattle and Portland manufacturers and clubs eagerly supported a new sport that quickly caught on.

During the bottom of the Depression the new snow sport, like horse racetracks and screwball comedy pictures, provided new excitement and relief from the pressures of daily life. In April 1934, the first of the annual Silver Skis races—a downhill race from Camp Muir to Paradise, and just short of a vertical mile—took place above Paradise, and this event continued through 1941 (excepting 1937), publicized, some years, by the *Seattle Post-Intelligencer* and C B S Live Coverage. Late that year, the National Ski Association approved using part of the Silver Skis course for national slalom and downhill races the following spring. The course dropped from Camp Muir to a finish line near the Paradise Inn. Because this event served as Olympic ski team trials, it drew thousands of visitors—and potential new skiers. The National Ski Association's interest and sponsorship inevitably boosted skiing's glamour. Within four winters, Paradise proved the hottest spot in the region for skiing.[31]

The region's leading pair of volcanoes reveal opposed responses to the sport of skiing. Speed of access, it turns out, anticipates the happy speed of skiing. Ski resorts usually recapitulate the funnel design, with hill traffic—whatever the fan of runs and terrain—converging at the bases of chairlifts, themselves nearby the central lodge and parking lots beyond. Downhill skiing represents a high-density use of restricted terrain, and with its six resorts, Mount Hood is the region's most skied volcano. At Mount Rainier downhill skiing surged in popularity until the winter of Pearl Harbor. By then N P S philosophy nixed further infrastructure supporting the sport, since this institutionalized sport created crowds committed to their sport rather than the terrain beyond the area boundaries. In some cases skiers headed north to Mount Baker's ski hill, on its northeast side, where snowfalls were (and remain) legendary.

Before and after World War II, skiers flocking to Mount Hood had a choice of slopes. On its southwest side the Multorpor ski area's first facilities opened in 1928, merging with Ski Bowl in 1964. On the north side, the Cooper Spur ski area opened in 1949: a "Jump Hill" had been built by 1938. On the east side, Mount Hood Meadows, which grew to become Oregon's second largest ski resort, opened in 1966, its phases of expansion marked by continual controversy with conservationist groups and the MHNF.[32] And at Timberline, Northwest downhill skiing pioneer Otto Lang—handsome young Austrian-American whose example captured the European glamour of the new sport—founded a ski school in 1938, just two years after doing so at Paradise.[33]

Mount Hood displays, as no other volcano, antithetical traditions of low-density and high-density uses. Symbol of Mount Hood skiing, Timberline's Palmer chairlift, extended to the 8500-foot level in 1978 and rebuilt in 1996, is the most conspicuous, and highest, chairlift on the flanks of a Northwest volcano. The chairlift ends near the standard, south climb route and by the mid-1990s, conflicts between the skiers and climbers resulted in the standard route moving to the east of the groomed ski runs above Silcox Hut. In the twenty-first century's first decade, almost two million people visited Timberline annually for skiing, dining, and sightseeing; approximately 154 thousand drove to Ski Bowl, Summit, and Cooper Spur ski areas; and over double that number patronized Mount Hood Meadows.[34] Almost half a million annual participants demonstrates that skiing is far and away the most popular activity on Oregon's most popular mountain: an activity showing, at times, an urban density within an "arctic island" otherwise remote, sparsely populated, and set aside. In the past generation, Hood has also been a key site in the fast growth of snowboarding. Particularly during winter season, a few slices of Hood reveal traffic patterns similar to that of Portland's Pearl District, or downtown Eugene.

At Mount Hood, however, lower-density is relative. Mount

Hood's standard climbing routes are less daunting than Rainier's (e.g., much less elevation gain), and for a variety of reasons it has been climbed en masse longer than Rainier. But for decades, Hood's standard, southern route, with a bottleneck near the summit, has been subject to a range of traffic problems, given the volume of climbers ascending and descending. The picture sometimes resembles the Timberline ski runs below: evidence of the twentieth-century story of regional mountaineering, which echoed the rush of skiing.

Better roads and faster cars led to fast skiing and far more climbing. The downhill skiing scene in its first generation foreshadowed the surging popularity of climbing soon thereafter. During the Depression, while Civilian Conservation Corps crews built much of MRNP's infrastructure, a faction of the Mountaineers—initially a minority group, made up of younger, talented climbers who chaffed at social protocols—began to assume control of the Mountaineers' programming and philosophy (prominent among this group was Lloyd Anderson, who founded REI in 1938), and what is sometimes called the Northwest school of mountaineering was born. Climbers sought European equipment, new challenges (such as new routes), and much smaller climbing parties of two to four people.

In the following generation, more and more graduates of the Mountaineers' climbing course took to the other volcanoes and nearby non-volcanic peaks. More climbers from elsewhere flocked to the Cascades and Olympics. The Mazamas' climbing course, begun later, grew similarly. Climbing the Mountaineers' "Six Peaks," (the five volcanoes plus Mount Olympus), once a status badge within the club, became only a prerequisite, a list to surpass as soon as possible. Common routes saw more traffic.

Of all user groups, climbers (whether Mountaineers or not) take on the biggest, most physical challenge at the volcanoes. Summiting numerous peaks embodies the status tourism that became primary as the mass sport evolved.

The acceleration of mountaineering's popularity, in the Northwest and elsewhere, goes hand-in-hand with the story of shifting technologies and ever-improving equipment: lighter, stronger, safer, just like local ski manufacturing. And in the oldest advertising parable, newer means better; older is suspect at best. The complexion of climbing shifted as the baby boomer generation pursued the "glacier gospel," and by the 1960s, with new gear and new techniques, the definition of "average" climber and "average" achievement had risen a notch. By the 1980s both the number and affluence of climbers had fundamentally increased.[35] Sharp population increases, which included hordes of "gear hounds" and "gear geeks," resulted in standard routes on Northwest volcanoes sometimes mimicking congested highways. And among these hordes, more tackled the volcanoes' hardest routes: Rainier's Willis Wall or Hood's Sandy Glacier, for example.

In a crowd it's hard to savor private experience, let alone feelings of conversion or personal transformation. At the volcanoes and elsewhere, something basic shifted. Over thirty years ago one scholar rued the drastic change in scale, claiming that "figuratively speaking, we are all standing in a widening circle of yellow snow": "On a holiday weekend more people now climb Mount Rainier, Washington, than climbed it during a whole season in the 1950s. It is estimated that over 5,000 climb Mount Hood, Oregon, every year."[36] Nowadays the number exceeds ten thousand per year on these bellwether volcanoes. That widening circle of yellow snow describes the primary management challenge in the twenty-first century for popular routes on Northwest volcanoes, as it bespeaks a density of use unimagined half a century ago.

As metaphor "yellow snow" symbolizes mountaineering as a mass sport since hordes, many of whom wouldn't have tried the snowpeaks generations ago, have eagerly caught volcano fever. The late twentieth-century legacy of "mountain glory" has meant unprecedented numbers of boots and crampons on mountains including Northwest volcanoes. Given these numbers, many have suggested carrying capacity limits, permit systems, and rationing, but such notions remain deeply unpopular.

After the 1963 American Everest expedition led by Jim Whittaker, one half of the most famous twins in American mountaineering, the popularity of Northwest mountaineering surged, and climbing became a firm feature of status tourism. Whittaker—who started as a Rainier climbing guide and was the first American to summit Everest, planting a U.S. flag atop the mountain—became a celebrity with White House access. Willi Unsoeld and Tom Hornbein, also Mount Rainier guides, were the first to climb Everest via its West Ridge route; another Rainier guide, Lute Jerstad, also summited (with sponsor *National Geographic* staffer, Barry Bishop). That those 1963 American climbers trained primarily on Rainier, coupled with the subsequent claim repeated by many Northwest or other alpinists bound for Everest that it provided the best stepping stone, spotlighted Rainier in a way it had not been before.

The effects of new prestige were quickly felt at Mount Rainier and, indirectly, elsewhere. Over two thousand climbers tackled Rainier in 1967; by 1974, over five thousand a year climbed; by 1994, over ten thousand per year. In 1969, 1647 climbers summited, over eleven hundred via the standard, Ingraham Glacier-Disappointment Cleaver route that includes Camp Muir; by 1982, the figure topped four thousand per year. Within one generation, from 1965 to 1985, over fifty thousand summited via the two standard routes.[37] Unsurprisingly, some strong climbers pursued (and still climb) more technical routes to avoid crowds or meet new challenges, thereby mimicking the gold standard proclaimed by early climbers. That astounding figure from the Northwest's most dominant mountain tells the tale of mass mountaineering. Presumably those thousands experienced in muted, diminished form the personal transformation that early climbers celebrated. If a profound sense of renewal or rebirth depends upon conditions other than crowds, it has become, on standard routes at least, much more elusive.

The Everest-Rainier linkage, chronicled by several histories, underscored Rainier's status as Washington's number one tourist attraction in a new way, one that has changed the sociology of climbing as greater numbers of amateurs, who could buy gear and sometimes guides, took to the mountains. In the past two generations, a new breed of occasional climber, who can afford the ever more sophisticated equipment, has tackled Rainier as though gaining a foretaste of the world's highest mountain. Almost half the time, this newbie hires guides either through the venerable Rainier Mountaineering, Inc. (which Lou Whittaker co-founded in 1968), Alpine Ascents International, or International Mountain Guides. Numbers draw greater numbers.

The number of climbers summiting Rainier continued to grow in the 1990s and early 2000s. Its surging popularity continues, as the numbers show. In the new century's first decade, the year 2000 proved the high point, with 13,114 registered climbers and 6083 successful summits, a 46 percent success rate. Curiously, the numbers on Rainier dropped about 30 percent between then and 2006, when 9154 climbers registered and 5785 summited (63%). There are several possible explanations for the downward trend, including the regional dot-com bust after 1999, but in 2006 almost as many summited as during the peak year of 2000. The October 2008–September 2009 climbing year saw 10,616 on the mountain, about a 5 percent increase over the preceding season: of these, practically 80 percent commenced at Paradise and 65 percent climbed via the standard route.[38] Traffic on the most common routes above Camps Muir and Schurman (on the northeast side) has decreased little, "low impact" or otherwise. In one recent year, about two thirds of all climbers massed on one route—that narrow throat—and Camp Muir (like Emmons Flat, on the northeast) resembled a bulging, transient campground. This despite the fact that more climbers climbed harder, less common routes than ever.

Most visitors or climbers exercise care, but some ignore or flaunt the guidelines of low-impact alpine hiking, camping, or climbing. Above those full parking lots and trash barrels at Paradise or Sunset and elsewhere, a more noxious problem flourishes. Climbers are supposed to deposit their poop in double blue plastic bags and toss the bags into conspicuous fifty-five-gallon barrels. Most do but some are careless about their shit and other deposits. An online "Mount Rainier National Park, 2006" document reports, unsurprisingly, increased problems with poop.[39] In addition it states, "climbing rangers also dismantled 71 rock walls [built for tent protection] and newly established [i.e., unsanctioned] campsites."[40] The report contains a parable of mass mountaineering, which doesn't just mean gathering rocks and building horseshoe-shaped walls for tents or bivouac sites. Those two figures—nearly seven hundred pounds of portable trash and over one hundred discarded blue bags or piles of poop from one season—describe mass mountaineering. Instead of cleaning up after ourselves, we leave deposits of our passing and others—for example, climbing rangers—must clean up our messes.

Industrial tourism, which environmentalist Edward Abbey repeatedly inveighed against and which has become an accepted critical and popular term, describes a scale and style of travel that presumes high volume (like cruise ships) and a variably elaborate infrastructure that tends to standardize the experience of touring. In an age of industrial tourism, masses come not just *to* but also *on* the volcanoes, and standard routes resemble the Chilkoot Pass scenes in Charlie Chaplin's *The Gold Rush* (1925), where the climbing prospectors, stepping hard upon one another, look like a line of ants. Some mountaineers climb for status more than personal transformation: in an era of mass mountaineering, there has been a paradigm shift. With increasing crowds climbing volcanoes, others want to join and not feel left behind.

In addition to these issues, the scene at volcano bases or high camps imitates mall food courts, and this condition rubs against the dictates of wilderness area management. Climbing parties bump against one another and tents cluster close. Such camps don't necessarily appear along more technical routes, but signs of use remain because so little decomposes. In the parable of concentration, we accumulate evidence of ourselves. The strange yet increasingly commonplace picture of worn, crowded high camps reveals a crucial dilemma, as access to volcanoes trumps protection of resources. As one scholar remarked some years ago, this picture "is an urban problem requiring an urban solution, but the politics of wilderness cannot accommodate this solution."[41]

The pressure towards standardized experience also reconceives a volcano climb as a measurable outcome, or product. Industrial tourism captures the braided regional story of auto tourism, skiing, and climbing as the human presence at volcanoes has shifted in scale. Such scale overlaps considerably with the prevalent paradigm of status tourism, wherein tourists collect experiences more for outer (i.e., social) than inner reference.

Mount Rainier or Mount Hood, as physical facts and spiritual presences, far exceed our human footprint near or on them, of course. But that imprint increasingly damages the Northwest's most exceptional mountains, whether measured through nearby auto pollution, clogged mountain roads or full parking lots, or dirty snow or frayed plastic at higher altitudes. Most contemporary hikers or climbers, raised according to the idealism of the Wilderness Act, expect some degree of "wilderness experience," however fuzzy the definition. For most, it means small groups or an individual experience. In some regards Dan Evans was correct in his late twentieth-century assessment: "We . . . are in mortal danger of loving [Mount Rainier] to death."[42] Clearly, the public must change their habits when visiting or climbing, just as management policy must be revised to provide urban solutions to what is primarily and ironically an urban dilemma. The Mount Hood National Forest's Strategic Stewardship Plan (2006) repeatedly proclaims the need for new public collaborations in addressing a range of management challenges. Agency personnel cannot revise public habits on the federally protected snowpeaks without extensive public input and assistance. The solutions and restrictions that will prove most palatable and effective have not yet emerged. Given the pressures of constriction, the funnel effect, viable alternatives are hard to imagine, let alone implement.

3 CITIES AND THEIR VOLCANOES

> Looking across the forests over which the mellow light of the sunset
> was streaming, I soon discovered the source of my friend's ex-
> citement. There stood Mount Hood in all the glory of the Alpen
> glow looming immensely high, beaming with intelligence, and so
> impressive that one was overawed as if suddenly brought before
> some superior Being newly arrived from the sky.
>
> —John Muir, *Pacific Monthly*

Despite the lessons of history—Pompeii in AD 79 or Saint-Pierre,
Martinique, in 1902, for example—several Northwest cities take
great proprietary pride in nearby volcanoes that help constitute
their identities. Bellingham has claimed Mount Baker, Portland
has claimed Mount Hood, Bend claims several, and both Seattle
and Tacoma claim Mount Rainier as their own. They do so for
reasons intimated by John Muir in his "Mt. Hood from Portland,"
published more than a century ago. Muir's Mount Hood glows and
towers over the city just as William Samuel Parrott's painting of
Hood glows and towers over that subalpine lake without human
presence, evoking (a generation earlier than Muir) some mythic
time without Native Americans or cities. Muir's animism more
explicitly invokes the secular testimonies voiced at the twentieth
century's end. No one sold Portland better than Muir, who closes
the distance between the city and the volcano looming to the east:
"Mount Hood is in full view, with the summits of Mounts Jef-

ferson, St. Helens, Adams and Rainier in the distance. The City of Portland is at our feet, covering a large area along both banks of the Willamette . . . a telling picture of busy, aspiring civilization in the midst of the green wilderness in which it is planted."[1]

Muir's metaphor renders Portland an organically rooted entity like the conifer foothills beyond and Mount Hood just beyond them. The fact that Mount Hood presents itself north of Clark County, Washington, or farther south in the Willamette Valley, or way up the Columbia River Gorge, becomes ultimately irrelevant against the claims of Oregon's largest city. Since the nineteenth century as volcano and city coexist in intimate relation, Mount Hood has belonged to Portland. In Robin Cody's novel *Ricochet River* (1992), he writes, "The white mountain loomed like Truth itself, or a bad painting." And historian Carl Abbott underlines the bond, echoing Muir: "Usually the mountain is playground and backdrop, silhouetted against a sharp blue dawn on occasional clear winter mornings, tinged pink in summer evening sunsets."[2] The intimacy was confirmed by the iconic crowd scene of the Mazamas' founding at Mount Hood's crater, many of those climbers from Portland.

Muir's characteristically painterly composition framed Mount Hood as the climax of the view of and from Portland—the view "from" is contained within the view "of." He was likely positioned at Council Crest Park, named only four years before his article and the high point of the city's West Hills. More than a thousand feet above sea level, Council Crest Park displays views of five volcanoes, and trees are pruned or cut to preserve the viewsheds. Of these, Mount Hood dominates. Though distinctly removed from Portland proper by distance and history, it remains atop the city's self-portrait and psyche. That fact twice prompted the city—in the 1970s and in 1991—to issue building restrictions to preserve the vista corridors.[3] Thus, the modern history of Oregon's most famous volcano is, in some respects, an urban history, one that echoes and refracts the material and cultural changes in a particular cityscape.

FIG. 5. A Washington State ferry in the San Juan Islands with Mount Baker in evening sun. Baker's crater is in the dip just below and to the right of the summit. Courtesy of "Hyak approaching Lopez Island 02" by Compdude123 is licensed under CC BY 3.0, https://commons.wikimedia.org/wiki/File:Hyak _approaching_Lopez_Island_02.jpg.

Figure and ground are essential components of landscape composition, and in the unfolding aesthetic of nineteenth-century American landscape painting and photography, mountains became standard fare as monumental background. In some instances, cities attached themselves to a nearby mountain, and in the Northwest, volcanoes were handy. In such landscape composition people intuitively define themselves by association, as background showcases foreground—and vice versa, according to some human scales. As a municipal identity coalesced and matured, the volcano crowned that identity and afforded a number of bragging rights. The story of cities and their volcanoes includes a series of appropriations in many guises.

This is a story of connection and disconnection since geological history, of course, unfolds apart from human history, only randomly intruding upon the latter. Mount Hood no more "belongs" to Portland than the Three Sisters "belong" to Bend. Yet residents often feel they do. The powerful illusion of juxtaposition creates a series of habits and consequences, some pleasurable and some perilous. Juxtaposition means much more than potential eruption—the threat of lahars from Mount Rainier for Pierce County communities along the historic floodplains above Tacoma's Commencement Bay, for instance. The ambivalence of juxtaposition explains one strand of regional identity and documents, from an urban vantage, the shifting chronicle of modern human interactions on the snowpeaks.

This chapter plots the ambivalent history suggested by the possessive adjective *their* in its title. The adjective poses a complex pretense—which fact has never slowed marketing or brand identification. The chapter addresses two questions: in what respects can it be said that Eugene, Salem, Portland, Tacoma, Seattle, Yakima, or Bellingham own their particular volcanoes? And what are the dangers of proprietorship given the proximity of particular volcanoes? The Portland–Mount Hood symbiosis, for example, manifests itself through a startling range of behaviors over the past 150 years or more. Though Oregon claims more volcanoes than Washington, more than half its population lives within Multnomah and Washington Counties—in or near Portland, which includes more volcanic vents and cinder cones than any other city on the continent. Geologically, Portland bears a special affinity with those volcanoes in its Council Crest Park panorama. And Mount Hood poses a clear case of the legacy of proximity and the fiction of identification.

Many commentators have echoed Theodore Winthrop's extravagant claim that the Northwest comprises a bigger, better New England, with one historian, Carlos Schwantes, recently borrowing the first lines of "America the Beautiful": "the opening stanza . . . could well describe its mountain peaks and amber waves of grain."[4] Though Katharine Lee Bates had Colorado's Pikes Peak in view when she penned "purple mountains' majesty," the epithet belongs to the Cascades as well. The quasi-Christian testimony of residents, many of them urban or suburban, again confirms the snowpeaks as godlike entities. According to this fond looking glass, we live in a heavenly place (see Winthrop or novelist Thomas Wolfe). Physical proximity or contiguity engenders an imaginative ownership, as several volcanoes form the indispensable core if not climax of the panoramic urban landscapes. Furthermore, such imaginative ownership engenders a conviction of privilege in the regional ethos, as background enhances and enlarges foreground.

In the Northwest proximity feeds and seals identity, one version being the juxtaposition of city or suburb with backcountry, or "hinterland." "Hinterland" sends mixed semantic signals in its historical sense of being land remote from urban areas, particularly insofar as "remote" connotes "behind"—behind the times. In the nineteenth century, of course, all the "old Oregon territory" was hinterland from mostly white population centers, and the volcano-strewn Cascades epitomized hinterland for a period after the Oregon Trail accelerated settlement. Certainly meanings of hinterland overlap with those of wilderness, and in the last century its status steadily and dramatically tilted. Backcountry presumes front country, the growing cities of the region. Paradoxically, hinterland gains value as we draw near and settle in—it seems to reach closer to us. The juxtaposition of arctic islands with young cities sharpens the paradox and increases its lure.[5]

Juxtaposition depends on accessibility and some minimum of affluence. Hinterland's enhanced value is manifested through our road system. In recent years, for example, Washington's Alpine Lakes Wilderness Area, in its annual data of user days, has proven one of the country's busiest. In high season trails in the South Fork of the Snoqualmie River valley, along the I-90 corridor, imitate Seattle's big parks (e.g., Discovery, Volunteer, or Woodland Parks) in foot traffic. To reach these or other highly prized, wild places near Seattle, we just grab the right gear and hop in the car—and battle jammed I-5, or I-90 beyond North Bend. Regional residents—those seeking outdoors pursuits—want to have their cake and eat it too, and they do. Urbanites want high culture and high mountains, and for many the best wild places are the volcanoes. In "only an hour" they reach "an ocean of freedom," as stock a metaphor as any to define alpine country.[6] The endless freedom of high country close by reconciles many to urban life, an old story. Our vehicles and highways close the physical gap between city and volcano that has been repeatedly bridged through acts of imaginative appropriation.

The fact that high hinterland affords spacious personal freedom—see Mountaineers writer Harvey Manning's title, *Mountaineering: The Freedom of the Hills*—sustains the oldest testimony in mountaineering. As is well known, friendships become both more fluid and enduring in the mountains. This social value of being, for instance, on a volcano above eight thousand feet enlarges the possibility (and traditional value) of personal transformation. Acquaintances can turn into trusted friends, and old friends grow closer. The alpine benefit of juxtaposition and accessibility seems beyond dispute, as the individual temporarily sheds her normal life and discovers—or rediscovers—new, abiding connections in high places.

So the value of the volcanoes' proximity also resides in their alpine setting that democratizes human interactions—in some respects—and cements friendships differently from the low-altitude zones where most people cluster. Mountaineers have always known that being roped up often engenders close bonds that long outlast the pitches. The rope literalizes intimate connection. On the snow-peaks friendships old and new differ in quality and depth. Guides on Rainier or Hood have known for generations that, for their clients at least, the temporary guide-client friendship endures beyond the climb, in part because of the "aha" moments when the clients undergo the kind of transformation climbers have always extolled. For most that transformation has always been shared, at least with one or a few others. It's private *and* social. Though the volcanoes own a central place in these cities' composed landscapes, part of their value inheres in their spectacular difference: a difference that can seal deep bonds.

Volcano proximity—arctic islands near at hand—defines, in part, Northwest status since weekend climbers can summit a volcano with no disruption to their weekday work schedules. This brag rings true for many urban- or suburbanites and undergirds Northwest exceptionalism as it manifests the good life, an optimal mix of urban lifestyles and glaciers. That crammed scenario, unimaginable to the first generations of climbers, had become commonplace by the 1980s. One sign of mountaineering as a mass sport in the twentieth century's closing decades, this scenario represented an undisputed quality-of-life benchmark. It can't get better than this rapid-fire, city-summit-city plot: we can have a quickie with a volcano, with sufficient funds and leisure. The contiguity of hinterlands to metro centers lends the latter their particular *frisson* and fuels their boasts of a superior ethos. We've got it all, the regional mantra goes. What had emerged by the 1880s, from both local inhabitants and railroad promoters (like Northern Pacific), abides through the present.

As the narrator in a recent Seattle novel chauvinistically comments, "even pedestrians glided by without hats or umbrellas in fleece jackets and ultralight hiking boots, as if they might scale Rainier that afternoon if the weather cleared."[7] Juxtaposition makes Northwest cities exceptional since lots of folks did (and do) devote their weekends to the mountains, even as their styles and dress have shifted over generations. The Cascades as last frontier prompted an urban-suburban pattern of use.

A city with volcano views confirms a happy choice of location for old and recent residents, whose imaginative claims follow their eyes. Most don't close the gap like climbers, thankfully; they remain content with "their" volcano in view, like Mount Hood and the other four volcanoes from Portland's Council Crest Park. The term *viewshed* implies some proprietary relationship, however imagined or bogus, between viewer and viewed. Viewshed occupies some uneasy conceptual place between landscape theory and real estate practice. No doubt it derives from the nineteenth-century romantic sublime, when the monumental and alpine provided the backdrop in ideal landscape composition. If casual viewers, sighting one or more volcanoes, receive a charge as Muir insists regarding Mount Hood, then cities built nearby inflate their civic pride through their imaginative annexation of the proximate snowpeak.

As Lou Whittaker, the other half of the United States' most famous mountaineering twins, commented about Rainier, "It's almost like an ownership for people around here."[8] If a given volcano is defined in sacred terms, in Northwest literary tradition, the claim is at root religious: it "belongs" to us because we need it. Acts of annexation reveal one kind of regional history according to its urban cores: a history that affirms the volcanoes' grip in the regional imaginary.

The first half of the twentieth century disclosed a regional and national population shift away from towns and rural communities into cities and that increasingly prevalent, contiguous hybrid, suburbs. In the latter half of the century, "Greater" Seattle connected north to Everett and south to Tacoma and Olympia beyond: most Washingtonians live within this urban-suburban-rural corridor along southeastern Puget Sound. Rainier, premiere visual icon, rises just beyond it, as close as one's windows or windshield. Driving to Paradise, or to Timberline Lodge on Mount Hood's south slopes, simply closed the gap from Tacoma's Point Defiance Park or Portland's Washington Park, respectively. But the gap is real, despite the fond eyes of city dwellers and promoters who have always used a telephoto lens to pull a volcano close.

In the Northwest several cities, during their early adolescence, seized upon the proximate volcano to solidify their municipal identity and brand. They broadcast, in myriad forms and venues, the figure-ground landscape composition. Just as Council Crest Park, at the turn of the twentieth century, confirmed Portland's attachment to Mount Hood, Seattle's 1909 Alaska-Yukon-Pacific Exposition, built on the University of Washington (U W) campus, confirmed Rainier's place in its viewshed. The most famous vista at the exposition, and the most famous campus view for over one century, runs southeast from the central quadrangle to Drumheller Fountain in the center foreground and beyond it, the Montlake Cut, sections of Lake Washington and Mercer Island, and in the center background, Rainier. A traditional landscape composition, one endlessly reproduced.

In images from 1909 through the present, Rainier is often pulled closer to the city than it really is. Once the campus was moved, decades earlier, from the central business district northeast to the tract bordering the Montlake Cut and Lake Washington's Montlake Bay, Rainier assumed a visual and psychological place at Washington's first university, one confirmed by the subsequent design of the fountain and view corridor. Thus the premiere university is linked with the premiere mountain, which "presided" over the fair just as it presides over UW and Seattle. This particular fit into campus design, like other views of Rainier from the central business district or various neighborhoods north and south, matches the placement of Mount Hood as visual center of interest in eastward Portland vistas. Rainier's broad dome lends itself to foreshortened perspectives as though it bulges closer than it is—as though, in words taken from a recent novel, "the looming snowball of Mount Rainier had rolled a little closer to downtown."[9]

Viewsheds dramatize the value of contiguity. With Mount Rainier the implications of juxtaposition are foreshadowed in the very title of the environmental history of Mount Rainier National Park, *National Park, City Playground* (2006).[10] The juxtaposition suggests that the former extends and frames the latter: that the biggest volcano (and its park) derives much of its value from its contiguity with one or more cities, rather than in and of itself. In any long view Rainier is apart, but it is also a part—that's the essential paradox, for both are true. In this story, the *meanings* of Rainier overlap and depend upon the *meanings* of Tacoma or Seattle. As "city playground," MRNP in its history has been pushed and pulled according to changing paradigms in natural amenity economics, and "use" "embraces both recreation and exploitation [and] includes the packaging, sale, and consumption of nature as an aesthetic experience."[11]

Portland's Council Crest Park epitomizes this strand of Northwest urban history, of myriad acts of imaginative appropriation. Northwest volcanoes have been branded and sold for a long time, as regional marketing, painting, and photography, for example, attest. The late nineteenth-century journalism, ranging from personal testimonies to those *Wonderland* guides in the case of Rainier, recommended a visit or climb as an optimal product. A visit, hike, or climb promises great personal gain in limited time: heavy time constraints bound and frame one's "mountain fever." More recently, the "commodification of nature as an aesthetic experience" has become a commonplace among contemporary environmental historians, those who chronicle the long history of a physical landscape or landscapes (and the built environments therein).

The volcanoes, crowns of the regional geography, enjoy a rich virtual reality far removed from their specific locations through endless reproduction in many visual media. When movies came to the volcanoes—*The Call of the Wild* (1935) or Jerome Hill's *Ski Flight* (1936) or Stanley Kubrick's *The Shining*, which used Timberline Lodge for exterior shots (1980)—the latter acquired a new cachet far beyond the region, one parallel to the mountain photography pioneered by Northwest photographer Asahel Curtis and in the next generation, photographers Ray Atkinson and Bob and Ira Spring.

Such filmmakers or photographers pulled the volcanoes in far closer than city parks or prospects do. They boost the work of appropriation. As a result of such reproduction the volcanoes reappeared inside, on the walls of art galleries or homes, or on coffee tables in large format books. They were domesticated, brought down to size through myriad marketing strategies and brands. And in the past generation, endless images appear on countless websites, many of those urban websites, as though the volcanoes' virtual presence eclipses their actual positions.

Arguably, the habit of commodification comes from the city, home of the marketplace. Volcano-as-playground confirms the tendency to commodify them. For Seattle and Tacoma leaders past and present, packaging Rainier means construing it as an extension of their respective park systems, themselves sites of complex landscape design and domestication. Given its overwhelming viewshed values, the volcano is annexed as if it belongs to both cities. These spectacular views elevate us, and they sell. Always have.

So volcanoes serve not only as brands but also as unique playgrounds, extensions of municipal park spaces. Mount Rainier as recreational space figured into the municipal identities of Seattle and Tacoma from their earliest years. In the era of auto tourism this mind-set gained force due to the quickly established pattern of weekend visits. The pattern has only been modified, not changed, since then. Visiting a volcano grew out of the Sunday afternoon drive, as motorists sought out countryside no longer present in their daily lives. In their initial decades of growth, both Seattleites and Tacomans regarded Rainier as a culminating symbol of their good fortune. Early city planners capitalized on residents' symbolic appropriation, claiming Rainier "had a tonic effect on the cities' residents": it's good for you.[12] The boast has not changed, as it applies Winthrop's airy prediction for the Northwest as a Chosen Land. Both cities exercised proprietary claims over Rainier, believing the mountain symbolized "the scenic beauty, quality of living, and regional superiority" of each.[13] In this view, volcano proximity confirmed each city's happy story of itself, one that still flourishes. The Evergreen State's two largest cities thrive in the glow of the biggest volcano.

As an environmental historian has written of Seattleites, "catching fish, climbing mountains, or picnicking in the city's parks were more than idyllic escapes; they were also matters of politics and power."[14] The fact that picnicking was linked with fishing and mountaineering illustrates the historical consequences of Rainier's urban glow, as the volcano was scripted as an extension of the city's recreational credo. Each activity figures as part of urban presumption. Here and in other cities, the wishes of the prosperous prevailed. Financial interests in nearby cities called the shots and determined the human footprint on several volcanoes, removing other kinds of claims. For example, the so-called "consensus view," primarily white upper and middle class, pressured the removal of mining claims in Glacier Basin on Rainier's northeast side and the retirement of any extant grazing practices. Neither mining nor cattle grazing belonged in the playground, nor did Native Americans.

Of much graver consequence, the ancient lifeways of tribal peoples were swept aside. With Mount Rainier, traditional tribal (e.g., Nisqually or Yakama) claims or presence nearby the volcano— seasonal hunting and berry picking, for example—were denied. The fact that snowpeaks themselves were taboo zones for most tribes in no way precluded their seasonal use of alpine parks and drainages below timberline, of course. In some instances, because of the contiguity of reservations (e.g., Mount Adams or Mount Jefferson), enforced exclusion did not take place.

The exclusion of old Nisqually or Yakama practices around Rainier is a local example of a pervasive pattern in the late nineteenth and early twentieth centuries of forced tribal removal from newly designated parks.[15] By the nineteenth century's end, urban proponents of the park, descendants of Theodore Winthrop's own racism and blindness to tribal degradation, presumed Native Americans would either assimilate or die, the prevailing white paradigm until the early twentieth century. Drawing park boundaries or, later, wilderness area boundaries tended to discount or downright ignore ancient human traffic—traffic symbolized by Native names for particular volcanoes as well as the accompanying creation stories. Native absence from Rainier's environs matched the prevalent, twilight-of-the-gods credo. The question of whose park, or more broadly, whose volcano, was being answered by mostly urban, mostly privileged classes.

Urban viewsheds, then, excluded other, older views and connections. In the figure-ground composition, a glaciated volcano served (and serves) as spectacular ground for the built environment front and center. Of course the built environment, in early stages, didn't look pretty. When Sanford Gifford and Albert Bierstadt painted Mount Rainier from the southeast tip of Vashon Island in 1874 and 1889, respectively, they entirely omitted the "figure," the raw, young industrial city of Tacoma—an early instance of what has been recently called ecopornography, that tendency to "greenwash" or airbrush a given landscape to the point of significant factual (or documentary) distortion. The fact that Gifford placed two sea canoes in the right foreground instead (ten figures in the larger canoe, four in the smaller) illustrates the very old Nisqually habitation under Tahoma just at the time of its eclipse. The canvas affirmed the "vanishing race" mind-set, assigning the Natives to a mythic past that in the 1870s was disappearing. Subsequent tribal history gives the lie to that late nineteenth- and early twentieth-century, racist ethos. The desired city-volcano symbiosis didn't always fit prevailing criteria for optimal landscape composition, though those criteria soon shifted to include facets of the foreground.

Seattleites and Tacomans jostled for decades over the notion that Rainier belonged to one or the other, but not both—like two young bucks fighting for the exclusive favors of a girl who belongs to neither. Tacoma's closer but Seattle's bigger, etc. Not only that, but different values jockeyed for preeminent position. The competition grew most heated over the volcano's "proper" name, Tacomans and some others stressing the fact that city and volcano shared the same native name. Yet during the fin de siècle lobbying for a national park, rivalries disappeared as both preservationists and commercial interests joined hands in common cause. As always, the cities had the numbers. Both constituencies were primarily urban, the former as members of the Washington Alpine Club or its successors, the Mazamas and the Mountaineers.

Though Congress settled the name issue in 1899, the intercity rivalry appears, in retrospect, less important than that between preservationists and developers. The region's dominant volcano serves as bellwether since it has always appealed to contradictory values, potential personal transformation or potential dollars. MRNP's history of commodification (e.g., Rainier National Park Company) reveals an uneasy compromise between a host of spiritual and aesthetic claims and the eternal lure of the bottom line. In the past century the latter has increasingly preempted the former. Private experiences have grown increasingly prepackaged if not diluted by sheer numbers and the usually irresistible glow of status tourism. Additionally, *use* has a messy history in which "recreation" sometimes leaks as "exploitation," and experience leaves deposits.

In the last century's first four decades, no one embodied those mutually exclusive outcomes as conspicuously as Asahel Curtis, co-founder of the Mountaineers in 1906, founder of its Seattle-Tacoma Rainier National Park Committee in 1910 (renamed the Rainier National Park Advisory Board in 1916), and promoter extraordinaire. Curtis was, with his older brother, Edward, as famous a homegrown photographer as the region has seen, and his body of work, above all his camera eye, documented, in miniature, the urban Sound's appropriation of Rainier. For all his mountaineering, he wanted infrastructure and lots of it. His ring road proposal for Mount Rainier, one imaginative annexation of a volcano, denies its status as fundamentally apart, other.[16]

In NPS history, MRNP was the first park located near two cities, a crucial fact in the story of cities and "their" volcanoes, particularly to the extent that Rainier has been a lead example of imaginative appropriation. The urban history of Rainier—an apparent paradox—not only inscribes the deep ambivalence of city-volcano juxtaposition, but represents one increasingly important facet of NPS history: the legacy of proximity in thickening patterns of short-term visitation. The history also unsurprisingly reveals the dominance of upper- and middle-class white interests—their standards of decorum—dictating park policy and development to the exclusion of other groups. Those interests derived from late nineteenth-century park aesthetics inspired by Frederic Law Olmsted, the nineteenth century's most famous city parks designer who also worked in Seattle, and his peers. The Olmsted Plan, adopted by Seattle and developed by Olmsted's sons after 1903, featured amenities such as ball fields and tennis courts, which would be underused by Seattle's working class and racial minority populations.

Analogously, those with more money wanted their volcano park according to their wishes. Working class folks and racial and ethnic minorities from the cities were less welcome, as the brief history of the Cooperative Campers movement (1916–22) evidences.[17] That Stephen Mather and the MRNP superintendent jointly decided to remove the Coop Campers suggests a socio-economic class war.

The Coop Campers felt the Rainier National Park Company did not accommodate poor people; the monopoly concessionaire regarded the coop's services as a violation of its park contract. It is no coincidence that the Coop Campers flourished during the period of Seattle's general strike and that its most famous leader, Anna Louise Strong, was an active socialist. But with the NPS backing the Rainier National Park Company, the outcome was foretold. Only gradually was the grip of the leisured classes lessened at MRNP and other volcanoes.[18] To this day, of course, visiting, hiking, or climbing remains a financial privilege that precludes many members of nearby urban populations.

Highways enabled municipalities to imaginatively annex nearby volcanoes, thus enhancing the proprietary illusion. Private vehicles sealed the case for cities and "their" volcanoes, as they extend the habits of domestication. Mounts Hood, Rainier, Baker, and others became and remain weekend leisure goals. Just as urbanites use their neighborhood parks to stroll, picnic, or toss a Frisbee, many do the same at the volcano in their viewshed. Mount Rainier especially served as an outstanding "reservoir of the primitive," the best of hinterland, for a region increasingly urban (and suburban) rather than rural.[19] In the Northwest, perhaps the best form of nearby hinterland remains the volcanoes, supremely reservoirs of the primitive. This rich metaphor, along with the notion of the arctic island, defines the volcanoes' acute appeal. The juxtaposition of arctic and primitive with temperate, sea-level built environments stamps Northwest urban identity. The juxtaposition also explains why so many town or city dwellers love nearby volcanoes, because they like to imaginatively or literally touch the primitive, however fleetingly.

Of course, most visitors cherish their iconic volcano for its differences from, rather than similarities to parks in Seattle, Tacoma, Portland, or Bend. They delight in their brief, felt encounters with this geologic version of primitivism. The appeal of the primitive invokes a thick, ironic history of interpretation in the past two to three centuries among groups who identified themselves as variously First World, progressive, affluent, intellectual, or cultured. The image of Theodore Winthrop mocking the three natives who paddled or guided him in 1853 instances one stereotypical, nineteenth-century narrative of First World affluence encountering what it labeled primitive. Of course, not only indigenes but exotic landscapes, including the U.S. West's monumental mountains and canyons, were thus labeled and patronized. In the twentieth-century Northwest the lure of nearby volcanoes underscored people's lifelong fascination with their elemental nature.

That people construe a nearby arctic island as part and parcel of their urban landscapes and lives is wishful thinking, an illusion whose nuances have been happily ignored by urban architects, boosters, and marketers, though not by vulcanologists or poets (e.g., Marianne Moore, Denise Levertov, Gary Snyder).

Cities establish their claims through publicity stunts and annual traditions. In north Puget Sound, Whatcom County in the early twentieth century developed in its urban core a volcano identity similar to those communities along Puget Sound's southeast shores or in the lower Willamette Valley. That appropriation manifests itself through a celebrated foot (and ski) race and destination ski resort, the latter capitalizing on big winter snowfalls. Though Mount Baker easily lies within sightlines from Washington's Island and San Juan Counties, the northern Olympic Peninsula, and British Columbia's two primary cities, Bellingham has long claimed it as its own. During the same period when road builders punched Chuckanut Drive along the cliffs bordering Samish Bay, thereby providing an overland link to Whatcom County for the first time, the Bellingham Chamber of Commerce joined forces with the Mount Baker Club in an unusual publicity ploy that connected the young city with the graceful volcano just to the east.

The city conceived a palpable link according to individual human effort via an annual seashore-to-summit race. This ultra-marathon commenced in 1911 and lasted only three years due to accidents and chronic dangers. But this fund-raising stunt spawned a sound-to-summit tradition that, after a sixty-year hiatus, reversed direction, reinvented as the Ski to Sea Race: a relay linking crater to sound, dropping two vertical miles. In the increasingly outdoor recreational present, this annual event flourishes.[20] As a robust publicity engine the race further solidifies the city-volcano link: Baker belongs to Bellingham.[21]

Of course relatively few run to or ski off a volcano; most want personal comfort and convenience, the usual suspects. So Bell-ingham, like other regional cities, consciously promoted itself as a gateway community. "Gateway" enhances the appropriation and deepens the municipal identity. A century ago, a spur railroad line ran partway up the Nooksack River valley to the settlement of Glacier, just northwest of the volcano. The story of development, here and around Mount Adams, precluded national park status: mining companies, for example, bested local preservation interests. In Bellingham mountain and city clubs joined forces as in Seattle and Tacoma and lobbied hard for a Mount Baker national park in the 1910s. But in 1917 the mining lobby squelched a bill that had been well supported by a congressional committee.[22]

Bellingham, like Portland, proved a test case in national park lobbying, but local mountain clubs and chambers of commerce in both, along with those in Yakima and even Spokane, failed to follow Seattle's and Tacoma's successful example. They pushed hard against Mather and Albright of the NPS. In the eleven years following 1908, nine bills establishing a Mount Baker national park were introduced. Between 1919 and 1921, three bills were introduced establishing a Yakima national park focused on Mount Adams.[23] Three cities joined the bandwagon but their lobbying came to naught: for the Park Service, three volcano-based parks (including Mount Lassen) in the range was enough. Urban lobbying indirectly created what became Washington State Route 542 and the ski resort on the northeast side: a regional story of urban identification and self-aggrandizement. Failing a national park, Bellingham and Yakima—and Portland, Salem, Eugene, and Bend—developed other expressions of proximity as gateway communities. In each case, they have extended their identity to the nearby volcano (or volcanoes) through their marketing and promise of quick access.

In the 1920s Mount Baker was subject to diverse recreation and development agendas including a destination resort based on the new sport of downhill skiing. As at Rainier's Paradise, Mount St. Helens' Spirit Lake, Mount Hood's Timberline, and other locales, destination resorts provided luxurious creature comforts adjacent to the exotic, a snowpeak—the pleasing tension of stark contrast. In 1926, 74,859 acres around the volcano were designated (by the secretary of agriculture) for recreation *and* resource extraction, and the USFS designated a 188,000-acre game preserve.[24] But the resort attracted far more money and attention: Congress appropriated monies and a road was built to Heather Meadows and Austin Pass, along the divide between the volcano and the ever-photographed Mount Shuksan immediately east. In 1927 Mount Baker resort, with 100 rooms, opened, and four years later an improved highway was finished.[25]

Downhill skiing at Baker appeared pre-destined, as at select other volcanoes: fresh snow only an hour east from sea level! The early 1930s saw the same growth hosted by local interests (e.g., Mount Baker Ski Club) and the lure of tournaments and races as far south as Mount Rainier and Mount Hood. Furthermore, in 1934–35, the film adaptation of Jack London's popular novel, *The Call of the Wild,* was shot at the ski resort. Hollywood comes to the volcanoes! Stars Clark Gable, Loretta Young, and Reginald Owen were photographed on skis, and these glossies and press reports linked the new sport with the location. The PR could not have been better for Bellingham, a gateway community reconfirmed each generation according to new media outlets and packaging.[26]

The argument for contiguity and appropriation was sealed in a mid-twentieth century anthology, *The Cascades: Mountains of the Pacific Northwest* (1949). In its introduction editor Roderick Peattie, using one of American history's hoariest metaphors, defined the Cascades as "the last frontier" and "essentially a wilderness." The former conception revealed a combination of myopic thinking, wistful desire, and local chauvinism. Peattie, a mountains geographer, unsurprisingly ignored the long history of tribal uses of the snowpeaks. Instead, he immediately affirmed the region's proprietary relation to its most exceptional mountains: "I know of no mountain area more completely, pridefully, and possessively claimed by a people than the mountains of the Pacific Northwest."[27] This affinity sustained Winthrop's symbolic appropriation of Mount Rainier nearly a century earlier. A writer like Peattie repeats the well-worn civilization-frontier trope ever recurring in American literature. In his uncritical boast, northwesterners presumed ownership, but especially those in its larger towns and cities who found a snowpeak within their viewshed. There is nothing new about towns or cities borrowing a nearby mountain to complete their idealized self-portraits, yet an energetic urban identification with particular volcanoes proves an ambivalent legacy at best.

"Last frontiers," whatever their conceptual legitimacy, exist to be entered and, to varying degrees, changed into something other than themselves, according to our history. In the Northwest the westering narrative of nineteenth-century white history met up with the prediction of cultivation and settlement voiced by George Vancouver at the end of the eighteenth century. A later chapter of this narrative, one devoted to alpine recreation, is highlighted by the ballooning memberships in local mountain clubs, especially those based in the cities. The Mazamas had already celebrated their golden anniversary in 1944 and the Mountaineers would soon celebrate theirs. By this time, the advantages of nearby hinterland were clear and the pattern of weekend exodus was set, as alpinists pursued their special, private places. This prideful comment defines, in a local context, recreational tourism. The weekend-exodus-and-return pattern represents a more general version of the climber's vaunted city-crater-city plot mentioned earlier. Those with sufficient income, desire, and skill can enjoy expensive cuisines and snowpeaks all in the space of forty-eight or seventy-two hours. Or less.

The 1950s arguably proved the last decade before explosive growth in the mountains and particularly on the volcanoes. Within a decade or two, the notion of private places in the mountains proved increasingly elusive. Appearing near the beginning of the baby boom generation, *The Cascades* beckoned people with their cars and their boots, and the "steady stream" of visitors accelerated. "Front line" volcanoes—Baker, Rainier, St. Helens, Hood, Jefferson, Washington, and the Sisters, for instance—functioned as mirrors of their self-regard and symbols of their desire, and they streamed to them like Alice stepping through her looking glass. In the process they embodied a combination of recreational and status tourism—a shifting combination.

By the late twentieth century, though city park visitation patterns—such as food or information kiosks, picnic, short paved walk—remained in place, a sizable group increasingly valued their close-up encounter for its overwhelming differences from their lowland lives. On the snowpeaks they endorsed poet Gary Snyder's Zen Buddhist credo of climbs as walking prayers and summits as sites for self-transcendence.

During this period that steady stream, coupled with the population concentration in or near the west slope cities, resulted in air pollution impacting volcanoes and occasionally viewsheds—an additional source of obscurity besides the seasonal low cloud cover. What, then, might be concluded about the juxtaposition of cities and volcanoes in the early twenty-first century? Those moving to the Northwest in the past twenty years often cite its extraordinary landscapes as a primary indicator in quality of life, and among those, the volcanoes are of course hard to miss.[28] Northwest urbanites always want rich choices even if they choose outdoors over indoors, or high altitude over sea level. Increasingly, some folks want all of the above.

Increasing numbers alternately head for the mountains or the cities' leading cultural institutions, given the popularity of Seattle's Macaw and Benaroya Halls and the Seattle Art Museum (s a m), or Portland's Opera, Symphony, or Art Museum, as well as countless other cultural offerings. The splendid geographical endowment complements the cultural institutions of the built environment. Urban (or suburban) northwesterners don't necessarily prefer a volcano to their opera, but they want both options convenient (if not always affordable) just as they demand Starbucks or Seattle's Best or Tully's. Contemporary urban expectations depend upon a rapid shift between sea level and ten thousand feet (or higher). It's no surprise that the region's superb natural setting has advertised itself for generations and that, as its urban cores spread in the twentieth century's closing decades, more newcomers expected and satisfied a wide spectrum of quality options, one that linked coffee houses and jazz clubs with nearby volcanoes. In the flattering self-portrait, the background completes the urban foreground.

Of course, this luxury of choice characterizing the affluent ignores those legions who barely make it and rarely patronize a playhouse, let alone get out to the mountains. In sheer numbers, the majority of city dwellers lack the wherewithal to visit or climb volcanoes. Or more crucially, volcanoes don't fire their imaginations, barely existing on the margins of their radar or desire. They would not visit or hike or climb even if they had the money and time. And given increasingly common congestion in greater Portland (for example, I-5 between Tigard and Vancouver) or between Tacoma and Everett, the road system, above all I-5 and its spurs, is approaching or has reached saturation: a glaring dark side to the good life, as many local critics (e.g., Knute Berger, in *Pugetopolis*) have written.

The dark side poses an unintended legacy of the usual endless growth model. In Seattle history "Greater Seattle" became a fixed mantra by the 1960s, and dissenting voices such as journalist Emmett Watson's—leader of the mocking "Lesser Seattle" movement whose motto was KBO, or "Keep The Bastards Out"—knew they wouldn't prevail against the bigger-is-better paradigm and in-migration. As cities (and suburbs) grow, so does human traffic on the volcanoes.

By the twentieth century's end, the volcanoes' proximity was being redefined again—stretched, as increasing numbers spent increasing time driving to trailheads. Thick traffic, like an organism's clogged arteries, now forces residents to question the region's declining ecological health, or at least the infrastructure or their unreflective private auto habits, particularly if it's taking longer to reach Timberline Lodge or the Cascade Lakes highway above Bend, or Rainier's Paradise or Sunrise. In the twenty-first century, it might take longer to reach that volcano at the other end of the view. In the old parable of local demand and supply, proximity feeds growth and profits. But the transportation infrastructure, with its clotting surface traffic, measures the cost of our vaunted juxtaposition.

In many respects, then, nearby volcanoes cap urban self-portraits, and the habits of play upon the volcanoes extend residents' recreation in city parks. Residents happily enact Winthrop's self-aggrandizing prediction of a century and a half ago. In ideal Northwest landscape composition, a snowpeak as "ground" fulfills the foreground "figure," the city. Bend, Oregon, for example, occupies center stage, and the Three Sisters, Mount Bachelor, Belknap Crater, and the other clustered volcanoes exist primarily to enhance its "arrived" status. This wish fulfillment is splendidly confirmed from panoramic Pilot Butte State Scenic Viewpoint, itself an old cinder cone within Bend's city limits. But a city-volcano intimacy presumes a non-existent interdependency. However much certain natives memorize "their" volcano's shape and colors through four seasons or over a lifetime, or however frequently it is photographed or painted or sculpted or written, it remains *apart* far more than any *part* of us.

The futile desire to somehow belong to volcanoes, which underlies the wide habits of branding and the psychology of viewsheds, is corroborated by one who recently knew Mount Rainier close up more than most anyone else. Mike Gauthier, native Washingtonian, spent eighteen and a half years (1990–2008) as a climber ranger at MRNP, the final five years serving as Supervisory Climbing Ranger. Gauthier represents the masses who want Northwest volcanoes, particularly Rainier, under their boots, soaring just above. He worked as an ultimate foreground figure in the middle of our telephoto views, as he spent several summer seasons at 9500 feet while posted at Camp Schurman on Rainier's northeast flank. An intimate of Rainier, Gauthier epitomizes our proprietary heritage and fond gaze.

Studying the ridges and glaciers above and below him, Gauthier stated, "There's a real sense that I'm part of what's happening and it's part of my life. I don't think of leaving the mountain and going home. I actually think of the mountain as my home."[29] This sentiment expresses a well-worn credo of mountaineering, in fact an archetype that precedes, in some manifestations, the nineteenth-century growth of European and American alpinism, ancient local habits of aversion (e.g., Yakama and Nisqually) notwithstanding. Despite John Muir's skepticism atop Mount Rainier in 1888 (Chapter 1), "mountain glory" meant that summit craters also figure as a home place: a concept that developed in late nineteenth-century mountaineering ideology and prevailed through much of the twentieth. As an extension of urban space we have used front-range volcanoes as light show spectacles (e.g., Mount Hood in 1887) or cemeteries or, more recently, as sites for fundraisers and corporate self-improvement schemes.[30] A Gauthier, with Rainier at his doorstep, serves as spokesman for the population. Those snowpeaks in our backyard belong to us.

But the limits of that tempting illusion are also voiced by Gauthier, who concedes, "I've come to learn that the mountain plain doesn't care. It doesn't care about me or anyone else."[31] Rainier's indifference denies not only all urban claims to a given volcano but all sense of human identification stretching back beyond Theodore Winthrop. The geological reality of the volcanoes utterly apart from human life embodies a biocentric rather than anthropocentric perspective, and however standard the former has become in recent environmental theory and praxis, that paradigm shift cannot discount the Northwest history of cultural ownership.

In centuries past, though most tribes kept their distance, they embraced nearby volcanoes through names and origin stories that figured in the central fabric of their histories. The volcanoes existed in storied relation to them. Many among the more recent regional population desire some sustained relation, which takes many forms.

In fact, recent and contemporary patterns of volcano use of necessity exist between these eternal contraries of connection yet disconnection, even as the volcanoes' geologic status always trumps the signs of the former. Figure and ground, built environment and volcano backdrop, constitute a false relation, and the indifference of the latter, like any landscape, exposes the vanity of human longing—our romantic conceit. Gauthier voices our dilemma wherein a volcano feels like a home place yet never is. The latter recognition links him with John Muir's concession about Rainier's summit. "Home" is not home; ground remains disconnected from fond figure—Bellingham's preferred version of itself, for example, with Bellingham Bay in foreground and Mount Baker in back. As conspicuous visual icons signifying a region, the volcanoes remain open to imaginative appropriation and elaborate self-definition, yet remain indifferent to human presence. Our behavior near or on them must reflect both the imaginative truth of belonging and the factual truth of existing forever apart and below.

4 GREEN CONSUMERISM AND THE VOLCANOES

I joined the ranks of the REI Army, that legion of gear-obsessed soldiers who suit up every weekend and drive into the hills to hunt down and kill their God-given portion of wilderness transcendence. . . . At REI a humorless sense of moral superiority seemed de rigueur, fostered by the belief that those who stomp the natural world under their Vibram soles are healing Gaea, while the rest of the world tears her asunder.

—Bruce Barcott, *The Measure of the Mountain*

Climbing volcanoes has always separated a self-chosen segment from the rest. That fin de siècle group of Rainier summiteers, chanting in alpine costume on a Tacoma street, epitomizes its status. Only the costumes and venues have changed. Successful volcano climbers don't dress any more for spontaneous street theater and applause, but the assumption of status—the conferral of cool—has not lessened. Quite the contrary: The possibility of personal transformation is connected to, and increasingly replaced by, some recognition of achievement, however modest; private experience is contingent upon public response of some form. No a priori connection exists between private and social realms, but for many the promise of a status otherwise unavailable signifies a primary rationale for tackling one or more of the snowpeaks. By the late twentieth century, thousands sought that status. Private experience also seems increasingly contingent upon sundry habits of commodification, which often eclipse it. Activity at or on the snowpeaks becomes subject to endless quantification, which all too frequently renders mountaineering a species of status tourism—a highly competitive high altitude sport.

The genre of persuasive testimonials has not disappeared; instead, more peer pressure has upped the ante. In its "Northwest Weekend" section (February 4, 2010), *The Seattle Times* ran an article titled "Is this your year to summit Rainier?" Aside from its internal rhyme, the title suggests that the second verb of mountaineering—to summit—has become an everyday term. The bylines, in block letters above the title, read, "FOR WASHINGTON MOUNTAINEERS, MOUNT RAINIER IS THE ICONIC CHALLENGE. NOW'S THE TIME TO COMMIT FOR A SUMMER CLIMB—OR TO START PLANNING FOR 2011. IT'S A MAJOR FEAT. IT'S A BIG MOUNTAIN. HERE'S A BACKGROUNDER TO HELP YOU DECIDE." The swollen ranks make the crater more desirable and possible for more people. Those testimonials tease wannabes and others to strap on crampons, get on the mountain, and show your ambition. Usually more demanding than the others, Rainier remains the biggest prize.

For Washington's leading newspaper, its biggest mountain remains a regularly visited subject. The same long-standing relation exists between *The Oregonian* and Mount Hood. This particular story marks the current relation of the mountain to the paper's readership: it invites the uninitiated to summit as so many others, from near and far, have. Bagging the snowpeaks confers both privilege and esteem, and the reward of altitude signifies a potent mode of tourism marked by perceived status. The lack of amenities characteristic of mountain trips—the old tradition of temporarily doing without, or with less—paradoxically increases their value. The combination of status and scale, notably industrial scale, becomes an apt filter through which to scrutinize the shifting narrative of regional mountaineering, particularly once mountaineering became a mass sport.[1]

This is a sociological narrative in which prevalent habits of mind and behavior turn, in many regards, increasingly consumerist. In the big business of regional mountaineering everyone gets a shot—if enough money is ponied up: as one mountaineer-critic observes, "Today's mass mountaineering offers democratic opportunities for elite achievement, commodified services for individual ambitions."[2] In it a volcano climb increasingly resembles a commodity, a pre-packaged entity with a careful script and usually swift execution. A summit becomes an intersection point between the ambivalent attractions of risk recreation—the inherent dangers of snowfield and glacier and rock climbing—and creature comforts expected by novice adventurers typically more affluent than not. "Dirtbag" climbers, proudly averse to convenience, lower that accepted level. Volcanoes as commodity, available to those with disposable income, assumed signal importance, economic and otherwise, by the late twentieth century. If the snowpeaks climax the region's self-portrait, increasing numbers climb to their tops, stretching their own stature in the process. Quick trips atop arctic islands earn a lot of points on anyone's chart. For beginners, buying a climb, an increasingly popular option, manifests the "accepted level of convenience" and a mercenary basis of that potentially transformative private experience. With so many climbing, traditional values like potent freedom and a sense of rebirth often take a back seat to the status game—the spur of competition.

The regional history of mountaineering reveals variations upon the theme of status tourism. It also reveals a shift from clubs—the long history of the Mazamas and the Mountaineers—to crowds. In the twentieth century's first half, both clubs organized and championed large trips, particularly through their annual summer outings—leisurely expedition climbs. In later decades, as one measure of a mass sport, guiding services served increasingly diverse clienteles. This suggests one pervasive trend wherein potential climbers purchase their experience through rented expertise if not gear. New climbers and wannabes faced increasing choices in alpine clothing and gear as fashion became a predictable means to buy the right look—mass-market descendants of those long ago Rainier climbers. The volcanoes became a primary destination for and expression of environmental consumerism, as a volcano climb (and its accompanying gear) became, in large part, a trophy like a big, chased-silver rodeo belt buckle. Trophies visually separate achievers from the rest and exert pressure on some beholders. Through the summit-as-trophy, many chant their achievement like those early, costumed summiteers. And they expect applause of some form.

The "right stuff," like that rodeo belt buckle, marks the individual bagging the summit. Whether the climber-as-consumer wholly "transcend[s] this commodified relation to the peak" by climbing it, as one critic asserts, is therefore open to question.[3] When volcanoes are insistently used as product brands, most consumers never entirely sever the linkage between image and product. Or they blur the imagery with the actual mountain. While most who summit the volcanoes experience some measure of personal growth and indelible change, it becomes tricky to distinguish feelings of humility or desire, for instance, from the status accrued from clothing or gear: the outer vesture of achievement. The climb-as-package, an end in itself, enables one to be more studly—another notch in the belt.

The Mountaineers' history is inextricably linked with not only with Mount Rainier, "the home base of the Mountaineers" in its early years, but also the history of the regional outdoors gear industry, as is the case with the Mazamas.[4] Experience in the Cascades means gear, and over the twentieth century the gear market exploded, becoming an end in itself. The market grew expensive and clothes often eclipsed gear. With the right look, individuals appear as virtual volcano climbers, their actual snow experience secondary or fictitious. Northwest icons—for example the late Kurt Cobain, leader of Seattle's band Nirvana, a bellwether of grunge rock music—sealed a trendy, rough look, one in which expensive flannels or anoraks, for example, should appear worn or even slightly torn. Part of Northwest chic consists of the outdoors, especially alpine, look. We wear who we are—or want to be, the latter always tugging the former. By the 1990s REI's flagship stores, for example, were ripe for social criticism of the sort voiced by journalist Bruce Barcott (see epigraph). As an outdoor industry leader, REI branded itself as some high altar of green elitism along with alpine opportunity—for a hefty price. Like other outdoor gear vendors, REI's website illustrates the tight weave of experience and commodity; of environmentalism and consumerism.

The history of mountaineering, northwest or otherwise, is not only inextricably linked with the outdoor gear/clothes industry. As a mostly social history it chronicles widely changing fashions in group size and scale. The promise of personal transformation manifested itself in a social context (except with solo climbing) that varied dramatically over time.

The founding scene of the Mazamas ironically forecast the contemporary pressures of industrial tourism. In its beginnings, group affirmation counted more than personal achievement. The first page of *We Climb High* (1969), the 75th anniversary almanac-history of the club, chronicles the day the club was formed: "Despite a formidable thunder and sleet storm," "155 men and 38 women gained the summit" with "105 climbers [subsequently] sign[ing] up as charter members."[5] The Mazamas began as a big party, in several senses of the term. In this ceremonial scene, climbers summited en masse, and almost 60 percent of them pledged themselves to this large-group identity. The back cover photo of *We Climb High* depicts a quintet of climbers on the flat summit awaiting the arrival, one by one, of a string of nineteen others similarly dressed. A gentleman on the summit, left arm behind his back as though bowing, courteously extends his right arm and plants his short

FIG. 6. An early Mazamas expedition climb approaches the crater and summit of Mount Baker. Oregon State University Libraries, Wikimedia Commons.

FIG. 7. A Mazamas encampment near Mount Rainier. This represented a form of high-impact camping unacceptable in recent decades. Oregon State University Libraries, Wikimedia Commons.

alpenstock to help the first of the nineteen hoist his torso over the snowy lip. The image and gesture, both formal and humorous, provided comic relief for club members over many decades.[6] The Mountaineers' founding scene (1906), a Mazamas Mount Baker climb led by Asahel Curtis and a Seattle businessman named C. Montelius Price, involved a large party, though nowhere as large. According to these founding scenes, most early climbers were in this thing together as tiny parts of a large social organism. If anything, group success mattered more than individual success.

Large clubs can become victims of their own success as outsiders intrude or younger members wield their influence and change the club's direction. Like California's Sierra Club, both the Mazamas and the Mountaineers employed quasi-military structures in their mass ascents. Other forces challenged those structures at times. Crowds attract crowds, and in the early twentieth century non-members joined Mazamas climbers on Mount Hood, particularly on the annual Fourth of July climb that commenced in 1914.[7] On this holiday national, regional (and state), and club identities fused, providing rich frames of reference for the individual climber. Despite this tradition, the Mazamas didn't establish a mountaineering school until 1950, years after the Mountaineers; two years later the club changed its programming to more climbs and smaller groups.[8]

For the Mountaineers, the annual summer outing focused club climbing instruction for the first three decades. Despite its name, mountaineering was not the main agenda. The "outing," primary expression of the club as a climbing club, signaled collective achievement. That annual climbing instruction unsurprisingly proved a strait jacket soon enough, since climbers wanted more climbing and new policies at the Mountaineers' Snoqualmie Lodge.[9] After the first generation, the values of climbing increasingly diverged from the values of the outing: by the 1930s climbing gained center stage. The Mountaineers didn't discontinue the outing until 1980, and by then big group climbs had been anachronistic for a generation. The scales of status had shifted.

FIG. 8. An early Mazamas hiking trip on Mount Rainier (south side). Oregon State University Libraries. Wikimedia Commons.

These clubs defined a particular style of being in the mountains, one that institutionalized recreational tourism into a particular structure. It was all about common cause, not individual will, as early Mazamas combined personal energy with "public service and regional development" ideals and group discipline. Regional mountaineers of this period fancied themselves high-minded public citizens who prized elaborate organization—a far cry from mountain identity in later generations. Both Mazamas and Mountaineers flourished because of a specific blending and balancing of goals—goals that, in a few decades, seemed quaint, anachronistic. Club identity—a mix of "physical exertion, social idealism, and humor"—trumped personal achievement.[10] Their commitment to "social idealism" matched their practice of bringing their club principles to subalpine or alpine encampments that combined challenge with creature comforts. Such camps flourished through a devotion to club rules and ideals, along with a modicum of amenities.

With the club emphasis upon the annual summer outing, the volcano climb became clearly commodified, accompanied by an elaborate infrastructure and expeditionary planning. Reaching a crater signaled group achievement and affirmed one's identity as a member. Shifts in emphases and fluctuations in membership, as outlaw groups succeeded mainstream clubbers, reflected changes in mountaineering, particularly as climbing lost its coterie reputation by the mid-twentieth century. A changing membership alters club fashions if not philosophy. The clubs' success in opening access to the volcanoes and other peaks led to their loss of exclusive control of that access. Though the Mazamas remains a primary mountain club in Oregon, it is not the only act, nor has it been for a long time. Both venerable clubs have revised themselves repeatedly to recruit or retain younger members who might see the venerable clubs as uncool.

The Mountaineers' identity was indelibly stamped by the personality of its early president, University of Washington historian Edmond S. Meany, who served 1908–35—according to several historians, several years longer than he should have. Meany dressed the part of famous professor and Seattleite, with pipe and tie and tweeds, and he didn't change when climbing. He recited poetry and led Sunday morning interdenominational services, climbs, and the evening campfire entertainment, often with his freshly penned mountain poems. Judging from one sample, "Glacier Peak," Meany's hackneyed, nineteenth-century romanticism showed him in common cause with Theodore Winthrop's effusions. He thought this style still valid in 1930. He presumed himself, a versifying scholar-scrambler, the pre-eminent role model, and in Meany's version of a day in the mountains, summiting mattered little.[11]

Meany embodied a broad view of being in the mountains, one in which summits are not primary. His leadership was confirmed by the land purchase and construction of Meany Ski Hut near Stampede Pass in 1928, as well as by the naming of Mount Meany in the Olympics and Meany Crest near Mount Rainier's Little Tahoma.[12] But dissent loomed as inevitably as winter snowpack.

In his later years, younger Mountaineers rebelled against his style as well as the Mountaineers' check-in rules regarding the "ten peaks" and "second ten" in the Snoqualmie Pass region. Arguably to encourage use of the Mountaineers' Snoqualmie Lodge, the club developed a list of ten peaks in the Snoqualmie Pass area that club members were supposed to tick off. They quickly developed a second ten also in the pass area.

According to one critic, "When you got through that you were supposed to do them all over again. And I looked at the various maps of the Cascades, and there seemed to me many more interesting places than Snoqualmie Pass. But the Mountaineers were devoted to keeping this lodge going financially and they didn't want to climb anywhere else."[13]

Meany's personality and value system did not represent younger members more interested in climbing, and if you didn't like his poems and quasi-military standards, too bad. But late-Victorian sensibility and gentlemanly conduct, like the paramilitary structure and size, had become anachronisms.

By the 1930s, alternate definitions of status in the mountains were emerging that challenged the centrality of club identity. The early generations valued fellowship over peak bagging, one representative member fondly recalling Mount Rainier ski trips, the summer outing, and the club plays.[14] Mary Anderson, co-founder of REI, spoke nostalgically about the camaraderie in her old age: "It was the one way people could get out into the wilderness. There was singing and the goodnight song. I don't even think the Mountaineers know the Goodnight Song anymore. The summer outings finally died out when roads and cars made places more accessible, and maybe because no one wanted to take over the responsibility."[15] Nothing new about such cycles in a club's life, as formality, for example, is succeeded by informality. Most social features of the old Mountaineers went the way of the alpenstock, to no one's surprise.

Anderson pointed to the changing infrastructure as a primary cause for the annual outing's decline and fall. Private cars meant decentralized climbing. No one organized and led large, expeditionary climbs since smaller groups gained favor. The size of parties coming to the volcanoes dropped even as the numbers shot up. And they usually came with new gear bought at the new co-op: REI.

In the oldest story of generational conflict, the younger rebels against the older and asserts itself as contrary. Against the residue of Victorian gentility, younger Mountaineers figured as populist outlaws. Mary Anderson's husband Lloyd Anderson, leading climber and co-founder of REI, deemed himself an outlaw, as did his friend, Harvey Manning, the club's most famous writer. In Meany's final years, climbers like Anderson and Wolf Bauer were pushing the envelope—willing, for example, to use pitons (metal spikes hammered into rock cracks, to which ropes are attached), which old-timers considered heresy. Looking back, Anderson said that he joined the Mountaineers from the "Tillicum organization" at the University of Washington, "a radical organization." He shook it up as part of a radical group that forced a revolution within the club. As his friend Manning said of the Andersons, "both came from farm families": they were not middle class urbanites.[16]

Populists revolted against excessive manners both in the club-house and on the peaks: too formal, too stuffy. The outlaw climbers group, or 35 members (7%) of the club, first met September 25, 1934, but were not officially sanctioned until 1937; the first climbing course, taught by Wolf Bauer, was likely the first in the country. According to the Mountaineers' historian, the climbing course designed by Anderson endured, with minor modifications, until the century's end.[17] Anderson and Bauer placed their own climbing careers second and leadership in the climbing courses first. For such pioneers, the revolt concentrated the club's energy on climbing, not social traditions.

By 1938, the "Climbing Committee" in effect controlled the Mountaineers just as regional styles fundamentally changed. As always, older climbers viewed younger as brash. As European climbing styles and hardware proliferated, route difficulty gained central status as did first ascents. Mount Hood's west side and Rainier's north face, the latter with its huge Willis Wall and challenging routes like Curtis and Liberty ridges, played a central role in regional mountaineering as it accelerated in popularity, difficulty, and accomplishment. All volcanoes remained proving grounds as a spirit of competition entered the sport.

With the new focus, summiting per se was not the complete prize; route selection gained value, and being in the mountains meant climbing peaks via increasingly difficult routes. The harder, the better. Additionally, the climbing emphasis spread to other domains including search and rescue, and publishing. The Mountaineers' first climbing course was split into basic and intermediate sections after World War II, graduates of the latter usually staffing the former. By 1939, the Mountaineers Rescue Patrol had formed; by 1948, the Mountain Rescue Council had formed, and by 1959, the regional idea had spread when the national Mountain Rescue Association (MRA) was established. The MRA, the oldest search and rescue association in the United States, has carried out its double mission of mountain safety education and rescue for over half a century.[18] The Mountaineers' climbing courses were codified in Manning's *Mountaineering: The Freedom of the Hills* (1960; 7th ed., 2003), which launched its highly profitable publishing division.

With the advent of World War II, Mount Rainier became the site of another use, one strikingly different from increasingly hard climbing. The Mountaineers offered their first ski mountaineering course the month of the attack on Pearl Harbor; soon thereafter ski troops from Fort Lewis were training on Rainier. The Army's purposes differed fundamentally from those behind the Mountaineers' course. These troops later formed a core of the Army's famous 10th Mountain Infantry Division, which saw dense action in the Apennines of Italy. For the first time, a volcano served as a base for sustained military training: a temporary institutional use, one antithetical to the pleasures of cross-country or downhill skiing.

In the post-Meany era, another individual defined a contrary climbing ethos. Seattle native Fred Beckey, by the late 1930s, began a series of first ascents that made him the most famous name among regional mountaineers. Compared to the proletarian rebels who dominated the Mountaineers, Beckey symbolized a loud, anti-establishment credo that, over decades, itself became establishment among increasing numbers of acolytes and fans. To this day Beckey remains a living legend, one whom writers seek to profile (e.g., Tim Egan in *The Good Rain*). In his heyday he simply covered more ground than other climbers: he defined the status of first ascents, long the gold standard in climbing. Beckey could be called the godfather of dirtbag climbers—a species that emerged in the past generation or two and accrued great status through their worn clothing and outrageous proficiency.

Ever an iconoclast, Beckey epitomized a different drummer, a single-minded devotion to climbing. He lived for climbing, taking a series of random, casual jobs (or product endorsements) to support his habit, according to a friend of mine who has climbed with Beckey and knows his story. In this world, the rest of one's life is incidental. Beckey underlined his authority as an author—an alternative to the Mountaineers' Harvey Manning—by writing (and revising) the three-volume, definitive climbing guides to the Washington Cascades and producing other books, notably the elaborate *Range of Glaciers*, a beautifully produced history (geologic and human) of the North Cascades (2003). Beckey embodies an anti-club philosophy and was famously not invited to be part of the 1963 American Everest expedition: possibly he'd irritated too many people.

With such variable role models as Anderson, Bauer, and Beckey, the new sport developed an intimate connection with business. Anderson served as president of the Mountaineers (1946–48) while simultaneously being paid a part-time commission (1945–59) for staffing the REI co-op he and his wife had founded in 1938. A symbiotic relationship between activity and supply house unfolded, in part because in the postwar years the Mountaineers climbing course became famous locally and nationally.[19] Local "wilderness mountaineering," not imported from the Alps, helped refine climbing techniques.

The Northwest led, inspired as well by a new focus in mountain photography developed by twins Bob and Ira Spring—a focus markedly different from the work of an Ansel Adams. Early mountaineering photography proved great business: as Ira Spring reminisced, "No one was doing anything on U.S. climbing. So we appeared in all the popular magazines of the era with our mountain stories and they led to a lot of other things."[20] As the Springs, Portland's Roy Atkeson, and others proved, the photography business, like the supply business, accelerated public interest in the snowpeaks, and in turn alpine values spread into auxiliary domains of reproduced images, gear, and clothing.

The post–World War II boom in mountaineering proved a harbinger. During the 1950s regional climbers helped change the sport just as Americans, mostly upper and middle class, took to the mountains as never before. The numbers suggested mountaineering would continue to grow exponentially. In the very period when the Northwest's reputation as a region gained stature, mountaineering proved one dramatic manifestation of it. Many joined one of the two clubs, though the ratio of members to overall climbers declined as more lost interest in club structure. Club control lessened.

Though the west-slope population centers commanded most club membership, mountaineering clubs sprang up on the east side of the Cascades as well. One spinoff club, the Sherpas based in Ellensburg Washington, kept it small, loose, and informal, their anti-rules bent posing an alternative to the more institutionalized, older clubs.

Though the Sherpas ran their meetings similarly to their climbs, some of them participated in a Yakima-based mass climb of Mount Adams—Yakima's volcano. A mass climb tradition was tied to local, east-slope boosterism and promotion, not unlike the Mount Baker–Bellingham summit-sea race. According to longtime climber Dave Mahre, "On one of the climbs we took five-hundred people to the summit. . . . The little town of Yakima wanted to have some type of festival. I was one of the guys who was on the committee when it formed. . . . [the] Sun Fair climb on Mount Adams . . . went on for thirteen years until the Sierra Club and the Lloyd family shut us down. We were ruining the perpetual snow fields on the mountains."[21] The Sun Fair climb not only sealed the Yakima-Mount Adams bond but also signaled the final act of regional large-group climbs—though, in another respect, it precisely forecast the ongoing dilemma of massive volcano climbs. Sherpas climbers like Mahre knew firsthand the damage wrought by large-group climbs, and he no doubt concurred with verdict of the Sierra Club, which after all had originated the large group climb in the 1890s. These disappeared in part because of a rising environmentalism: many members found old camping habits and sizes increasingly detrimental to alpine landscapes.

The post–World War II greening of the Northwest, which the baby boomer generation grew up with and expanded, must be plotted against the rise of the outdoor clothing and gear industry, for their stories are tightly braided. To a considerable extent, our relationships with the volcanoes became increasingly commodified in the later twentieth century, and environmental consumerism has become both commonplace and unquestioned. Part of this trend can be seen in the paradox reflected in the mission statements of the Mazamas and the Mountaineers, who have consistently advocated for conservation *and* access—the same conflicting dilemma faced by the NPS in its maturity.

From their beginning the Mountaineers wanted mass access and preservation, and their naïveté forecast our own. Its first president, Henry Landes, believed the club should actively oppose environmental destruction, but also make the mountains available to all who might want to be there.[22] As the twentieth century progressed the friction between these contrary ideals grew apace. At the same time, accessibility provided a raison d'être for the booming outdoors industry, which embodies another fundamental conflict. The volcano climb as package deal was easily extended to the appurtenances surrounding it.

The Northwest also proved itself a national leader in outdoor gear, since the story of regional climbing indelibly links itself with the story of new stuff. During the 1920s and early 1930s, for example, Eddie Bauer, Inc. expanded by supplying gear for the new sport of downhill skiing.[23] A product of the late Depression years (1938), REI remains not only another Northwest icon like the volcanoes, but a U.S. leader in outdoors clothing and equipment. The fact that its founder, Lloyd Anderson, was called "the most persistent climber of the prewar period" implies a complex interplay between the promise of alpine experience and the fact of equipment.[24] REI's story symbolizes the big business of mountaineering, among other sports, and one conspicuous version of environmental consumerism. Over the decades REI imitated and defined shifts in the regional ethos, and it provides an accurate barometer of changing values in Northwest mountaineering.

Harvey Manning's REI: *Fifty Years of Climbing Together* (1987) reflected the industry/alpine experience symbiosis in its title. Who was *not* climbing with REI, after all (aside from the fact that REI per se does not climb)? It became difficult to distinguish being in the mountains from being properly outfitted, and the latter definition shifted in terms of safety, comfort, and cost. Manning, playing the part of irascible curmudgeon with gusto, pointed out that REI was born amidst a pervasive co-operative movement in Seattle. The nascent co-op was barely distinguishable from the club, as climbers preferred to check out new gear rather than remain in the clubrooms. For a period during World War II, co-op and club shared common space and name, with the former "commonly referred to as 'The Mountaineers Co-op.'"[25] For members of either they functioned de facto as one. Soon enough the business far outstripped the club because it changed its look (and its goods) much quicker. Eventually, wearing the right stuff didn't necessarily imply being on the volcanoes as alpine fashion took on a robust life of its own.

The evolution of an outdoor gear business like REI, which quickly outgrew its blue-collar roots, traces a common trajectory, one that arcs through non-profit to big profit(s). Growing affluence meant growing demand and rising price tags. Numbers tell part of the story: in 1949–59, REI membership grew by 900 percent; in 1959–69, by 1600 percent; in 1969–79, by 700 percent, to just short of one million members, and sales increased 900 percent in that decade.[26] By 1987 there were over two million REI members, and compared to its rolls, the club proved a footnote. Within one generation, the Mountaineers-REI nexus had mostly disappeared, as by the late 1960s over half of REI's active members lived outside Washington state.[27]

Regional residency no longer mattered, its skiing and clothing lines catering to socio-economically ambitious markets. And who didn't self-identify as "upwardly-mobile" in the generation following World War II? At the same time, REI fostered a Northwest chic, as 1960s staffers dressed in outdoors if not alpine clothes and spread the cool vibe to the swelling ranks of customers.[28] When the upwardly mobile met the fit, outdoorsy crew, the former bought the latter's look in hopes of buying its status. In this business's rapidly changing identity, fancy replaced functional and an earlier close-knit community dissipated.

The story of the regional alpine gear industry suggests that status tourism eclipses the traditional, private reasons for climbing volcanoes or other peaks. Being "properly" outfitted helped novices and others fit in on increasingly crowded trails or standard routes above them. Affluence alienated the older generations who thrived on war surplus gear that was cheap; by contrast, 1960s mountaineers wanted the newest, top-of-the-line gear some of the old timers, who'd been poor, despised. In a standard plot, "cheap stuff" is replaced by "expensive crap" as a business morphs from its humble origins into a corporate giant dedicated to "fancy," and for many volcano climbing (or other climbing) is construed as a packaged (or pre-packaged) experience. For some, "top-of-the-line" has become disassociated from its primary functions in the field. Anderson himself voiced the same contempt regarding later REI catalogues and climbing equipment.[29] Apart from their unsurprising grouchiness, the Harvey Mannings and Lloyd Andersons fingered the baby-boomer shift in values. Once one's relatively low REI member number became cool, the store's product lines became status symbols in themselves, as though one buys reputation apart from actual experience on glaciers or in steep gullies.

If Fred Beckey remains the godfather of regional dirtbag climbers, the Whittaker twins, seven years younger, symbolize establishment climbing for the general population as no others. Their rugged, long faces are more recognizable than Beckey's seamed face.

Especially since 1963, Jim Whittaker has embodied alpine cool more than most regional (or even national) mountaineers, and his career closed the gap between alpine experience and commodity, between Northwest volcanoes and peaks and gear, as had no one else's. This West Seattle native made it real big. He ran REI for twenty-four years (1955–79) and oversaw its growth from a local shop into an international business.

Looking back upon his reign, he sounded an upbeat note: "There are some things I see that I don't like, but all in all it's serving a lot of people. What we tried to do was get people out and give them a good product for a good price. That ties into my philosophy. You can educate people about how to take care of the out-of-doors, but you've got to get them out. It's like a church. If you get them out, they're going to know it and like it."[30] With the invocation of "church," Whittaker voiced the traditional value of volcanoes (or other mountains) as sites for personal transformation, but now the transformative potential is neatly packaged and priced. In the old allegory, supply meets demand.

Alpine gear companies effortlessly link experience with equipment as if they are the same, equipment being the ineluctable vesture, in this self-serving rationale, of experience. The familiar invocation of personal growth is tied to equipment—"a good product," the "good price" being debatable. Whittaker voiced the credo of industrial tourism, of alpine experience as bulk commodity, in preaching the indisputable gospel of the mountains: "I'm taking a lot of people up mountains who haven't climbed before. They're older, they're rich. They're seeing that their lives are going to end without any adventure. A lot of people want to experience the mountains."[31] More want a taste of that unique ocean of freedom found in high altitudes and along a rope, and pay good money for it. The scale of alpine desire has changed, particularly to the extent that that desire is wrapped up with perceived prestige as a primary outcome of summiting.

The heady 1960s turned up the status game. Mountaineering gained a new prestige and masses wanted in on the action. As always, the volcanoes lured as the highest peaks and biggest trophies. After the 1963 Mount Everest expedition, Mount Rainier, as the training mountain, enjoyed new celebrity as did REI, and Whittaker discovered himself an overnight hero, familiar to *Time* magazine readers and the Kennedy White House. He fraternized with Bobby Kennedy and led him on climbs just as his twin brother, Lou, led Robert McNamara up Mount Rainier. As Harvey Manning astutely commented, Whittaker "would gain fame as the biggest bum in the history of Northwest mountaineering, and then would run things by making bumming respectable."[32]

"Making bumming respectable" defines the seismic shift in the scale of regional mountaineering just as it explains cycles of offshoots such as dirtbag climbers. The phrase captures the lure of mountaineering for masses who might not crave summits but who gravitate to the ostensibly socially disreputable or marginal. The gravitational pull alters the supposed stigma and renders climbing-as-bumming not only respectable and mainstream, but also highly prized. In 1969 about midway through Jim's reign at REI, Lou Whittaker co-founded Rainier Mountaineering, Inc. (RMI), by far the oldest guiding service at Mount Rainier. For decades R M I enjoyed a monopoly, and such a service formalizes the climb as packaged experience. Their literature stresses Rainier as gateway volcano, prerequisite for higher, harder peaks in Alaska and on other continents. The Whittakers institutionalized bumming and made it chic, upscale, as Beckey, ultimate bum, did not. Dirtbaggers resist institutionalization even as they bag endorsements from North Face, Mountain Safety Research, and other alpine gear biggies.

One Northwest mountaineering chronicler, Malcolm Bates, spoke for many coming of age in the 1960s: "President Kennedy promoted fitness, and those of us who weren't playing touch football were trying 50-mile day hikes around Lake Washington. And the hills were alive with the sound of lug-soled feet tramping along mountain trails, no doubt irritating old-timers who had grown used to having the Cascades all to themselves." Hiking and climbing posed valid alternatives to the usual mass audience team sports. Bates unsurprisingly praised the emerging climbing community he joined because of their commitment to expanding the sport even as styles shifted from "siege variety" expeditionary climbing to lighter, faster, smaller teams.[33] New equipment drove new values: lightness and speed. Technology extended the landscape of the possible and pushed mountaineers to ever more difficult routes and challenges. Routes considered unclimbable a few years earlier were routinely tackled, in part because of new kinds of climbing hardware. Or routes that hitherto required ropes and hardware were being free climbed (i.e., unroped). This period also birthed speed climbing, a dubious contemporary gold standard that further defines a climb as a swiftly executed package experience.

Legions both local and itinerant responded to Whittaker's call, and numbers on the volcanoes and other peaks imitated, on an admittedly far smaller scale, the accelerating numbers of R E I members. Northwest climbers found strangers on their favorite Cascades peaks and routes, and there were plenty of strangers in the generation after 1963. Nowhere was this truer than on the volcanoes' standard routes—those white funnels. Ironically, just as the numbers of REI members and climbers surged, a new environmental advocacy, growing since World War II, took hold as hikers and climbers joined preservationist organizations opposing further resource extraction. They hit the trails and wanted to protect what they saw. At the same time they bought increasing amounts of new clothes and gear. Environmental advocacy grew into the political mainstream just as environmental consumerism turned into big business. Advocacy and consumerism go hand-in-hand, and in the Northwest that fact easily extended itself onto the volcanoes.

Jim Whittaker, Mount Everest summiteer, longtime REI CEO, and one symbol of the experience-equipment nexus, also epitomized REI's shift to environmental advocacy. Not only did he preside over big expeditions and big growth (e.g., the REI mail order business), and but he also led REI's grassroots activism. Reminiscing later, he embodied the change to green thinking: "We used to climb and drop tin cans and juice cans down the wall to hear it tinkle. Then we began to bury the tin cans and orange peels under the summit rocks. You'd pick up the rocks, there'd be stuff under them, and you began thinking, 'Geez we'd better carry some of this out.' That's how it started, and it didn't really start until the late 1960s."[34] The gradual shift came about from the increasing numbers at summit cairns as much as any factor.

This three-stage plot expressed, in miniature, salient changes in Northwest behavior in the mountains in the twentieth century's second half. This recent history chronicles the growth from childish irresponsibility—the fun "tinkle" of falling cans or shallow burying of the climbers' leavings—to environmental responsibility. Whittaker recalled directing many REI initiatives including cleanup climbs in the Snoqualmie Pass region as well as tree planting at the Seattle store. Yet even as the "pack it out" credo gained wide acceptance, increasing numbers of abusers left their trash signatures. More cleanup, more trash: this tough symbiosis marks the regional love affair with hiking and climbing.

And it matches the consumerism/environmental advocacy symbiosis that figures centrally in the alpine status game. REI's "pack it out" mantra was visibly supported by Governor Dan Evans (1965–77), a longtime member. Whittaker's celebrity enhanced his effect as a CEO lobbyist and REI, as an outdoors industry leader, used its position to teach and practice stewardship. In the past forty years, REI's commitment to outdoors education and grassroots conservation has been steady. At the same time, its facile linkage of "outdoors" and "outfitted" has been insufficiently critiqued. Education bleeds into consumerism. Alpine experience as commodity is accompanied by increasing layers of fancy rather than cheap clothes and gear.

Mountaineering has changed beyond recognition within a century, core "shared values" having tilted or been obscured. In the past generation the pace of technological refinements matched the burgeoning numbers. The current generation can be defined by quantity and autonomy, with large numbers of cutting-edge climbers continually raising the bar of what's possible. Behind these leaders, thousands of wannabes trudge or admire from a distance. The new breed willfully disconnects itself from the past. According to one older observer, they look and act differently, "dressed in feather-light, skin-tight waterproof (almost) outfits made of the latest synthetic fiber. Today's climber seems stronger, faster, brasher, more irreverent, less interested in ties to his and her mountaineering past."[35] Of course an older generation often views the newer with anger and incredulity. Mountaineering competition in many guises has been considerably notched up, and as is true in many sports, the so-called leaders throw down gauntlets for legions of imitators.

One contemporary gauntlet, speed climbing, replaces craters (or other summits) with finish lines, the climb being reduced to a race against the clock. In speed climbing, speed becomes seemingly the sole reason for being on mountains. That criterion fits one adolescent mind-set broadcast by loud tight clothes: watch me because I'm faster/better than you'll ever be. For some climbers not speed climbing, a climb is measured by the door-to-door time (lapse). In some respects speed climbing, wherein a route becomes a race, represents the extreme example of a climb-as-commodity, as if the quickest time on a mountain equals the best time. In the status game, speed climbing implies that being on (or in) mountains represents a race, like slalom or downhill skiing competitions. This is a mixed heritage at best. Speed climbing represents a perverse reduction of being in the mountains, as though speed best distills that traditional ocean of freedom and potential for personal trans-formation. Those values accrue from deliberate pace and a reach of time, not the opposite.

Speed climbing constitutes an odd gold standard. By the late twentieth century, the "mountain glory" of old was thoroughly tinc-tured with mountain boast, speed climbing posing a loud example.

Sociologically, it's a different landscape. Many contemporary climbers exult in their gear-driven abilities and often lack historical sensibility—or more than casual social bonds. For some of them, mountaineering by the 1990s represented the sexiest of sports—one that led many in the corporate world to adopt the Hood climb or other climbs as models for management training. The well-publicized dot-com bubble that burst at the twentieth century's end temporarily dampened this reputation, but it has rebounded. Mountaineering carries great status for cadres of buff men and women seeking new expressions of cool, and the volcanoes call.

Proportionally fewer of them belong to clubs, but we're not talking about a mass climbing-alone phenomenon. The Mazamas, the Mountaineers, and their many offshoots thrive through stra-tegic adaptation even as their earlier, dominant presence on the volcanoes diminished. In the case of the Mountaineers, their mem-bership dropped by one third in the past generation, similar to national patterns for recreational clubs, but leaders ambitiously plan to expand membership far above this drop during the current decade.[36] While such clubs occupy solid market niches (Mountaineers claims itself the third largest such club in the United States), increasing numbers choose to be in the mountains but not be in clubs.

In some respects, club identity has been diffused by corporate behavior. Most serious or casual climbers including myself prefer small, fluid groupings rather than anything fixed or organized. They want neither rituals nor restrictions. To expand their niche, club leadership has tilted towards the corporate world. In the Mountaineers in recent decades, its leaders come from business backgrounds. Recruiting ranks of amateurs to the volcanoes requires marketing savvy that typically advertises the experience as a unique, tightly run package deal. Club identity is further diffused by the scale of industrial tourism, with thousands contracting their climb through a guide service. In doing so, the climber-consumer does not "transcend this commodified relation to the peak," as critic Gordon Sayre argues, but rather completes or seals it. After all, the scripted schedules offer a clear beginning, middle, and end, like buying a short narrative in which the consumer figures prominently. And she does so wearing the same light, tight, synthetic clothes as those worn by the contemporary pros.

The popularity of volcano and rock climbing has surfaced in regional cities and suburbs in a new way during the past generation. Increasing numbers, many of them accomplished climbers, want the feel of climbing short of actually going to the mountains. Just as many wear the alpine look away from the volcanoes, so a type of virtual climbing enables the contemporary generation to climb indoors, in cities or suburbs. It's hard to simulate glaciers and ice walls, and no artificial mini-volcanoes have erupted on the landscape. Yet climbing on indoor (or, occasionally, outdoor) "rock" walls flourishes despite its literal and philosophical distance from actual mountains.

Whether stairstep to snowpeaks or an end in itself, indoor

climbing has gained great vogue in one generation. Practical considerations—proximity, comfort, brief time commitment, convenience—explain its surging regional growth. Walls can be climbed during school or lunch hours, after school, or in the evening. "Routes" are usually top-roped (i.e., secured with a rope fixed from above), which increases the safety margin. Speed of access and use, then, account in large part for the popularity of facsimile climbing: a trend that matches the increasingly short, quick visitation patterns in MRNP or MHNF wilderness areas. Folks want to climb in the city.

The Mountaineers, for example, has promoted its own climbing wall, erected to mimic a rock face and visible for many city blocks. Simulation and visibility are crucial to the club's new headquarters' crowning feature. The wall and courtyard boulders (from a November 2003 North Cascades Highway rockslide) market the club and bring the mountains to the city. A fake rock face has exposed itself inside Seattle, just a mile or two from the real boulder 1930s Mountaineers practiced on—yet another expression of a city incorporating nearby mountains.

Climbing walls' visibility account, in part, for their high status (pun intended). For many, a wall constitutes the first pitches that eventuate in a route on a volcano or rocky peak; for others, it has become an end in itself, faux bouldering. Why go to the mountains when a wall rises much closer and stays dry and warm? Climbing walls/gyms appear a quick and easy adaptation of commodified climbing. It's so much cheaper and quicker and nearby—as long as you're willing to pay your money and wait your turn (the latter like popular big rock wall routes). Although its skill sets anticipate those of rock climbing, the notion that they are synonymous is an illusion. As a trusted climbing instructor and friend claims, climbing walls often set up dangerous expectations about one's ability and the transference of skill sets onto actual rock.

Though climbing walls do not prepare one for rock faces or volcanoes, they usually include audiences, however small. Climbing walls exist in part as status symbols so that the climber can be watched. Of course this happens below real rock faces, or sections of standard routes, but probably it occurs more frequently at climbing walls as others, perhaps waiting their turn, watch a climber's every move.

The current REI wall in Seattle's flagship store rises immediately west of the southbound lanes of I-5, on the north edge of Seattle's downtown. The wall is fittingly called the Big One, on the edge of "Hiketown"—a term used by more than one environmental writer to describe a Seattle neighborhood populated by "granolas" and others who wear the alpine look in town, like many REI staffers. REI Seattle's website homepage boasts, "More than a store, we rank among the Emerald City's top sightseeing attractions," a continually updated mart/shrine to regional mountaineering. The Big One represents a new stage of bringing the outdoors inside and of blurring the boundaries between artificial and real. Hundreds of passing motorists glance momentarily, some enviously, at individuals on various stages of "the Pinnacle," as it's also called, taller than anything else of its kind. The glimpse is fleeting, unlike studying Rainier farther south on I-5. Lots of eyes, not just those in the store, flicker over the Pinnacle behind the four-story windows. At this mini-Matterhorn much shorter than Walt Disney's at Disneyland, snow is only a memory.[37]

In the past two generations, the gear industry has grown sophisticated in the equipment-experience nexus, inextricably linking its institutional green commitments (e.g., programming and philanthropic support of local grassroots causes) with advertising. For some, clothing has eclipsed gear in proliferating venues. Cost and affluence have obscured outdoor equipment's older, functional basis characteristic of REI's first generation. In this simple social addition, buying the right stuff is prerequisite for bagging a summit, itself prerequisite for alpine status. At that flagship REI store, home of the Big One, climbing gear spreads over several aisles and racks rather than being clustered in low-level or out-of-the-way cubbyholes. The scene is suffused with clothes and regional cool ripe for satire.

Journalist Bruce Barcott's indictment of the "REI Army" (see epigraph) portrays both self-righteous military mission and earnest green elitism. To what extent do those wearing REI windpants or gaiters or crampons carry some trace of "moral superiority" onto steep snowfields or glaciers? Social critic David Brooks has called REI "a store that sells leisure stuff to people who spend their leisure hours strenuously, or at least would like to look like they do," which features a hieroglyphic "code of gear connoisseurship."[38] The codes—the right labels—are potent. In the old status game, wannabes outnumber those seeking steep snow but hypocritically dress the part as though they also use crampons. A critic like Brooks exposes the gap between the codes known only to the cognoscenti and the rest of us. Like a pilgrim in an Eco-Consumer's Progress, he mocks the perceived status of the codes and critiques the whole enterprise, feigning interest in "a titanium Omnitech parka with double-rip-stop nylon supplemented with ceramic particles and polyurethane-coat welded seams." Feeling "like a character is a Jon Krakauer book," he loses "the will to live" even before reaching the "'performance underwear section."[39] Environmental consumerism offers a broad target, but the satire exposes the stakes in alpine status competition. Dressing the outdoors part confers alpine identity upon the newly garbed. Now that part costs far more than it used to.

The Whittaker twins, famed Northwest climbers and guides, are not the only paradigm of alpine cool in the Northwest, and neither is the dirtbag persona pioneered by Fred Beckey. Poet Gary Snyder, who climbed all the snowpeaks early in his career, represents another model: that of one who marries alpinism with poetry and Zen Buddhism, thus equipping the high-altitude identity seeker with some hip culture. Patagonia, Inc., brainchild of famed mountaineer Yvon Choinard, manufactured more climbing hardware than anyone else in the late 1960s; by the following decade it marketed clothing made from synthetics such as Capilene. Like REI in some regards, Patagonia has made a big name for itself in outdoor clothing for every season. Patagonia marketers saw a big value in Snyder.

The fall 2000 Patagonia catalog featured Snyder, a linkage that has been studied by at least one critic of environmental consumerism, Michael Lundblad.[40] Lundblad contends Patagonia, a socially progressive corporation, sophisticatedly assuages the potential purchasing guilt of its progressive, often affluent customers by supporting and featuring famous environmental writers with whom those customers identify. After all, Patagonia underwrote and published a book of commissioned photographs and essays (*Patagonia: Notes From The Field,* 1999) by prominent contemporary writers like Tom McGuane, Paul Theroux, Gretel Ehrlich, and Rick Bass. The book suggests these artists endorse Patagonia and so should the reader. Such brand recognition is extremely profitable.

Snyder and other writers bring an enormous cultural cachet to the big business of green purchase power. Snyder effectively loaned his career and aura to Patagonia. Patagonia creates intense brand loyalty through privileging the dirtbag climber ethos and seamlessly blending that with upscale, outdoors consumerism. Slightly scuffed but outfitted and poised. Mountains enthusiasts entering Patagonia stores need not feel any guilt about affluence because, as former dirtbags or wannabes, they're still in touch and buy only what they need. But need is trumped by desire, of course.

The Patagonia catalog, like comparable publications, itself morphed into an ambitious form of environmental journalism, a subgenre of green pop literature. In this subgenre the status game enacts itself as forcefully and "naturally" as the unquestioned weave of buying and being. As one scholar recently remarked, the Patagonia catalog "was a work of art and an articulation of an emerging philosophy of outdoor recreation and environmentalism."[41] Whether print or online, such publications meld environmentalism with environmental consumerism into a product resembling an art museum catalog, one strewn with photos of bodacious climbers or skiers on steep faces. Seasonal Patagonia catalogues feature stunning full-page photos showing attractive young climbers or extreme skiers, male and female, enacting our alpine fantasies in jaw-dropping settings—the Patagonia runway. In between these pages one finds the usual rollout of new clothing lines from which we may buy in order to enact our own fantasies. The stickiness phenomenon ("Readers/consumers who like this have also liked/bought . . .") pioneered by Jeff Bezos, founder of the Amazon.com empire, focuses green desire and consumption in the mountains.

The Patagonia catalog, like the climbing wall, represents a robust example of virtual alpine consumerism flourishing at a distance from actual volcanoes or other Cascades. Like its counterparts, the catalog functions as a dream mirror in which a viewer, who will never resemble one of those featured climbers or skiers, pretends to close the gap by buying some of the same Patagonia fleece layers or shells. We buy because Patagonia endorses writers we like; even more often, we buy to supposedly step closer to those awe-inspiring vertical mountainscapes inhabited by those idealized model athletes—faux mountain glory.

In the evolution of alpine cool, the experience-equipment nexus provides one litmus test of green buying. The REI website, for example, promises "frequent educational clinics and expert advice at our retail stores and at REI.com from trusted REI staff," but outreach always serves consumption: "Above all, we provide a convenient and seamless shopping experience, whether at an REI retail store, online, by phone or by mail order."[42] Knowledge does not exist apart from purchase. According to advertising's credo of eternal disequilibrium, wherein consumers never reach complete satisfaction with their possessions, what REI describes as the browser's "passion for the outdoors" never reaches stasis because of ever new product lines.

The apparent marriage of high-altitude experience (on the volcanoes or elsewhere) with the latter is assured. Who could resist the appeal of such educational outreach and "environmental stewardship"? But institutional environmentalism is inextricably linked with unchecked consumerism. One cannot disentangle "products" from "expertise" any more than one can separate "inspire" and "educate" from "outfit." Nouns and verbs blur, and the right gear promotes if not guarantees the right stuff for summiting. The difference between buying into high altitudes and being in high altitudes grows indistinct.

The tide has again shifted in the big business of Northwest outdoors recreation, as REI has recently reached a new level of fame. With 127 stores in thirty-one states, the *New York Times* described the company as "the nation's largest consumer cooperative." In the winter of 2013, Sally Jewell, its CEO, became the secretary of the interior. This choice suggests a likely new prominence of the outdoor gear industry in the federal government, particularly since this industry means bigger business than the gas and oil industries, as it supports three times as many jobs—over six million jobs. Additionally, Jewell, a Seattleite and serious climber, skier, and kayaker, symbolizes the twenty-first-century American West resident.[43] She has climbed Mount Rainier seven times. Arguably, the Sally Jewells comprise the majority of affluent northwesterners who, whether holding an REI card or not, take to the snowpeaks and other peaks or rivers in waves. Those waves often interpret and experience spectacular Northwest landscapes through commodified modes—the guided overnight climb or half-day whitewater trip, for example.

The reign of fancy clothes and gear has distanced, in some respects, earlier generations' values in regional mountaineering. And glitz has become an end in itself, like indoors climbing. It is difficult to detach the regional outdoor rec industry from the evolution of status tourism in the mountains. These changes palpably express maturing regional self-identity insofar as it is distinguished by a sense of privilege and complacency. As a sport, climbing is sexy in some of the same ways that regional residents define themselves because of location. Recently, nothing advertises mountain glamour more than speed climbing.

The definition of alpine cool has shifted gears to the extent that volcano climbs have become, for most everyone, fast and packaged. Social relationships have changed in some ways as well even as bagging peaks and buying gear overlap as consumer actions. In an online article, "Mount Rainier, 100 Years Later," Donn Venema, a young, prototypical millennial-generation climber, contrasts his twenty-fifth Rainier climb—via Sunset Ridge on its west side in 2004—with his grandfather's 1908 climb via the then-standard, Gibraltar route.[44] Harry Venema was part of a group of twenty-five from the Seattle Y M C A; grandson Donn climbed with three partners, two of whom he'd initially met online, and one he had never met before the first morning of the climb. Since his grandfather's time, equipment had changed almost completely, and climbing partners—physical strangers—were found on the Internet. Such casual partners might morph into the close friendships traditionally promised on a rope, but not necessarily.

As Venema and his partners summited from the west, they saw dozens of climbers atop the standard, northeast (Emmons Glacier) route approaching the Columbia Crest summit, and several small groups ascending from southern routes. Everyone took pictures with small, lightweight digital cameras. A nearby climber was on a cell phone announcing his location to family back home. The scene is urban, a string of small groups unknown to one another, not one group of twenty-five Y M C A men who had known each other, in most cases, for years. Today's summit scene resembles a transitory picnic on snow and without tables. While Venema's group of four camped on the mountain two nights during their ascent, the 1908 party ascended from and descended to timberline in one day. Though the 1908 climbers spent less time on the mountain, they spent much more time arriving and returning. They stayed together. Presumably many were longtime friends at the Y M C A.

Their camaraderie differed substantively from the quickly arranged quartet in 2004.

By contrast, within several hours of his twenty-fifth summiting, Donn Venema was back in his Portland home uploading his climb photos onto his computer. Digital cameras and cell phones measure the swift climb. He quickly posted photos, standard contemporary expression of summit status but concludes, "I would love to tell my grandfather how much more impressive his climb was in 1908 than mine in 2004." The contrast in ninety-six years concerns more than transportation and equipment, though no twenty-first-century climber would trade places with an early twentieth-century climber in that regard. Maybe speed climbing represents the ultimate expression of the approach-ascend-descend-return plot, since "quick" constitutes the sine qua non of convenience and esteem. Like the price tags of gear and clothing labels, the fast climb, or climb-as-race, is easily quantifiable. The habit of measurement belittles or ignores older traditions of being at high altitudes—traditions captured in the nineteenth-century notion of mountain glory. Experiences tantamount to conversion or personal transformation resist easy assessment.

In the early twenty-first century, regional mountaineering is big business and a popular sport, and because of status and industrial tourism, the growth represents an ambivalent bounty. Amidst sizable shifts in scale and mountains of clothing and gear, much social idealism has disappeared along with traditions of club or fraternity interdependency. Climbing parties are small, casual, and frequent, clotting standard routes, and although climbing partners may stay together for decades, in many cases relationships have become as temporary as the financial one between client and guide. Camaraderie can be more fleeting and evanescent. The increasingly macho contemporary generation of professional climbers ratchets up the ethos of alpine cool. Taking our measure on volcanoes has become, too often, subject to measure, whether car-to-car times or gear costs.

The relentless quantification of alpine experience lessens the experience. But the trophies lure as never before, and the quantification extends from the climbs back onto the products one wears and uses. Outdoors marketing deliberately targets all who seek to reduce our carbon footprint and minimize our impact on rock and snow. The appeal to personal stewardship in no way lessens our purchasing or our numbers on the peaks, and the latter creates problems in some places. Green buying shadows green climbing. Environmentalism and environmental consumerism dance together like longtime partners, and the snowpeaks prove one sturdy setting for their dance.

5 WILDERNESS AND VOLCANOES

A small share of the American people have an overpowering longing
to retire periodically from the encompassing clutch of mechanistic
civilization. . . . To them, the enjoyment of solitude, complete independence, and the beauty of undefiled panoramas is absolutely
essential to happiness.

—Robert Marshall

In the United States, mountains have proven a primary domain
for our changing understanding and valuation of wilderness, in
part because mountains comprised our first wilderness areas.
Mountains possess a psychological and symbolic remoteness as
realms removed from usual human affairs, even if occasional cities
or towns spread close to particular peaks. Iconic sites above and
beyond human settlement, mountains are historically associated
with deities and serve as threshold for divine communication if
not epiphany. Late Northwest composer Alan Hovhaness, who
wrote symphonies dedicated to two of Washington's five volcanoes (Symphony #50, *Mount St. Helens*; and Symphony #66,
Hymn to Glacier Peak), endorsed this archetypal view: "Mountains are symbols, like pyramids, of man's attempt to know God"
(Notes to "Mysterious Mountain," 1955). Hovhaness defines the
familiar motive for climbing as a fundamental desire for physical
places far above the mundane. The sociability of climbing in no
way lessens (though it might obscure) the old value of personal

transformation, or the appeal of volcanoes or other mountains as pilgrimage sites.

Wilderness and remoteness overlap considerably as human constructs in the Northwest, as the region's volcanoes evidence. Mount Rainier was first set aside in the Pacific Forest Reserve in 1893; Mount Hood, in the Bull Run Forest Reserve in 1892. The Forest Reserve Act of 1891 was not designed solely to set aside acreage "for the protection of timber and watersheds." Rather, scenic values and preservation of spectacular landscapes were primary criteria years before either the USFS (1905) or NPS (1916) came into being. As President Benjamin Harrison's secretary of the interior, John Noble, argued in a letter to the President on March 25, 1891, reserves should include areas "of great interest to our people because of their natural beauty, or remarkable features."[1] The impulse to set aside public lands in the fin-de-siècle western United States arose, in part, out of deepening appreciation of mountainscapes inspired by landscape painting and photography. Certainly, the Pacific Northwest's most exceptional mountains provide a fascinating case history of evolving ideas about wilderness because of their status as "reservoirs of the primitive."[2]

In the Northwest the notion of "wilderness volcano" developed as a result of urban growth: those snowpeaks farthest from cities or their viewsheds epitomized remoteness. As hinterland they rise in the "back" range, not the front, farther from the collective human gaze—and trailheads. These include Washington's Glacier Peak and Oregon's Mount Jefferson—which ironically rises right along the Cascade Crest. But no highway cuts close to it. Such judgments have abided through the past two centuries. For example, in *The Northwest Coast* (1857), pioneering ethnographer and diarist James G. Swan twice omits mention of Glacier Peak among Washington Territory's five volcanoes. It existed outside his purview and that of the territory's young, seaside towns. He underlines Glacier Peak's remoteness by ignoring it: Glacier Peak lies farther east than Washington's other four, a distance from Puget Sound and the Chehalis and Cowlitz River valleys. Though not a wilderness volcano like Mount Jefferson, in modern regional history Mount Adams has been labeled "the forgotten giant" because of its distance or absence from urban viewsheds (excepting Yakima's). In the twentieth century, volcanic wilderness tends to mean distance from cars.

The formation and naming of many wilderness areas along the Cascade Crest reveals the centrality of volcanoes. Of Washington's thirty-one wilderness areas, half are located in the Cascades and ten are either named after or next to volcanoes, or are themselves volcanic in origin (e.g., Goat Rocks Wilderness Area). Washington includes Mount Baker, Glacier Peak (third largest), Mount Rainier, and Mount Adams Wilderness Areas. Mount St. Helens poses a special case as a USFS-run National Monument since its 1982 genesis.[3] Almost half of Oregon's forty-seven wilderness areas (much smaller than Washington's) are located in the Cascades, and thirteen tie in directly with volcanoes or are volcanic in origin. Oregon includes the Mount Hood, Mount Jefferson, Mount Washington, Three Sisters (second largest), Diamond Peak, Mount Thielsen, and Mountain Lakes (including Mount McLoughlin) Wilderness Areas.

Most Northwest volcanoes exist within a wilderness area that took its name, if not identity, from it. In the Northwest, the evolution and codification of wilderness has derived, in large measure, from the visual and psychological dominance of volcanoes. Thus, their modern history also chronicles our changing definitions and practices regarding wilderness. In recent decades volcano wilderness areas serve as a litmus test of new scholarly and popular understandings of wilderness: understandings that distort even as they revise the mid-twentieth-century philosophy of wilderness.

The volcanoes prove as much as any regional wilderness areas do that nature and culture have always existed along a continuum of habitation, and that set-aside lands never exist apart from a range of human uses. It is folly to ignore the long view of such uses prior to the twentieth century—the deep perspective of environmental history—even though, for many indigenes, volcano craters or glaciers constituted taboo zones.

The history of federally set aside lands and the evolving philosophy of wilderness also disclose a history of quantification, one result of which is a series of behaviors that quantify some if not most facets of wilderness experience. If wilderness experience, particularly within a designated wilderness area, resembles a product (or set of measurable outcomes) more than, say, a sensibility, then visitors are cast in the role of consumers. A packaged volcano climb provides one instance of pervasive wilderness consumerism since, according to one scholar, recent understandings of wilderness derive from "the logos of consumption": human actions in wilderness resemble a form of environmental consumerism.[4]

In the twentieth century, the Wilderness Act of 1964 represents the great divide separating wilderness system lobbying from a legally enacted system that has been steadily added to in the past half century. After the Wilderness Act, wilderness became named and commodified through the National Wilderness Preservation System (NWPS). The Wilderness Act climaxed our tendency to conceive time spent in officially designated preserves as a highly sought product, since the legislation marked off a wide range of precisely measured enclosures—Wilderness Areas—that lured outdoors enthusiasts as do no other landscapes.[5] The act spawned a tradition of exclusivity, one which the a priori exclusivity of volcanoes enhances. Since passage of the act, the Northwest has witnessed half a century of additions and extensions. The legal mandates of wilderness (with a capital *W*), which the relevant agencies are charged to enforce, often do not match ground conditions in particular backcountry or alpine zones (e.g., standard routes) on Northwest volcanoes. A yawning gap exists between legal wilderness and ground reality. What climbers or backpackers find sometimes doesn't match what they buy into.

The habit of perceiving wilderness area experience as commodity derives in part from a much older tradition, endemic among indigenous peoples, of animating landscapes, of treating them as storied. Stories or myths arising from a given wilderness become the best means of identification—and, in contemporary thinking, consumption—as they comprise the deepest level of attachment. One environmental historian, Thomas R. Vale, argues that wilderness areas need stories because they lack the rich legacy of "place recognition" typical of most western national parks. While wilderness areas tend to be generic, many Northwest wildernesses centered on a volcano enjoy supreme place recognition. Others need stories and storytellers to stamp their identity and render them unique.[6] Ideally each climber attaches personal stories to the cumulative script of a volcano. The attachment of particular lore to particular wilderness areas expresses a human history in designated wild places. With volcano wilderness areas, the obvious examples come from native stories of origins, for example the braided tale of courtship and jealousy explaining Loowit (Mount St. Helens), Pahto (Mount Adams), and Wy'East (Mount Hood) narrated by the Multnomah tribe. Certainly story embeds place recognition; it also sharpens our conception of wilderness as commodity.

The modern story of California's Sierra Nevada range is tied to the rhapsodic journalism of John Muir and the origins of the Sierra Club, the United States' most venerable environmental organization. Arguably the best American exemplar of the nineteenth-century gospel of mountain sublime, John Muir also best demonstrated the fundamental bond between mountains and wilderness. Muir ranged the continent's west coast, celebrating and climbing Cascadian volcanoes (e.g., Mounts Shasta and Rainier). In his final two decades he insistently proclaimed the mountains-wilderness identity, the religion of alpine retreat and restoration, through his books and the Sierra Club that he founded in 1892 with its triple (recreational, educational, and conservationist) purposes in its charter. In his credo, he sang, "Come up into the mountains, and hear their good tidings," mountain environments figuring as a tonic, a source of endless joy and spiritual renewal. That ethos still prevails, with varying emphases. The Northwest spinoff clubs linked mountaineering with wilderness preservation as though both activities go hand in hand. Climber Jim Whittaker's parable of green growth, from dropping tin cans to packing everything out, epitomizes the overlap.

The wilderness history of Northwest volcanoes includes a modern story of rivalry that does not explain volcanic origins in anthropocentric terms. Instead, USFS-NPS interagency rivalry, a sometimes-nasty tale, includes the history of several contentious terms, above all "use." The use game chronicles, as much as anything, the region's wilderness history. In the twentieth century's first half, the USFS led the federal effort to articulate and expand wilderness, though government regulations were often in conflict with premier mountaineering clubs. In the second half of the century, the NPS took the lead position in the articulation and establishment of wilderness, as the USFS was perceived to be the handmaiden of the timber industry giants such as Weyerhaeuser and Boise Cascade. The modern story of wilderness includes, at its core, the famous term, "untrammeled"—which Howard Zahniser, chief architect of the Wilderness Act, borrowed from his friend, Northwest activist Polly Dyer—and the subsequent concepts of "wilderness *thresholds*" and "*de facto* wilderness": recent variations on a theme that carries special regional resonance.[7]

On their website the Mazamas, founded only two years after the Sierra Club, proclaim their longstanding legacy of conservation lobbying. In their first decades they became known as "pragmatic environmentalists and regional boosters" who, in keeping with a prevailing national ethos, regarded the mountains as a primarily moral force. This late nineteenth-century ethos survived, with modifications, for generations because of growing concerns about perceived (or actual) ill effects of cities, categorized as "the other."[8] A century ago anxieties about urban life, for old and new urbanites, derived from their physical distance from natural landscapes such as mountains or forests or rivers. Growing numbers of outdoors advocates celebrated natural environments as a vital corrective to the increasingly crowded, mechanical conditions, if not debilitating influences, of the city.

The migration to the city (and after World War II, the suburb) explains, as much as anything, the accelerating attention to and advocacy of wilderness as set-aside domains removed (and remote) from one's normal life. The biggest single engine behind wilderness preserves was the massive road-building program accompanying mass-produced automobiles in the period after World War I. Many feared that roads would penetrate the forests and climb the shoulders of mountains—precisely what born-again developers such as Seattle's Asahel Curtis, famed photographer and co-founder of the Mountaineers, wished.[9] And roads were built accordingly—for example, the Mowich Lake and West Side roads in MRNP, the state highway to Austin Pass on Mount Baker, or the McKenzie Pass highway in central Oregon—but they didn't reach mountain fastnesses or volcano craters (with a couple of exceptions like CLNP's Rim Drive, or Newberry Crater just to the east in Oregon).

The wilderness lobby included more than middle- or upper-class urbanites, furthermore. Other forces made the case for curbing road building precisely as Americans took to the roads—and the mountains—in their Model As and Ts. The growing popularity of auto tourism in the 1920s forced the issue of access: in a familiar pattern, often those most recently on the road argued most loudly for limits to road building in the mountains. Auto tourism created a new American democracy and a new debate about car access and appropriate restrictions in the mountains. Critics included labor unionists who motored and camped along the Columbia Gorge–Mount Hood loop as eagerly as any other tourists. Unsurprisingly, blue-collar workers advocated for wilderness alongside more affluent city and town residents. Revolted by increasing evidence of trash, many unionists, in the words of a labor historian, "helped create a new debate about wilderness" because they wanted early USFS restricted areas "preserved for those who were willing to invest the time and energy into packing their way in."[10] This "new debate" rested upon a dilemma, as preservationist voices were themselves part of a new, mass affluence codified by the 1928 Republican campaign ad claiming their policies had put "a chicken in every pot. And a car in every backyard, to boot."[11] And with that car, everyday folks took to the mountains even as some among them argued that cars should be parked and backpacks mounted.

The Northwest history of wilderness ironically records a receding remoteness as the road system thickened. The volcanoes got closer thanks to the thick, capillary system of USFS roads built to support massive logging; at the same time, the sense of wilderness receded in some locales because of greater proximity occasioned by those very roads. For some, quicker access diluted the perceived purity of wilderness. The Mountaineers sounded warnings about an expanded road system in MRNP, for example, almost a century ago, precisely as Model As and Model Ts chugged up the Ricksecker road en masse. After all, MRNP was the first national park to allow cars. One member, George Vanderbilt Caesar, published an article in the October 1927 *Saturday Evening Post* against NPS road building: "Why . . . should the Government incur enormous expense to encircle the wilderness with roads?" That question resonated across the century, gathering force as it pointed up apparent contradictions between road access and wilderness.

In 1928 another Mountaineer, Edward Allen, drafted a position paper calling for designated wilderness areas within MRNP. Allen subsequently claimed the Department of the Interior accepted his paper and designated seven areas within the Park as "wilderness territory," which precluded infrastructure and allowed hiking and horse packing. But there is no evidence of Interior adopting and implementing any such plan: it existed only on paper.[12] Nearly half a century would pass before wilderness areas had legal definition and force at Mount Rainier and other volcanoes. That lag is tragically commonplace. The Caesars and Allens comprised minority voices until the 1960s.

The foregrounding of wilderness provides a vehicle through which to assess development pressures in MRNP and elsewhere. Additionally, the appeal of wilderness explains early USFS "primitive areas" within national forests and, through their changed mission after World War II, the diluted categories, "wild area" and "limited area," which could be redefined or shrunk given sufficient economic (e.g., logging) pressure. For example, the USFS "created a Glacier Peak-Cascades Recreation Unit of 233,600 acres, or 360 square miles" back in 1931, but primary extraction activities like mining and logging were still allowed.[13] Preservation interests battled "getting the cut out" particularly as timber harvests spiked before midcentury.

Within MRNP, the Mountaineers insistently opposed resort plans championed by founding NPS director Stephen Mather along Mount Rainier's base. Some voices directly opposed the early NPS program to bring the crowds to the parks in their own "motors." Such dissent flew in the face of NPS promotional philosophy. Mather wanted to bring the masses to the parks to build advocacy; at MRNP the Mountaineers feared the damage wrought by crowds (such as evidenced at the early Camp of the Clouds) and regarded Asahel Curtis's proposal for perimeter highways as a disaster. The fact that MRNP adopted a master plan in 1929 (the first national park with such a development plan) did not lessen the anxiety of those favoring preservation and opposing extensive amenities infrastructure. The master plan expanded the Rainier National Park Company's (RNPC) monopoly concessions role in three locations and included investment by at least four railroads. There was little reason to believe that a big hotel-and-cabins resort at what became known as Sunrise (on Mount Rainier's northeast side) would not be built, but Mather died, the railroad CEOs backed out of the deal, and the Great Depression ended any subsequent investment interest.[14]

Asahel Curtis as booster and the Mountaineers as preservationists embodied the conflicting voices of tourism and wilderness preservation, respectively: voices that contend through the present, given NPS and USFS foundational commitments to both access and resource preservation. By the late twentieth century, these commitments clashed in many alpine locations. The philosophy of open access—infrastructure intended to serve industrial tourism—presumes wilderness, and experience therein, as a consumable commodity; preservation resists consumerism in some respects even as it accedes to it in others. While the work of preservation entails detailed surveys and mapping a variety of resources and values, all the boundary-drawing holds out the possibility of unquantifiable experience "inside" intimated by John Muir, poet Gary Snyder, and many others.

One baleful offshoot of mountain auto tourism was tin can trash: the detritus of picnicking and camping that extended along trails and onto summits. For many, throw it out replaced pack it out. Those willing to pack their way in formed an increasingly articulate and powerful minority who governed the philosophy of wilderness in the next generation. For increasing numbers, access meant (and means) staying seated as much as possible.

The 1928 Republican campaign claim exposed a profound critique of consumerism and ambivalence about modernism—and solitude in the mountains. The emergent philosophy of wilderness constituted a "recreational critique" since forces of commercialization in the outdoors decreased the perceived "publicness" of natural spaces.[15] Of course "public natural spaces" were often domesticated to the extent of trails, bridges, campsites, and the like: the very act of drawing boundaries around wilderness quantified it, and rendered experiences inside as potential commodity. This infrastructure resulted in tin can trash *and* boosted the cause of wilderness advocates. Local advocates were represented in the USFS by Aldo Leopold and, even more, Bob Marshall: legendary hiker, one of the founders of the Wilderness Society (1935), and eloquent publicist for designated wilderness who led the agency in advocating and expanding USFS's early "primitive areas" and forest reserves.

Marshall's article, "The Wilderness as Minority Right" (1928), shaped American attitudes about wilderness as much as any document of this period because of his leadership position, even as his essential claim, based on his own solitary habits—"the enjoyment of solitude, complete independence"—ignored mountaineering realities of most climbers and legitimized an ambivalent idealism that later climaxed in the Wilderness Act. The history of regional mountaineering attests that climbers rarely achieved complete independence. Most are not solitaires stamped in the same mold as that virtuosic cross-country trekker and climber, Bob Marshall. That climbing is predominately social (however small the party) does not preclude the experience of solitude, if not complete independence. Yet solitude proved uncommon both on volcano routes and summits: though feelings of conversion or personal transformation remained individual, they typically unfolded within groups. The relation between the personal and the social context has grown far more elusive in the era of mass mountaineering.

The network of highways that transformed the American landscape in a generation accelerated the wilderness debate and further pressured the USFS to expand its poorly enforced system of primitive areas. In 1939, just months before his death at age thirty-nine from heart failure (on an overnight train from Washington DC to New York City), the visionary Marshall proposed a 795,000-acre Glacier Peak Wilderness, which was not acted upon; instead, the USFS proposed a smaller "limited area, identifying its natural values for future study." After the stall and delay it would take generations for this wilderness volcano and its environs to receive the protection Marshall proposed. Marshall and others of like mind mounted a critique against mechanized recreational access that continues unabated.

They faced what scholar Paul Sutter has called "the politics of mass consumption," which both focused the wilderness debate and exacerbated the anxieties of preservationists about mechanization in the mountains. Auto manufacturers indirectly aided and abetted the access debate, their endless products sharpening the perception that such modernizing pressures eroded that enduring mode of American freedom manifested in large, undeveloped tracts of land, whether in the mountains or elsewhere.[16] In this standard narrative, higher altitudes beyond mechanization offer individuals that ocean of freedom unavailable in their increasingly gridded lives. The wilderness vs. mechanization opposition still powerfully appeals to people who advocate quiet trails on public wildlands.

Mass visitation sometimes fueled mass illusion. Queues of recreationists, generations ago and now, approach Crater Lake, Mounts Hood, Rainier, Baker, and others in search, often, of a realm beyond themselves. The notion of wilderness as a remnant of freedom apart from modernizing pressures crystallized in the interwar generation and has remained intact, though cast in doubt by environmental historians and others. For many "the 'publicness' of natural spaces" meant excluding as many signs of materialistic society as possible. Thus the notion of wilderness areas as set-aside tracts that symbolize a less cluttered time, if not a timeless realm, took hold. This Theodore Winthrop legacy regards the volcanoes and their neighborhoods as time capsules removed from human agency.

A powerful though myopic nostalgia attached itself to those remote public lands. Vague notions of purity, for example of a golden age sans racial or ethnic minorities, sometimes clung to this blurry nostalgia as if these districts formed some sort of tabula rasa of national identity and promise: we *are* our spectacular landscapes and earliest days. Longtime tribal habitation does not exist in this subversive fantasy just as nineteenth- and early twentieth-century containment policies removed natives from most of the neighborhoods of volcanoes. The power of this nostalgia has long driven N P S policy in sundry parks. Visitors expect clean views and few or no signs of human habitation past or present, certainly nothing messy.

In their study of Yosemite National Park, for example, two scholars argue that landscape aesthetics have always trumped public health concerns: received notions of packaged scenery dictate that water reservoirs, sewage disposal systems, and landfills, for instance, be hidden, screened, or located off-site.[17] Visitors don't want to see what they depend on. Nor do backpackers or climbers expect to see any evidence of past mining or logging in Glacier Peak, Mount Adams, or Three Sisters Wilderness Areas, for example.

Americans in the mid-twentieth century endorsed the wilderness proposals of Aldo Leopold and Marshall in increasing numbers, and the preservationist lobby became a powerful voice, as witnessed in the careers of David Brower, first executive director (1952–69) of the Sierra Club, and Howard Zahniser, executive secretary of The Wilderness Society. For preservationists the USFS response to the desire for more set-aside lands was tepid at best. In 1942 the USFS created the Mount Adams Wild Area (the third "Wild Area" in the state), which excluded its flanking forests. Four years later it created a Mount St. Helens Limited Area. What was the difference? Environmentalists protested these designations for their artificial tree line boundaries and instability.

The odd story of ownership within the Mount St. Helens Limited Area reveals its false boundary. As one railroad apologist reminded us, "prior to the [1980] eruption . . . few people realized that the peak fell within the boundaries of the federal land grant awarded in 1864 to the Northern Pacific Railroad to help offset the cost of its construction."[18] Yet another example of the late nineteenth-century corporate land grab, the Northern Pacific—a big promoter of Northwest volcanoes tourism—owned the southwest quadrant (i.e., square mile) of the volcano itself, one quarter of the pie. The fact that part of the Northwest's most shapely (pre-1980) volcano, the one most active in the mid-nineteenth century, was partially owned by a railroad attested to the gutless status of this "Limited Area." The railroad traded parts of this slice to Weyerhaeuser, who logged extensively. From the green vantage of the late twentieth century, that a piece of volcano including its summit belonged to a corporation for over a century (1864–1982) seems beyond belief. In the Cold War generation, the USFS narrowed its vision of wildlands preservation to economic utility, other criteria (e.g., those articulated by Marshall) disappearing. The perception that the agency operated as servant of timber companies ignited environmental opposition in diverse forms. Many including the Mountaineers' Harvey Manning judged its categories of "protection" to be worthless since the USFS could reclassify them with no public input. In 1955 all the USFS classified areas in Oregon were redrawn, among them volcano preserves such as Diamond Peak and Mount Washington, which turned into smaller wild areas.[19] "Wild" meant more limited than "Limited." Smaller wild areas would provide more contained (consumable) experience. According to prevalent thought, those two volcanoes would be detached from the forests on their shoulders as though they could be defined apart.

The volcanoes themselves were not in dispute because they lacked "value"; the big trees below them, particularly along the west slopes, were always the targets, not higher elevation zones. The timber industry wanted open access to subalpine forests girding the volcanoes and played a central role in determining wilderness area boundaries. By midcentury, widespread environmental opposition drew lines in the sand by posing alternative definitions of *use*: recreational uses opposed extraction uses such as industrial-scale logging. These competing definitions created, as much as any forces, the extant wilderness system subsequent to the Wilderness Act of 1964.[20] Prevailing definitions control the agenda and the ground reality of wilderness, as the twentieth century's second half demonstrates.

Organized labor sometimes backed wilderness preservation, even at the possible risk of logging jobs. In Oregon, though some labor ranks had endorsed a tram proposal on Mount Hood in 1928, others opposed more road building. A generation later, labor endorsed further protections in the Three Sisters Wilderness

Area, one of central Oregon's most contested sites enacting the debate between logging and set-aside tracts. The president of the CIO-affiliated International Woodworkers of America and a local (Eugene OR) union secretary fought to preserve the lower elevation lands added earlier to that area.[21] But lumber demand reinforced the mind-set that detached the lush forests of the upper McKenzie River valley from the Three Sisters. When the USFS reclassified the Three Sisters Primitive Area into a Wilderness Area, the preserved tract shrunk by 52,000 acres, which were logged.[22] Up and down the Cascades volcanoes, tree line represented for a time a false boundary, and utility in lower-elevation lands was the only criterion. By midcentury in Oregon's Cascades, some labor interests had aligned themselves with the recreation lobby (largely middle-class urbanites) rather than the utility-driven timber companies. A broad socio-economic spectrum rallied against the powerful USFS-timber alliance that sought to "get the cut out" almost anywhere.

After midcentury, wilderness consumerism as a political lobby competed increasingly effectively against the more palpable consumerism of massive logging. As a result of the USFS's inclination favoring rapid clear-cutting, Northwest national forests resembled a weird hybrid of set-aside preserves surrounded by industrial tree farms.[23] "Tree farms," the metaphor unashamedly reducing forests to monocultural crop reproduction, became common in the midcentury. Recreationists including climbers found their familiar trails and approaches hacked and clear-cut, and protested this prevalent national forest use. Just as northwestern national forests were being logged on a hitherto unprecedented scale, mountaineering as a sport formed a new brand of environmental activism and political lobby.[24] Battle lines hardened. The three primary mountaineering clubs took on increasingly public roles as wilderness advocates, inheriting the old, failed USFS mission of expanding primitive areas. In 1952 the Sierra Club opened a Northwest chapter office in Seattle, and they fought the cramped mind-set that regarded forests as only potential lumber. Subalpine (and alpine) approaches to a volcano were increasingly understood as part of it: the wooded ridges and drainages belonged as much as glaciers and snowfields. The Cold War provided a new imagery for the volcanoes. The attraction to mountain wilderness that blossomed after World War II suggests a facile link between personal and national identity, as though climbing expresses one's patriotism since, according to scholar Susan Schlepfer, the nuclear family gained strength and identity in the mountains just as the nation sharpened its super-power identity: "While alpinism . . . retained its racial, national, gendered, and combative overtones through the 1950s . . . American climbers described themselves as closed-mouthed, self-contained, and self-controlled, a composite of the traditional British alpinist, the GI of WWII, and the hero of western movies."[25]

Though this equation downplays the status of women moun-taineers, it repositions the Marshall wilderness credo as part of the post–World War II American self-image as world leader. In this mind-set, Northwest volcanoes represent optimal remote sites where industrial modernism remains distant and the sense of re-birth prevails. Supreme Court Justice William O. Douglas's popular books (e.g., *My Wilderness*, 1960) preached this gospel in its cel-ebration of Washington's Glacier Peak, for instance. Testing one's mettle on a climb—whether one "conquers" or not—imitates an act of consumption, the approach-ascent-descent plot resembling a finite expenditure of planning and energy. This set of motives more closely links personal with national (or regional) identity.

Yet volcanoes were in danger of decimation below tree line, as though they could be stripped of their green skirts. Just as the USFS reduced Oregon's Three Sisters Primitive Area in converting it to a Wilderness Area, so it proposed that Washington's Glacier Peak Limited Area be similarly reclassified and significantly reduced in 1957. Those interchangeable terms—"primitive," "wilderness" or "wild," "limited"—lost currency as protected public lands. The wilderness volcano ethnographer James Swan had neglected to name a century earlier would have been stripped of its valleys and forests in what preservationists called "the starfish proposal" (1959). The proposed reduction resembled a starfish with the volcano at the center and the radiating spokes or fingers, glaciers and rock ridges: most anything below alpine parks was off the table. The Mountaineers, Mazamas, and Sierra Club mounted a national publicity campaign, advocating a holistic, ecosystem wilderness area a generation before this paradigm gained wide acceptance. They depicted the proposed Three Sisters and Glacier Peak Wilderness Areas in stark terms with fingers of snow (i.e., glacier) and rock, and everything below and between the fingers marked for logging. David Brower of the Sierra Club, with his gift for memorable phrase, called the Glacier Peak area "a Rorschach blot designed to bring out the worst in a highly guilty subconscious," and he forecast "a symphony of destruction."[26] The starfish shape constitutes an apogee of abstract thinking, of divorce from any recognition of any connectivity.

By the 1950s, both the national and regional population increasingly understood and endorsed the value of these volcanoes: value extending far beyond the trees below the glaciers. The fact that the Three Sisters and Glacier Peak existed far from any big city only increased their value as alpine hinterlands, thanks to the gathering national wilderness campaign. For example, the October 1959 *Sierra Club Bulletin* published David Simon's essay, "These Are the Shining Mountains," which contained "a proposal for a Cascades Volcanic National Park" based on central Oregon's rich volcanic region—the richest in the lower forty-eight states—and centered on the Three Sisters. But the young advocate died the following year and his proposal died faster than the "Ice Peaks National Park" proposal a generation earlier.[27] Such sentiment resurfaced, however, in the 1970s.[28] These volcanoes as hinterlands added to the generic appeal of mountains as remote settings. David Brower's baleful "Rorschach blot" interpretation of the Glacier Peak "starfish proposal" galvanized the wilderness lobby to further work to fulfill Robert Marshall's expansive wilderness area proposal. In Washington the North Cascades Conservation Council (N3C), founded in 1957 with a twenty-four-member board of directors, became the most effective local lobby advocating for Glacier Peak and Mount Baker as wilderness preserves.

Sierra Club and N3C lobbying strategies made a Northwest "wilderness" volcano a national cause célèbre. By the 1950s the Sierra Club had grown adept at using photography as a centerpiece in its lobbying strategies. In this case, its publications included aerial photographs of clear-cuts near the volcano as well as Ansel Adams art photos contrasting old growth forests with stump fields from recent logging and the glaciers and rock ridges just above. Environmentalists across the nation knew about Washington's Glacier Peak, in the fabled North Cascades, and continued logging and mining activity just below it.[29]

Anyone tramping in the Cascadian or Olympics foothills or the Oregon coastal ranges in the mid- or later twentieth century knew the visual scars of clear-cutting, let alone the comprehensive damage it occasioned. The USFS Glacier Peak Wilderness Area (1960), at nearly 450,000 acres—little over half of what Bob Marshall had proposed twenty-one years earlier—just didn't cut it. The lobby for a national park in the North Cascades grew in size and voice.

The Northwest volcanoes as optimal wilderness enjoyed a powerful Washington, DC ally in Supreme Court Justice William O. Douglas, a Yakima, Washington, native whose example and writing influenced the passage and extensions of the Wilderness Act, as many wilderness historians note. He extended the wilderness argument championed by Muir, Marshall, and others, and publicized Washington's two less visible volcanoes through his own frequent backcountry travels. Douglas knew his outdoors better than most DC insiders before or since, and his backpacking, books, and articles consolidated his influence. Because of his background, writings, and charisma, Douglas was known far beyond DC.

Douglas rhapsodized about Glacier Peak a la Muir, calling its glaciers and streams "pure distillation from a true wilderness." "Glacier Peak," he wrote, "is not visible from any major highway. Foothills hide the alpine area. The peaks are locked into a remote area that is a true recluse. This inner realm is remote and exquisite. Man did not plan it that way. The Glacier Peak area is a wilderness by sheer accident. Civilization so far has passed it by." His short sentences and metaphors boost his rhetorical effect and align his argument with standard early- and midcentury wilderness philosophy. Douglas recast Marshall's interwar ideal wilderness as sanctum sanctorum, site for solitude and independence: "The Glacier Peak area, if left roadless and intact, will offer perpetual physical and spiritual therapy. For its rugged nature—its steep canyons, forbidding glaciers, and knife-edged ridges—will be a magnet to those who have daring and fortitude."[30] Volcano wilderness as ideal testing site of selfhood links early climber testimonials with Cold War patriotism, and this macho-colored mentality survives in more muted forms.

Douglas appealed to all who construe public wildlands as domains beyond property and profit: "Glacier Peak nourishes restless man and helps keep him whole. This is a matter of the spirit beyond the expertise of appraisers of property."[31] That appeal underlines the abiding conviction that outdoors experience, volcano or otherwise, possesses values far beyond economic value. And that truth is repeatedly ironized by our contemporary habits of environmental and wilderness consumerism.

The backpacking Chief Justice proves an excellent case study for mid- and later-century regional wilderness lobbying, one whose advocacy made him a spokesman for baby boomers. His aptly titled *My Wilderness: The Pacific West* appeared midway (1960) through the eight-year gestation of the Wilderness Act. In it Douglas extolled Mount Adams, which he watched growing up and from a later home in Glenwood, Washington. He lamented that since his younger years, this alpine park had been desecrated: "The loss of Bird Creek Meadows to the wilderness is symptomatic of the transformation going on in most of our far-western forest areas. I have seen in my lifetime a wilderness of trails remade into a maze of roads. There is hardly a place these days a jeep will not reach. The network of roads is so vast and intricate that almost every wilderness area is threatened."[32] The demand for quick access trumped trail maintenance as USFS roads, like capillary roots, spread ever closer to tree line at several volcanoes.

The fact that these meadows, like all of Adams's eastern flanks, is Yakama Reservation land received no comment, as if their ownership or presence doesn't matter. That omission is in keeping with the regional tendency to erase longtime indigenous presence in volcano neighborhoods. In fact the Yakama Nation Mount Adams Recreation Area (1972), the only section of the reservation open to non-tribal members, includes recreational infrastructure such as trails and campgrounds that are maintained by the Nation for public use.

Douglas voiced a nature-culture dichotomy that in the past generation has been discarded by environmental historians (e.g., William Cronon, "The Trouble With Nature," 1995) and wilderness users. Yet his "machine age versus freedom" opposition, an inheritance from Marshall (among others), remains attractive for many however suspect its romanticism. An ardent preservationist, Douglas reacted instinctively against the coming "windshield wilderness," deeply fearing the network of USFS roads. Douglas understood that a tough choice needed to be made, given the culture of cars and convenience: "The struggle of our time is to maintain an economy of plenty and yet keep man's freedom intact." Like many since his time, he believed roadless areas the solution.[33] For Douglas "an economy of plenty" exists in opposition to "man's freedom" rather than along a continuum with it. Plenty of room for dispute, though Douglas may have been prescient given today's abundance of illegal ATV and ORV use.

The neo-romantic equation of wilderness with freedom matched that familiar alpine ocean of freedom and credo of personal trans-formation. But the machine versus freedom dichotomy created some popular misunderstandings about the meaning of "big-W" wilderness, whatever its legal definitions and management prac-tices. Some misconceptions, deriving from lists of restrictions, claim official wilderness precludes multiple uses. Those who equate wilderness with "locked up," for instance, insist that public lands, alpine or forested, should be accessible by machine—by staying seated, behind a windshield or not. Machine creep means using our bodies less.

For many, such machine creep signifies an unacceptable marker along the nature-culture continuum. According to his biographer Mark Harvey, Howard Zahniser, chief lobbyist for the Wilderness Act, realized that wilderness boundaries also meant sustaining what is wild inside them. In wilderness landscapes, natural processes—volcano ecosystems, for instance—should be more conspicuous than human activity. Zahniser championed wild lands for their spiritual as well as scientific values: modes of knowledge (e.g., mystical or animist) exceeding human measure. Those subscribing to his eclectic outlook know that natural processes include rather than exclude human cultural production. During the eight years Zahniser worked for the Wilderness bill (1956–64), he conceived wild lands not as static precincts apart from human activity, but primarily as "rich havens of biodiversity" that should remain "a home for the wild."[34] Mountain wilderness reveals, as much as any, systems in flux rather than some timeless realm, as popular misin-terpretations would claim. And the flux—the wildness—includes human beings in tune with their bodies and the natural world, as testimonials such as Gary Snyder's *The Practice of the Wild* (1990) eloquently insist.

The Wilderness Act's most famous sentence succinctly defines wilderness: "A wilderness, in contrast with those areas where man and his own works dominate the landscape, is hereby recognized as an area where the earth and community of life are untrammeled by man, where man himself is a visitor who does not remain." The act's most famous word came from Sierra Club officer (and Mountaineer) Polly Dyer, who described the ocean tracts of Olympic National Park as "untrammeled." Though the Makah lived here (and nearby) for centuries, human presence remains minimal in this vibrant seascape. The manifest geologic power of the contact zone, where the world's largest ocean meets the northwestern corner of the continental United States, represents a steadier version of the geologic power promised by the region's most exceptional mountains.

"Trammel" and "trammeled" show a long etymological history (OED), one in which metaphorical meanings emerged more recently in the nineteenth century. For Zahniser untrammeled meant unfettered, tracts beyond human control and social restriction "where one might tramp on foot for long periods of time" alone, and where one would not impact wild animals and plants.[35] The Wilderness Act captured an idealized notion of wilderness in which one hikes (or climbs) indefinitely apart from others, relishing solitude. This scenario ignores the long history of humans in mountain landscapes, and does not match route conditions for most Northwest volcano climbers. More often than not, climbers tramp where others have tramped before. And tramp on plants and too near animals.

In the relatively affluent 1960s, the Wilderness Act privileged one kind of public lands over others and unwittingly ramped up the habits of wilderness consumerism. The desire to buy the right gear effortlessly extended itself to actual experience within the exclusive, higher-altitude tracts of the mountain wilderness areas. The fact that backpackers (or day users) are visitors suggests we're much more absent than present, and absence increases our desire and the perceived value of our limited time "inside." Big-W wilderness areas, embodying that idealized, mostly sans-human view of wilderness, came to resemble a top-end product like a luxury car or five-star restaurant. Just as advertising ramped up diverse strategies to target increasingly affluent markets, the Wilderness Act, with its exclusive land tracts, created an analogous consumer desire for outdoors enthusiasts with at least some discretionary income.[36] The myriad additions to the original National Wilderness Preservation System (NWPS) only boost their collective status and allure. Given their promotional literature, consumer demand rises steadily. These places are special and so are those within them. People craving sustained hinterlands experience want the best, and high altitudes, with their guarantee of high status, are worth the cost.

The Wilderness Act included Washington's Glacier Peak, Mount Adams, and Goat Rocks Wildernesses in the National Wilderness Preservation System. Within this system, the zones surrounding Glacier Peak, Goat Rocks (centered on an ancient volcanic cone, the volcano prominent two million years ago), Mount Adams, Mount Hood, Mount Washington, Three Sisters, and Diamond Peak enjoyed protected status; Mount Jefferson was added in 1968 and Mount Baker, not until 1984. Among these, Three Sisters and Glacier Peak form the largest big-W areas, Three Sisters at 286,708 acres, and Glacier Peak including over half a million acres—roughly three quarters the size of Marshall's original proposal. Official wilderness areas replaced the spineless, three-category USFS system, as appropriate and illegal uses were clearly spelled out.

During the 1960s, as interagency rivalry heated up over wilderness leadership, the wilderness mission passed over to the NPS. Since World War II the USFS had lost its earlier leadership role in designating and enforcing forest preserves. Generally speaking, recreation, let alone preservation, mattered far less than resources extraction. With what appears as extraordinary myopia, the USFS tried to label recreational activities within wilderness a "single use" though they advocated "multiple use"—a cover for accelerating timber cuts. By the mid-1960s, wilderness advocates turned this rhetorical strategy on its head, defining various modes of wilderness recreation at Glacier Peak, Three Sisters or elsewhere as "multiple use" whereas logging constituted "single use." Environmentalists prevailed in the semantic battle once they owned "multiple use." This strategy remains a potent weapon.

Ironically, the North Cascades National Park (NCNP), signed into law in 1968, included neither northern volcano (Glacier Peak and Mount Baker), nor Washington's spectacular inland fjord, Lake Chelan. The intricate regional relationship between national parks and volcanoes had ended: once again Mount Baker and Glacier Peak failed to make the grade in the NPS. That year, the Glacier Peak Wilderness Area was expanded to include more forest in two west slope drainages (the Suiattle and White Chuck Rivers). Looking back in old age, longtime advocate Harvey Manning angrily recalled that "All of Mount Baker, the Cascades' whitest volcano up high and greenest volcano down low, and part of Mount Shuksan, often regarded as the most beautiful mountain in America, and most of their enclosing Nooksack River and Baker River valleys were left to multiple-use."[37]

Politics once again trumped long-term local planning, as Senator "Scoop" Jackson's NCNP boundaries had little to do with those of the leading preservationist lobbyists. Evidently another volcano national park in the Northwest mattered not at all in DC: "The Mountaineers, the Sierra Club, the N3C, and allies had devoted a dozen-odd years to a detailed, thoughtful proposal. There is no evidence Senator Jackson ever gave it a look." Manning borrowed a symbol from high classical art to record the outrage many felt in 1968: "A national park in the North Cascades that lacked its highest mountain was like Venus de Milo without a head. A national park lacking the entirety of 'the magnificent pair,' Glacier Peak *and* Mount Baker sculpted a very incomplete Venus."[38] It would take until 1984 for both volcanoes and environs to be officially protected as wilderness.

In practice, the new system of wilderness (NWPS) reflected as disjointed a series of agendas as the earlier USFS "system," though by contrast it retained statutory authority and ground power. Once wilderness became institutionalized in federal bureaucracies, both its philosophy and enforcement lacked single purpose though acreage grew steadily. We got a lot of official wilderness but no clear, unified system. If the pre-1964 history of wilderness under USFS authority revealed "conflicting political ideological meanings," the new National Wilderness Preservation System created a similarly decentralized, hodgepodge system without a clear administrative philosophy. As environmental historian Thomas R. Vale states, it "cobbles together wild landscape reserves overseen by different federal agencies with different administrative regulations. In spite of proclamations to the contrary (Wilderness Society 1984), it is no more coherent than the National Park System, and arguably less so."[39] Northwest wilderness areas sometimes reflect this de facto tradition of different federal agencies administering "their" acreage according to their own traditions and management philosophies. Most conspicuously, the Mount St. Helens National Volcanic Monument (1982) is administered by the USFS (one of a handful of national monuments) as a special category within the Gifford Pinchot National Forest.

Following the Wilderness Act debate sharpened between recreational interests and resource extraction interests, with Glacier Peak posing a case study. After all, as one mountaineering scholar has noted, mountains retained their "natural moral authority" just as wilderness carried rich cultural meanings.[40] These values have not changed. Those "cultural meanings" repeatedly played out on Northwest volcanoes since 1964.

In the Glacier Peak Wilderness Area, the act's mining exception grandfathered extant mining claims and allowed new claims (in any wilderness area) for twenty years—that is, 1984. The Kennecott Copper Corporation owned a big claim on the shoulder of Plummer Mountain, just northeast of the volcano. Company surveyors called their tract the "Golf Course" as though it were their own playground: a telltale metaphor that reveals the chasm between private, upper- or middle-class privilege and set-aside tracts around volcanoes. For increasing numbers, such a corporate inholding was unacceptable, even sacrilegious.

Eleven years after Douglas's *My Wilderness*, literary journalist John McPhee's *Encounters with the Archdruid* (1971) spotlit this wilderness volcano debate through its extended profile of Sierra Club's David Brower ("the archdruid"). The book provided balance in its three essays by pitting, in each, Brower with an ideological foe. Yet *Encounters* advanced the cause of wilderness. In "A Mountain," first panel of the triptych, McPhee, Brower, geologist Charles Park, and two others backpack east to west, from Holden and Lyman Lake to the Suiattle River Road just north of Glacier Peak. At the Wilderness Area boundary, McPhee reflects the dichotomy captured by the Wilderness Act, paraphrasing the sign: "'Take one more step and, by decree, you will enter a preserved and separate world, you will pass from civilization into wilderness.' Wilderness was now that definable, that demonstrable, and could be entered in the sense that one enters a room."[41] The ostensibly rigid distinction, which has been increasingly subverted in scholarly and popular understanding, makes the case for wilderness consumerism. When we hike past a Wilderness Act sign we enter the most fancy, most exquisitely appointed room, the one generally reserved for special occasions. McPhee's ironic paraphrase sets the stage for his essay's debate: should Kennecott Copper be allowed to drill and dig for copper inside the Wilderness Area (exercising the twenty-year exception for mining)?

Encounters memorably records the clash of contrary mind-sets and sensibilities and, while being fair to the Charles Parks, it tips the balance in favor of the David Browers. The book appeared just one year after the country's first Earth Day, as mainstream America turned greener. Before the mid-August 1969 backpack trip, McPhee had been advised by an NPS friend, "The Glacier Peak Wilderness is probably the most beautiful piece of country we've got. Mining copper there would be like hitting a pretty girl in the face with a shovel. It would be like strip-mining the Garden of Eden." Those brutal images stack the deck and reverberate in the set piece descriptions of the volcano the writer cannot avoid, from Cloudy and Suiattle Passes and then, from famed Image Lake—the latter, Glacier Peak's iconic view, matching Mount Hood from Lost Lake, or North and Middle Sisters from McKenzie Pass.

In the view from Cloudy Pass—one of those "scenic climaxes," in Brower's phrase—McPhee echoes his NPS friend: "In the central foreground of the view that we were looking at from Cloudy Pass—was the lode of copper that Kennecott would mine, and to do so the company would make an open pit at least two thousand four hundred feet from rim to rim."[42] Using standard lobbying hyperbole, Brower claims such a pit could be seen from the moon. The remainder of "A Mountain" plays variations on this dark "scenic climax": the image of a towering volcano skirted by glaciers, drainages, forests, and parks, with a potentially giant hole gaping front and center.

Through shifts in focus, McPhee writes a fairy tale scene that depicts our instinctive, archetypal greed for precious minerals. Against the insistent panoramas, the backpackers temporarily shift their gaze to a three-inch galvanized pipe, "Kennecott's Drill Site No. 3," amidst the alpine parks that comprise the corporation's "Golf Course." The canny writer plays panoramic and close-up views off one another allegorically, as the party had been scouting, like the corporation, for copper: "The beauty of the mountain across the valley was cool and absolute, but the beauty of the [copper] stone in Park's hand was warm and subjective. It affected us all. Human appetites, desires, ambitions, greed, and profound aesthetic and acquisitional instincts were concentrated between the stone and our eyes."[43]

Temptation and distraction, the hot beauty of copper diverts us from the cool beauty of white volcano. Under the Winthrop volcano, McPhee symbolized the painful challenge of the mining exception and exposed the mutually exclusive values of wilderness

FIG. 9. Glacier Peak from Image Lake. The most iconic view of Washington's "wilderness" volcano. Courtesy of "Image Lake and Glacier Peak" by Norm Hodges is licensed under CC BY 3.0, https://commons.wikimedia.org/wiki /File:Image_Lake_and_Glacier_Peak.jpg.

preservation and of resource extraction: the latter, abiding under the absurd, archaic provisions of the 1872 Mining Law and periodically appearing under the guise of "conservation," "multiple use" or, more recently, "wise use"—a semantic sleight of hand that sanctions continued extractive uses of hitherto designated wilderness. The twentieth-century regional history of wilderness, as idea and fact, shows the volcano's "beauty" increasingly dominating the "beauty" of a resource (forest stands as lumber, or a potentially rich copper vein).

In the parable, background insistently trumps foreground as the meaning of copper dissipates before the meaning of volcano. Under any volcano, everyone feels its pull. The glow of copper faded against Glacier Peak: "We were as close to it as we would ever be. It was right there—so enormous that it seemed to be on top of us, extending upward five thousand feet above our heads. 'That's the sort of thing that draws people into geology,' [Park] said. 'Geologists go into the field because of love of the earth and of the out-of-doors.' 'The irony is that they go into wilderness and change it,' Brower said."[44] Kennecott never developed an open pit copper mine near Washington's wilderness volcano: Washington Congressman Lloyd Meeds told N3C leader Phil Zalesky that its Miner Ridge claim and plans "would never happen." Too much political pressure had mounted against it. *Encounters* did not determine Kennecott's decision though it undoubtedly sharpened the debate even as it enhanced wilderness advocacy.

McPhee's nuanced presentation has proven a standard narrative in the intervening decades. The narrative includes ironic compromises, for instance, infrastructure within wilderness areas: folks want "untrammeled" but want trails, bridges, rock fire rings, pit toilets, etcetera. But not bulldozers, let alone open-pit mining. On the descent west along the Suiattle River, McPhee reduces the scarred images of a USFS trail "improvement project" to the sight and sound of a bulldozer, questioning the presence of the dozer tearing up ground within an established Wilderness Area. In Park and Brower's final clash about this Wilderness Area's optimal use, the former asserts "copper" and the latter, "blueberries"—food for bears and other critters including human visitors to the area.[45] The whimsical contrast defines fundamental differences in renewable vs. non-renewable resources and scale, copper symbolizing that "ascendency of the machine" derided by preservationists.

The notion of private property or ownership at the volcanoes strikes me as bizarre, yet with at least four of the peaks, including Glacier, competing claims in some periods reflected wildly diverse agendas. With two wilderness volcanoes, modern notions of wilderness superimposed themselves, with contrary results, over much older tribal jurisdictions and traditions. The fact that Washington's southern two volcanoes faced potential corporate development on or above their slopes strains credulity, given widespread regional sentiment about the snowpeaks and the seismic change in concern over wilderness protection after 1964. Yet a wedge of Mount St. Helens (mostly unforested, hence "useless") remained in corporate hands until 1982. And before the NWPS, Mount Adams was also under some mining threat, as its crater area contained sulphur deposits that had been prospected. The volcano was federally owned, and yet mining could have occurred near its summit.[46] In this absurd scenario, a volcano would have been mined at its crater, holes upon hole. This interest was not retired until 1984. In retrospect, this appears as far-fetched as the earlier tramway proposals for Mounts Hood and Rainier.

Yet the federal ownership of Adams is recent. Native American treaties signed in 1855 that recognized fourteen tribes established both the Yakama and Warm Springs Reservations. The former was created for the exclusive use of the Yakama; the latter was for the Warm Springs, Wasco, and Paiute tribes. The southwest border of the former includes at least 40 percent of Mount Adams, the boundary running through the false summit and summit. Almost all of Mount Adams's eastern side (including at least four glaciers, its hardest climbing routes, and William Douglas's beloved Bird Creek Meadows) belongs to the Yakama Nation. The Mount Adams Wilderness Area (1964) overlays it, so it and the Yakama Nation Mount Adams Recreation Area (i.e., the reservation's southwest corner) are co-administered as wilderness. Mount Adams—Pahto—has been part of Yakama lands for millennia. Ironically overlooked in the settlement of jurisdictions, this relatively recent wilderness philosophy overlaps tribal lifeways, many of which whites imitate and call "preservationist."

South of the Columbia River, Oregon's Warm Springs Reservation contains the eastern half of Mount Jefferson, the Mount Jefferson Wilderness Area (1968) bisecting the volcano. An older tribal claim bested the late 1960s effort to include all the Mount Jefferson environs within wilderness. The historical irony pits long tribal habitation against the recent commitment to volcano set-aside lands. From the vantage of Yakama or Warm Springs peoples, Pahto and Seekseekqua, respectively, are the opposite of hinterland, and wilderness volcano means nothing. In practice the tribal government manages its alpine zones in concert with wilderness area mandates. No discernable differences exist between Adams and Jefferson in terms of tribal management: in these cases, joint management does not reveal contrary agendas or activities.

With the region's most famous pair of volcanoes, wilderness legislation was superimposed over a national park and a premiere ski area that had seen myriad other uses, and these contrary traditions yielded contrary outcomes. In the 1970s popular support for the NWPS increased as advocates sought to enlarge extant wilderness areas and add new ones. In MRNP eight years after the Wilderness Act, NPS officials completed a wilderness proposal covering all park backcountry excepting the Paradise–Camp Muir corridor: the first half of the oldest, most popular climbing route and a popular day hike. This thin slice of the pie has for a century received greatest use. The proposal took sixteen years to pass Congress, but in the interim, staff proactively managed backcountry as de facto wilderness and tried to lessen ongoing development plans.[47]

"De facto wilderness," something tantamount to but less than official wilderness, became a common management designation in the region in the 1970s and 1980s, just as wilderness became a key component of "resource management." The policy palpably responded to public demand. By 1988, 97 percent of MRNP became categorized as wilderness: for one generation now, the park is almost entirely wilderness yet given its density of visitation, "wilderness" has been stretched, in some spots, well beyond the 1964 definition.

To get a handle on wilderness use in MRNP, researchers developed the concept of recreational carrying capacity, which included both ecological and psychological components.[48] The concept has crucial interdisciplinary reach but traditionally, field researchers had studied the former components but not the latter. The blend of ecological with psychological dimensions drove the backcountry plan circulated in 1973. Recreational carrying capacity factors us into the equation and reflects wilderness as a basic resource management issue, as though it were a measurable entity like big-W wilderness. This concept assesses specific traits ensuing from the act and attempts to quantify a moving target: how many is too many? The answers seem hopelessly variable and subjective, beyond the reach of some quantifying matrix. The plan primarily affected horse- and backpacking parties, and the restrictions resemble those subsequently adopted by wilderness areas throughout the region.

At Mount Hood, the codification of wilderness had to accommodate the long presence of downhill skiing, in which recreational carrying capacity features far higher numbers. Over 25 percent of Mount Hood National Forest is designated wilderness area and its core, the Mount Hood Wilderness Area (1964), currently 67,320 acres, encircles the volcano—with two exceptions. The differences in wilderness areas within MRNP and MHNF dramatize different agency (NPS vs. USFS) philosophies of use and traditions of lands protection or restriction. Most of the Mount Hood Wilderness Area extends westward from the summit (i.e., some of its hardest climbing routes), encompassing subalpine forests. On its south-southwest side, a narrow non-Wilderness Area corridor extends upwards nearly to Crater Rock. The high volume symbolized by Timberline Lodge and ski hill, with its high Palmer Chairlift, signifies uses antithetical to the act. Similarly, a larger wedge on Hood's southeast slopes, a slice of pie that also doesn't reach the summit, was and is excluded to accommodate big Mount Hood Meadows, a destination resort for several decades.

In the past generation, conflicts between wilderness advocates and commercial interests surface when Mount Hood Meadows has filed to expand. For example, in the 1980s it was "planning a city," in the words of venerable Mount Hood historian Jack Grauer, in a "wild, scenic" location within MHNF. The big environmental organizations (e.g., Sierra Club, Mazamas) stepped in to oppose and litigate if necessary; in 1988 a local organization, "Friends of

Mount Hood," was created in part to oppose any further resort expansion plans.[49] Study of the Mount Hood Meadows website, however, suggests that the resort has always been a leader in environmental stewardship. Antithetical narratives flourish. At Mount St. Helens a grassroots lobby contended with a regional timber giant but gained an unexpected boost after the 1980 eruption. Unsurprisingly, the argument for preservation emphasized its famed beauty (as the most shapely of the Northwest volcanoes) and its modern recreational history at the big lake below its north-slope forests. In the 1970s a local environmental group seeking to designate Mount St. Helens a national monument gained force. Two articles in *National Parks Magazine* (December 1963, May 1968) advocated for a national monument, since most local folks valued outstanding scenery and recreation over small timber revenues for the USFS.

Local environmentalists re-formed the Mount St. Helens Protective Association in February 1977, as Weyerhaeuser demanded continued access to the volcano's lush lowland forests—years after a comparable, timber-driven "starfish" proposal for Glacier Peak was rejected. Support expanded rapidly since several generations possessed indelible memories of youth camps or lodge vacations at Spirit Lake. To preserve the setting for future generations and halt further logging, many lobbied their congressional delegation.[50] The big lake, part of its identity, had functioned as a rustic destination resort for generations: a volcano and lake had together provided the kind of life-changing outdoors experience that shines undimmed in the memory of participants, who remain fiercely loyal to that experience and setting. Legions of regional residents were not about to see the woods near "their" lake and volcano stripped away. At yet another volcano, recreation battled resource extraction.

Recreation and logging had long existed in opposition below St. Helens. The former uses approximated 1960s wilderness philosophy (excepting motorized boats); the latter "single use" did not. In 1977, the USFS undertook "RARE II" ("Roadless Area Review and Evaluation II"), as mandated by the Wilderness Act and legal challenges to RARE I, and completed its work in January 1979, recommending an additional fifteen million acres be added to the NWPS. Because of subsequent legal challenges, RARE II was mostly voided. RARE II, incredibly enough, did not list St. Helens or environs for wilderness designation. By 1979, though, the era of massive clear-cutting was ending due to increasing environmental activism in the press and courtroom.

The May 18, 1980 eruption of St. Helens increased preservationist pressure, given the precedent of Mount Lassen National Park in northeast California, where massive eruptions in 1915 led to a national park in 1916. By 1981 the local protective association, with endorsements from several state and national environmental organizations, proposed a 216,000-acre monument; timber interests recommended a forty-thousand-acre monument in the blast zone only. Same old battle lines. The resulting National Monument compromise (May 1982), 110,000 acres, is closer in size to timber's small proposal than the protective association's expansive one. And ironically, the protected area would be managed by the USFS, which had lost its historic lead in wilderness preservation. Use regulations partially imitate Leave No Trace practice, though snowmobiles, for example, are permitted off-road. This National Monument contains, inconceivably, no official wilderness, which distinguishes St. Helens from almost every other Northwest volcano. Yet a restricted zone circumscribing the volcano is off limits due to St. Helens' rumbling and dome building in its center. This is de facto wilderness without people.

In the year of the United States Bicentennial the USFS underwent a paradigm shift in management philosophy due to passage of the National Forest Management Act. Because of this act ecosystem management rather than resource extraction became the primary criterion in forest planning. Finally, holistic planning began to replace the kind of abstracted line drawing that lacks every kind of knowledge except current extraction practices and profits. Ecosystem management overlaps considerably with wilderness preservation, and this act nudged the agency closer to its historic mission of preserves. Clear-cutting (e.g., below St. Helen's western slopes) would be out. Henceforth, the Service saw the forest, not just the trees. Since that seismic shift, mountain wilderness has increased. In 1984, because of bipartisan support from Washington's and Oregon's congressional delegations, Congress passed a supplemental Wilderness Act—the Washington and Oregon Wilderness Acts, respectively—which expanded Pacific Northwest Wilderness Areas acreage more than any year since 1964. For example, Oregon's Diamond Peak Wilderness Area was expanded to 52,337 acres.

In Washington, the northernmost volcano that also visually dominates southwestern British Columbia finally became official wilderness. The Mount Baker Wilderness Area, at 117,900 acres, unsurprisingly highlights the volcano as the icon of is southern portion. The wilderness area includes fourteen glaciers and over ten thousand acres of ice. The local grassroots lobby, the Mount Baker Wilderness Association, advocated for a 240,000—acre wilderness based on their extensive field research.[51] As at St. Helens, they got roughly half of what they asked for, sixty years after Washington National Forest was renamed Mount Baker National Forest and a decade after it had been combined with the Snoqualmie National Forest. A national forest, and later a wilderness area, again took their name and identity from a volcano. By 1984, then, virtually all Northwest volcanoes had become official wilderness.

Yet preservationist pressure increased as the majority population began to identify themselves as moderate environmentalists. Mountaineers writer Harvey Manning's *Washington Wilderness: The Unfinished Work* (1984), with gorgeous photography by Pat O'Hara, fit the winning Sierra Books coffee table format that in the preceding generation had proven as potent a lobbying weapon as any in middle-class America. Manning's inside cover featured a big state map and detailed thirty "proposed additions" to extant wilderness areas including acreage west of North Cascades National Park (NCNP); west, south, and east of Glacier Peak Wilderness Area; northwest, southwest-south, and east of MRNP; and north, west, and south of the small Mount Adams Wilderness Area (46, 353 acres). Congress got the message, at least a bit, since it enlarged Glacier Peak Wilderness Area (1984) for the third time in twenty years, adding acreage that had been controversial sixteen years earlier, when NCNP was created.[52] Within a generation the environmental lobby carried the day around Washington's wilderness volcano. A new Wilderness Area, which Congress named after the late Senator Henry Jackson, bordered the Glacier Peak Wilderness Area on the south. Factoring in the Alpine Lakes Wilderness Area just north of I-90 (Snoqualmie Pass), a big chunk of the Cascades north from Snoqualmie Pass to Canada became official wilderness. That's an extraordinary achievement that provides an alpine playground for several lifetimes. With the creation of the Wild Sky Wilderness Area in 2008, which is contiguous to the Henry Jackson Wilderness Area, and protects even more subalpine west slope forest (along the North Fork, Skykomish River), Robert Marshall's 1939 vision was finally realized. It only took three generations, as broad coalitions (and bipartisan support) "finished" the "work" in the North Cascades as elsewhere.

The greening of the regional population inspired additional categories of protection, "wilderness thresholds" and de facto wilderness (e.g., Mount St. Helens National Monument). Wilderness thresholds, or buffer zones, define national recreation areas and their relationship to contiguous national parks. These recreation areas provide the infrastructure for motorized visitors and recreationists.[53] With wilderness thresholds, high density recreation abuts big-W wilderness, as is the case on the south and southeastern flanks of Mount Hood. Though not legal wilderness, as management strategies wilderness thresholds present alternatives or buffers and, in the woods or above them, usually provide experience comparable to what backpackers expect in wilderness areas—even if not every wilderness area rule is observed.

In the Northwest, both preservationists and mining prospectors or timber cruisers focused increasingly on de facto wilderness: those areas adjacent to official wilderness.[54] This attention diffused, to a limited extent, the tradition of exclusivity characterizing big-W wilderness. Washington's Alpine Lakes Wilderness Area (1976) exemplifies de facto wilderness coupled with citizen initiative in its genesis. This mountainous region, directly east of the greater Seattle metro area, received broad-based citizen coalition support for permanent protection. When enough recreational and other interests demand wilderness protection for tracts contiguous to legal wilderness areas, de facto wilderness gains validity and becomes a transitional stage; a good example of this is what happened with almost all of MRNP between 1973 and 1988.

Farther north, North Cascades National Park (NCNP), which spreads east of Mount Baker and north of Glacier Peak, comprises a new national park entity, a "park complex" dependent upon "wilderness thresholds." At NCNP, a highway (Rte. 20, the North Cascades Highway, 1972) runs through it, bisecting the park and providing "scenic narrative" infrastructure—vista pullouts, signage—and amenities characteristic of mid-twentieth-century management emphases (e.g., NPS's Mission 66). Drivers transiting this threshold gain a slight taste of this park's identity. Most don't quit their vehicles for more than eight hours, and Mount Baker and Glacier Peak can't be seen from the highway: a relatively low-altitude corridor, an artery from which day hikers, backpackers, "through hikers" (i.e., Pacific Crest Trail backpackers) and climbers travel out and up, into the myriad lakes, glaciers, and jutting peaks of the "park complex." In 1988 Congress designated about 93 percent of the NCNP complex, along with the adjacent Glacier Peak (southwest) and Pasayten (east) Wilderness Areas, as the Stephen Mather Wilderness to ensure additional mandated protection. Though the percentage is not quite as high as in MRNP, almost all of this big block of mountainous, north-central Washington, including its two volcanoes, is dedicated wilderness. That's a significant grassroots and legislative accomplishment, a claim to fame in the Evergreen State. No windshield wilderness here. Wilderness thresholds and de facto wilderness function as contiguous buffer zones and quasi-wilderness, respectively. Yet in the 1980s consensus about both became suspect as Northwest logging entered a more frantic phase. At the same time, with ecosystem management as its mandate, the USFS was charged with enforcing northern spotted owl protection policies. In the 1980s and 1990s, the northern spotted owl, a threatened species that almost exclusively inhabits old-growth forests, became a lightning rod in Northwest timber wars. The subalpine zone below the volcanoes or other Cascades—or particularly Washington's Olympics and Oregon's coastal range—became a fiercely contested site of clashing values. At Glacier Peak, lines were drawn in the sand between environmentalists and loggers as spotted owl censuses declined. More and more people understood that extant national parks and wilderness areas—that welter of lines on maps—didn't sufficiently protect old-growth forest ecosystems, which include valleys and watersheds, not just what's above them.[55] Ecosystem management dictated what preservationists knew all along: high altitudes cannot be detached from low, as the resources in both always comprise an integrated whole. Northern spotted owls, like volcano glaciers, belong to the old forests below the latter.

The Northwest contained the lower forty-eight states' best stands of remaining old-growth forest and sometimes, old growth flourishes under the volcanoes. The logging industry, like many USFS old timers, was wedded to the metaphor and practice of tree "farming" as though foothills forests were a monocultural, renewable crop, like Palouse wheat or Hood River Valley apples. We're not talking Christmas tree farms. The zeal to log and replant up to wilderness area boundaries turned some de facto wilderness tracts into checkered cutover lands both ugly and sterile—horrific visual cliché of west slope lowlands. Additionally, such practices sometimes wiped out hiking trails or climbing approaches. Anyone flying over or hiking the Cascades or coast ranges knows the crazy-quilt legacy of industrial-scale harvesting in foothills up to 3500-foot elevation or higher. Though logging companies retained forest "curtains" adjacent to roads to dupe unsuspecting motorists, back-packers and climbers approaching volcanoes through subalpine stretches (just beyond wilderness area boundaries) knew better.

So did some professional foresters. On a September 1988 hike in the Three Sisters Wilderness, two individuals, one a USFS employee, decided to found a reform-minded employee organization.[56] The Association of Forest Service Employees for Environmental Ethics was born. Their experiences in one of Oregon's oldest and largest wilderness areas prompted the foresters to lobby the USFS to step up to the plate and manage forests holistically. A dozen years had already passed since the National Forest Management Act, and local enforcement lagged far behind, given the long, intimate relationship between the local national forests and logging com-panies. This internal USFS reform group played a key role in the regional debate about ecosystem management, sometimes joining forces with mainstream preservationist lobbies such as the Sierra Club, which opened a legal defense fund office in Seattle in 1987.

The notion of volcanoes as "arctic islands" misleads to the extent it splits integrated ecosystems; the precincts just below a volcano form part of it. Arctic islands constitute the backbone to regional ecosystems, with riparian zones connecting higher altitudes with sea level.[57] Riparian zones represent the most biologically rich re-gions, as field biologists, wilderness advocates, and timber interests have always known. The metaphor of higher and lower elevations as one complex organism exposes the artificial distinctions between legal wilderness and de facto wilderness.

For example, just beyond MRNP's southeast corner, the Highway 12 corridor is sandwiched between the Tatoosh and William O. Douglas Wilderness Areas. Ohanapecosh in MRNP's southeast corner—along with the Carbon River entrance in the northwest corner, the lowest elevation in the park—has long featured a "Grove of the Patriarchs" boardwalk trail that crosses the Ohanapecosh River and circles a small island. Ancient Douglas firs, western hemlocks, and western red cedars prompt responses like "cathedral," "magic kingdom," "a sacred place." The grove's irresistible, anthropomorphic title describes old habits of veneration. Visitors come not to learn about the area's one-time mineral baths or WPA camp; they come to experience the unique, intense atmosphere of old-growth forest, where tree girths and heights exceed common understanding. This island of time exists as part of Mount Rainier's eastside glaciers and drainages that have watered it for eons. In the Northwest, other groves of "patriarchs" grow under the volcanoes and exemplify old-growth forest. From the late twentieth-century vantage, such low-elevation riparian zones are integral to the glaciers and craters above them.

While the wilderness system enjoys broad support in the early twenty-first century, most of its supporters are urban or suburban, reflecting the demographic reality of the Willamette Valley and the Puget Sound basin. Increasingly, time inside a wilderness area is determined by the wired demands and alternatives of the city. It's a luxury. With some exceptions, use of wilderness appears an updated expansion of the traditional park picnic. Wilderness becomes quick and consumable, an outdoors alternative to high-end malls or art museums.

For example, the MHNF Strategic Stewardship Plan (2006), when highlighting the four Wilderness Areas around Mount Hood, comments upon the marked trend towards short visits. Wilderness experience in this "urban national forest" provides an odd mix, as Mount Hood "biographer" Jon Bell admits: "There are times, camped high up above Vista Ridge on the northwest side . . . when you feel solitude so wild that you forget a major metropolitan mess of more than 2 million people is little more than an hour's drive west. On other days, you run into familiar faces on the slopes as if you were just crossing paths at a coffee shop in town."[58] The former scenario defines wilderness experience; the latter does not, yet it occurs increasingly frequently inside designated wilderness.

The same trend prevails in other Northwest wilderness areas centered upon volcanoes, suggesting a profound and troubling lag, in the early twenty-first century, between *use* and *policy*. Decade by decade, *use* means different activities according to different constituencies. Wilderness *policy* contains clear expectations about experiences, at higher or lower altitudes, in small groups few and far between; wilderness *use* reflects, at times, numbers and habits characteristic of high-density populations in cities. Cities contain the primary wilderness lobby, along with most mountaineering clubs and alpine rec stores. Given the rate of urbanization, the region needs its big-W wilderness areas more than ever. The further contemporary technologies remove most of us from the alpine hinterlands, the more we need them.

The notion of a wilderness area as a "form of mental rebirth," as Howard Zahniser described it, sustains the familiar argument for climbing, especially volcano climbing. Experience on a "living volcano" or in a "living wilderness" area enhances individual and collective life. Whether such rebirth occurs during swift wilderness trips is unknown. A quickie is better than nothing, but it represents a fleeting glimpse in contrast to the backpacking or climbing celebrated by Northwest wilderness writers. Volcano climbs increasingly resemble a small, precious chunk of time we buy.

Anti-wilderness arguments past or present deride the whole notion of set-aside land as impractical and selfish, oddly enough. If wilderness boundaries create a system of public lands exclusivity, opponents claim exclusion as though official wilderness is "locked up," unavailable to "significant"—i.e., motorized—human use. In this mind-set, passing a particular wilderness area sign signifies entering a closed space, not a living, changing domain. Such arguments are embraced by many locally elected officials. Contemporary critics of 1960s wilderness thinking rightly condemn the fundamentally flawed ahistoricity sometimes accompanying the idea of set-aside tracts. Yet in the early 1960s Zahniser, the Wilderness Act's chief architect, sustained a more nuanced, dynamic view, noting in his diary that wilderness preservation should "remove the human trammels that keep the natural changes from taking place."[59]

For anti-wilderness folks, "locked up" usually means you can't enter or travel sitting down (excepting horseback). It rubs against a terminal love affair with vehicles, however small (e.g., ORVs and ATVs). In this respect the volcanoes (except Crater Lake/ Mount Mazama) remain locked up except for occasional approach routes. We uncritically laud our ease of access even as we recognize myriad problems accruing from motors, and we prize wilderness areas as domains apart. Not all who accept the fact of wilderness areas accept the preference for quiet trails, for example. Roads of any sort separate, more than anything else, the space of wilderness from other public lands since roads assume motors. And motors—the sound of "the machine age"—subvert, for most, the purposes of wilderness: purposes that demand different modes of access. Northwest volcanoes, by their very nature, symbolize optimal wilderness since they preclude motorized access particularly above tree line.

The very act of drawing (or extending) boundaries sets up distinctions between inside and out: inside entails more special provisions if not restrictions than outside. Such boundaries separate the special from the mundane, and sponsor habits of discriminating consumerism. Time in a wilderness area, like time on a snowpeak, is prized to the extent that it is limited, fleeting. An inverse scale exists. In the Northwest, the volcanoes have played a definitive role in the unfolding story of wilderness idealism and practice. Other set-aside traditions elsewhere interpret "locked up" literally, treating wilderness as a closed room. Reflecting a stringent wilderness area philosophy, Poland's Bialowieza National Park, in its core, illustrates a locked-up preserve far beyond our Wilderness Act, as nearly half of it is fenced and inaccessible without a park guide (it contains Europe's last bison herds and one of its last hardwood forests). By contrast, the Northwest's volcanoes resemble open rooms—or temples or cathedrals, to cite more apt metaphors—available via innumerable climbing routes and cross-country travel just below them. The problem, in the early twenty-first century, concerns both the density and distribution of human traffic, and that lag between traffic and the dictates of managing wilderness experience as a finite resource.

6 VOLCANOES AND CROWDS

Vehicles are a real problem for us. . . . 97 percent of [Mount Rainier
National] Park is wilderness. Yet within the next ten-fifteen years,
we will be surrounded by suburbs. And the pressure of people to
come and use the Park twelve months a year. It's that pressure,
pressure, pressure.

—National Park Service ranger John Madden,
   Rainier: The Mountain

The Wilderness Act (Section 2[c]), under "Definitions," calls for
"outstanding opportunities for solitude or a primitive and unconfined type of recreation" in wilderness areas. USFS and NPS management philosophy enforces "Leave No Trace" tenets, whether on
glaciers or rocks, or in alpine parks or drainages below. Yet traces in
many shapes and sizes get left, regularly. "Leave No Trace" includes
guidelines familiar to anyone entering big-W areas in the past
two generations, and compliance is assumed. The polite phrasing
on park signs assigns responsibility to visitors. But the colorful
plastic wrappers of varying shapes or wads of soggy white toilet
paper represent the outer, unintentional residues of wilderness
consumerism: casual trail discards of time expended within big-W
boundaries. The felt experience of the vast majority of Northwest
volcano visitors or climbers does not include "being unnoticed"
even if they use blue, double plastic bags. Quite the contrary, particularly on standard routes. Managing "wilderness experience" on

the volcanoes in the late twentieth and early twenty-first centuries places unreasonable if not untenable demands upon USFS or NPS agency personnel. Voluntary compliance with "Leave No Trace" tenets depends upon an informed and cooperative public, and the public is neither at all times and places.

There's a problem here. "Wilderness experience" since 1964 has solidified into an entity, something sought after and measured, a finite resource not unlike stream quality or particular wildlife censuses or migrations. Agency folks are supposed to monitor and protect this resource—the sign of access and use. This "resource" arguably comprises the fundamental management issue of the twenty-first century. Wilderness experience is both historical and contemporary, ineffable mountain glory and a set of measurable criteria, private subjective experience and legal mandate and management protocol. As a precious resource it is overdetermined, ideal more than real, and as Hamlet admits in another context, "Aye, there's the rub." Wilderness experience remains problematic, given the friction between these contrary tendencies.

Certainly the contemporary moment exists at odds with any historical view. The volcanoes have been taboo landscapes for eons, magnets for the past 150 years, and wilderness areas for the past fifty (or less). Now crowds come to the volcanoes and leave sundry imprints below and on the snow. Above timberline and the alpine parks, of course, those traces don't decompose so the signs of our passing linger indefinitely.

On the easiest climbing routes it's not hard to find discarded, frayed climbing slings or other trash. At the high camps along these routes, which imitate a bustling apartment complex in high season, it's hard to believe that camp spots or runoff aren't being degraded. Over three decades ago, one historian painted an indelible portrait of mass mountaineering's legacy: "Mountain slopes are often marred by paraphernalia left behind by exhausted climbers retreating from a summit conquest or from storms. . . . Abandoned polypropylene rope, aluminum cans . . . plastic wrappers, and nylon fabric become an almost permanent kind of defacement."[1] A bad habit in descents is evidenced by this kind of defacement as though a climb is psychologically diminished or neglected in its second half. The baleful legacy has not improved given the far greater numbers. Northwest volcanoes bear signs of this discard signature: a higher-elevation version of careless picnickers or walkers in the forests and meadows below.

Rainier hires crews of climbing rangers, of course, though climbers far exceed the number of such rangers; typically, few or no USFS personnel patrol on the other volcanoes. Climbing parties usually self-register, thereby pledging to observe local rules and Leave No Trace camping. That most elusive resource, wilderness experience, is a fiction unless one tackles obscure routes: the west-side routes above Sandy Glacier, for instance, on Mount Hood. Even routes famous for their technical challenges such as Rainier's Liberty Ridge, sharp on its northwest side, receive more than occasional parties due to increasing publicity. The numbers problem deeply erodes the letter and spirit of wilderness experience, and agency personnel face an impossible dilemma.

The Mount Baker–Snoqualmie National Forest website, like most national forest websites, deems "wilderness education" "the most important tool" in management. The site states the goal of preserving wilderness experience conditionally: "*If* people are aware of what is required of them in a . . . wilderness trip, *there is a chance* that they will behave appropriately. The *hope* is that people, by their own actions, will preserve the aesthetic experience. Management can be *anticipatory* rather than *reactive*, and a *traditional freedom of choice* will be maintained in wild land recreation" (emphasis added).[2] "There is a chance" sounds, at best, skeptical. Most hikers and climbers fulfill this best-case scenario, though day hikers litter more than backpackers. Published surveys from MRNP and MHNF within the past generation reveal a preponderance of increasingly short visits, and as the number of quick visitors rises, so inevitably does the fraction of "noncompliant users."[3] Trip brevity reinforces a carelessness typical of many in their regular, built environments, as though wilderness as *other* does not change behavior in the space of a few hours. The quick daytrip, or wilderness lite, prompts sloppy behavior by some who leave new versions of tin-can trash. This despite the fact that by the late twentieth century it became easier to pack it out.

Best-case scenarios presume a tendency to fall short, and an increasing minority remains blissfully ignorant of best practices on and below the volcanoes. In the old tradeoff between access and preservation, preservation plays second fiddle. Checks upon access are challenged and, at best, grudgingly tolerated—or ignored. Given the realities of mass mountaineering, the goal of agency management grows ever more elusive. Instead, personnel often practice damage control in the face of crowds: closure is not an option given likely public backlash. As one critic commented a generation ago, "insulation" increasingly trumps "intensity": "intensiveness of impact" pushes aside "intensiveness of experience."[4] In this sad tradeoff, the human boot print easily does damage.

In the past generation that thickening boot print at the volcanoes is accompanied by technology creep, but technology creep began decades before GPS systems, transponders, and smartphones. The ink was barely dry on President Johnson's signature on the 1964 Wilderness Bill before management challenges were manifest: the gap between the promise of solitude and on-the-ground traffic already existed in popular locales. When John McPhee reached the Glacier Peak Wilderness Area's Image Lake in August 1969, he encountered a suburban scene: "We walked past tents along the shore—blue tents, green tents, red tents, orange tents. The evening air was so still that we could hear voices all around the lake."[5]

The suburban scene is now repeated at base camps or along standard routes at all of the volcanoes. Lower-altitude parking lots are filled to overflowing, and NPS campgrounds fill within minutes of preceding campers' mid- or late-morning departures:

first-come, first-serve, with slowly cruising carloads warily eyeing imminent departures. NPS founding Director Stephen Mather's goal of nearly a century ago has been met with a vengeance. Leave No Trace didn't happen at Image Lake in the late 1960s. Arch-preservationist David Brower tried to soften the human impact, confidently claiming a longer view: "I've seen crowds in wilderness before. I know that they'll go away, and when they go they haven't really left anything."⁶ That claim depends upon the definition of "really." He was right and wrong, as the track record of the intervening four decades attests. Certainly the successive revolutions in the alpine gear and clothing industry have mitigated impacts to some extent. MSR (Mountain Safety Research) stoves and dehydrated foods, for example, have long replaced campfires, canned food, and #10 tins. Campsites below snowline are less depleted of wood. With some exceptions, gone are the days when saplings were hacked by dull hatchets.

The story has grown more complicated, though. Modern gear reinvents itself like those limitless brooms in *The Sorcerer's Apprentice*: an endlessly variable, alluring supply, continuous new models feeding an insatiable demand, the huge engine of environmental consumerism. Supply is the outer vesture of wilderness consumerism. Far more people bring far more gear—lighter weight and stronger alloys and synthetics—to the volcanoes and elsewhere, and while it lessens the impact of human trammels, the trammels still multiply. On standard routes, Leave No Trace competes against well-churned, braided trails and challenges climbers, for example, to find clean snow to melt for water.

Climbers wear plastic boots and tote transponders and portable communications devices including iPads for satellite feeds and instant access. They bring more pieces of the Web into the remote spaces of mountains as if more is better, rather than less. In the past two decades, "connectivity" increasingly means wired, dialed in at all times; the older, romantic meaning of mountain sublime, or even affinity with remote landscapes (or nearby outdoors), has receded.

Wired expectations and behaviors diminish the fundamentally different experiences and values epitomized by the snowpeaks.

The Internet creep represents, of course, part of the larger, wired twenty-first century. More Americans do visit wilderness areas though the percentage of visitors has declined in the past generation for many reasons, including the lure of the virtual world for the aptly named Net Generation and aging boomers.

The crowd at Glacier Peak's Image Lake or Mount Rainier's Emmons Flats or South Sister's standard route exacerbates the access vs. preservation dilemma endemic to the NWPS management, whatever the agency. Proposed rationing systems fly in the face of our democratic values governing public wildlands. But have we reached or passed "recreational carrying capacity," the point where the need for traffic control is paramount? In 1999 the USFS considered adopting a permit system limiting the number of Mount Hood climbers to twenty-five per peak weekend day, weekends proving the usual, disproportionate load. That number that might guarantee "wilderness experience," but the MHNF quickly backed off due to vociferous public protest. Journalist Jon Bell cautions, "It's an idea that's almost surely going to come back around. . . . As the Portland population continues to swell, the demands put upon the mountain increase, and an accident made worse by too many climbers on the South Side route morphs from potential to reality."[7]

Safety has been as issue for generations. Mount Hood's recent history includes a long series of disasters and deaths, and as more novices climb (on the southern route and elsewhere), the disasters grow in number. The longest chapter by far in Jack Grauer's *Mount Hood: A Complete History* is "Tragedy, Search, and Rescue," a recounting of climbing accidents on the volcano. Because Mount Hood represents the oldest example of mass mountaineering, it's no surprise that disasters on Hood form common copy—a predictable result of open access.

Even as definitions of and demands for "use" increase, the "resource" is finite. Volcano wilderness areas, with their diversity of climates and ecosystems, dramatize the fragility of wilderness as a resource in a country of over three hundred million inhabitants. The Northwest has exceeded the upward demographic curve of the past three generations, and many old and new alpinists with sufficient income and mobility take to the mountains, especially the volcanoes. Admittedly, most backcountry remains nearly deserted but that's not the case with the snowpeaks, particularly in those convergence zones where climbers have the best chance to summit. That sharp population increase pits access against preservation as never before. In too many spots, the former harms the latter, with various resources degraded. Some locations in local national parks, like volcano trailheads, imitate malls with limited parking: that wilderness "threshold" is tough to get beyond. One contemporary criticism of the National Park System concerns its privileging of recreation over protection, with one cynic claiming "NPS stands not for National Park Service but for National Parking Service."[8] In MRNP it's crowded at the top of the road, if not the crater, with Paradise employees working as traffic cops. That quip about the NPS exposes our enslavement by private vehicles and pursuit of the windshield wilderness.

The endemic tension between access and preservation in the agencies is, unsurprisingly, visible in the published agendas of more than one Northwest environmental organization. The Mazamas' Conservation Committee sometimes partners with up to two-dozen conservation organizations (such as "Friends of Mount Hood," founded more than two decades ago) to advance its preservationist agenda. In recent years it supported lobbying efforts that led to more than 127,000 additional acres in MHNF being designated wilderness (as part of the Omnibus Public Lands Management Act, March 2009). But its "Conservation Goal" defines a tough balancing act: "Mountain environments are protected and managed to balance their use for public enjoyment and their value as natural habitats." The first of its five strategies—"Advocate for open and fair access to alpine areas" (www.mazamas.org)—restates the gospel but potentially troubles that balance because open access has resulted in habitat degradation, both above and below snowline.

Thousands hike or climb Mount Hood every year but tens of thousands ski it (or near it). Mount Hood's skiing history explains its highest use (excepting Timberline as hotel), and accruing profits pit "wilderness experience" against the happy crowds of downhill (and, increasingly, cross-country) skiers and boarders. Occasionally, these contrary traditions exist side by side. The Mount Hood Meadows resort remains the biggest corporate player despite the history and fame of Timberline, and in its roughly forty-five year history it has frequently attempted to expand its special use permit through proposals submitted to MHNF—the old story of demand and corporate growth. Wilderness character was taking a back seat to this demand, and sundry environmental organizations opposed, by the 1980s, actions they deemed degrading to the vicinity of the Mount Hood Wilderness Area, for instance Timberline's heavy use of salt to sustain summer skiing.[9] A preservationist coalition (including Friends of Mount Hood) frequently opposed and litigated resort expansion plans both at Mount Hood Meadows and at Cooper Spur to the northeast.

In recent years "wilderness threshold" has proven a vexing concept around Mount Hood. The proposed Cooper Spur expansion would have given Hood a big ski resort on its northeast side, a counterpart to Timberline. The proposed resort plan demonstrates development pressures at the boundary of wilderness areas: pressures that reflect, in this case, a restricted and economically privileged definition of open access. This project would have allowed uses antithetical to de facto wilderness. Various nonprofits opposed expansion of the Cooper Spur Inn ski area into a four-season destination resort with golf course and new ski lifts and runs. The owners of Mount Hood Meadows, having acquired the Cooper Spur facility, wanted to complete a land exchange with Hood River County of over six hundred acres contiguous to the facility (156 acres already acquired) that contain old growth forests and pristine backcountry.

This proposal within the past generation proves that the early twentieth-century lure of volcano destination resorts does not fade, as the big business of Timberline Lodge and Mount Hood Meadows attests. Of course most people could not afford a fancy built environment abutting Mount Hood backcountry. The Mazamas' opposition appealed to various stewardship identities including its own. As its website proclaims, "The land and surrounding public and private land is an important part of Mazamas' history as well as an essential element of the natural heritage for the entire region and in particular the citizens of Hood River County, neighboring counties and the residents of Portland."[10] A high-density wilderness threshold was avoided through a negotiated settlement (2004), wherein the corporate entity gave up 770 acres northeast of Mount Hood for 120 acres in Government Camp primed for development.[11]

How can preservation survive open access near and on the volcanoes? Without a steady stream of visitors, the preservationist lobby—which fancies itself a prophet trying to convert those visitors to its doctrine of salvation in wilderness—would not grow and sway policy.[12] The dilemma updates the philosophy of founding NPS Director Stephen Mather and longtime REI CEO Jim Whittaker, who both believed in getting the crowds into the parks and onto the peaks. The massive recruitment, while converting many to the gospel of mountain glory and stewardship commitments, would lead to increasing problems on the ground due to sheer numbers.

Northwest environmental organizations advocate preservation but tend to ignore the tradeoff between crowds and degradation. Discover Your Northwest, a nonprofit founded in 1974 in Seattle, defines itself as a "social enterprise" that "promotes the discovery of Northwest public lands, enriches the experience of visitors, and builds community stewardship of these special places today and for generations to come." The group has fostered "community stewardship" through onsite "educational merchandise" such as MRNP trail maps. Those water-resistant trail maps, like the Mountaineers' hiking book series a generation earlier, facilitate mass use. Noting decreasing visitation in some public lands in the Northwest, this organization, like so many others, strives to increase the number of visitors to the volcanoes, improve their experience above and below snowline, and increase their environmental commitment.[13] The three-prong strategy of such a regional environmentalist organization, while laudable, does not address the access vs. preservation contradictions. Evidence such as overflowing parking lots and campgrounds around the volcanoes suggests that the first goal contradicts the second.

For virtually everyone, access means our cars, and we're unwilling to sacrifice personal preference for alternatives. How many who want to climb Rainier or at least get on the mountain would ride that old Tacoma Eastern railroad were it revived? The slow time of that old approach would be inconceivable for most who want to briefly visit MRNP or bag the summit. Or what about those vacationers who've planned one day (or less) for MHNF and Mount Hood? Yet a generation ago one historian, citing the usual problems of auto congestion, made the case for mandatory public transportation being the only approach to balance access with preservation.[14] The problem is succinctly stated but the proffered solution—tourist railroads—has not caught on, to put it mildly. Railroad infrastructure hardly exists for Northwest volcanoes, so it isn't a viable option. Other forms of shuttle, similar to Glacier National Park's 1930s-style open mini-busses, should be studied. Rocky Mountain National Park utilizes a moderately successful public transportation system that has been recently (2010) studied.[15] But most volcano visitors want a quick in-and-out experience, and aren't willing to sacrifice the personal convenience of driving themselves.

The issue of "recreational carrying capacity" sinks beneath the weight of diverse, subjective criteria including those variable definitions of "wilderness experience." It is extremely difficult to establish benchmarks that guarantee consensus about capacity and preserve that most elusive resource. Given mountaineering's popularity, the commitment to open access becomes harder to sustain as various systems of rationing or other controls are attempted.

Michael Frome, well-known environmental activist and author whose most famous book, *Battle for the Wilderness* (1974; 1997), is a late twentieth-century call to arms, reviewed some of the (use) permit systems in place in particular Washington and Oregon national forests. He concluded these systems lack size limits (i.e., number of people in one party), so do they have any teeth? Frome and like-minded writers want to advance the debate and force the agencies' hands, claiming the time has come for backcountry rationing systems since heavily used wilderness is not wilderness. He would claim that in high season, the "use capacity" of some wilderness areas has been exceeded.[16] That sentiment is common-place—but the measurements are problematic. Exactly how does "use capacity" define wilderness experience as a finite resource in a given area? Presumably the former cannot be standardized from one volcano wilderness to another. Certainly standard routes sorely test the notion of use capacity and pose a textbook case for re-stricting access. A range of restricted-access definitions has existed (with appropriate boundary signs) for many years and for many reasons in wilderness areas. But favorite approaches to standard routes show myriad signs of overuse, including trash along those braided boot trails on glacial moraines.

In particular backcountry locations, a sense of crisis accom-panies the lopsided contest between preservation, restoration, and increasing numbers of feet on and off the trails. What real choices do agencies have? In what specific ways should climbers or other wilderness users lower their wilderness expectations? Since the 1960s habitat restoration projects have stemmed or turned the tide of degradation. Certainly the alpine parks of MRNP's Paradise or Mount Hood's Timberline reflect the wear of mass tourism just as particular routes above them show chronic "traces." Other voices sound warnings. *The Mountaineers: A History* concludes that the

Northwest's extraordinary natural landscapes are under grave threat and that the kind of "responsible access to the backcountry" on which such clubs depend may be a thing of the past.[17] Though most backcountry—for example, North Cascades National Park—stays uncrowded, the volcanoes—Mount Baker, The Three Sisters—do not, for many reasons I've analyzed. While "responsible access" defines most climbers or other backcountry users, it doesn't define everyone, nor could it. Broad-brush wilderness area restrictions seem politically untenable and difficult at best to enforce.

Given the era of mass mountaineering, "wilderness experience" seems not only a receding target but, for some segments, a disincentive—precisely the opposite of its intent. In recent decades a changed sentiment is intermittently evident at trailheads and sometimes, above them. Some prefer not being far off by themselves; they live in crowds and seek people in the mountains, perhaps believing safety exists in numbers. This mind-set, accustomed to stadiums or gyms or electronic extensions of them, brings crowd expectations to national parks or national forests as though visiting a volcano comprises a species of one-stop shopping: a visitor center and gift shop, a short paved trail, a climb. Crowds are okay because that's what many people know and like. The presence of groups reassures them, and they won't get lost.

The ever-growing series of regional hiking, backpacking, and climbing guides heavily influences the sensibility that we're going the right way if we see other groups ahead or behind us. The flow validates our choice, rather than some "road less traveled" that offers wilderness experience. It's a different attitude towards the presence of others, one inimical to the Wilderness Act. In this mind-set, popularity promises a higher status. That fact, along with the ease (or difficulty) of a route, helps explain why, for example, a line of hikers and climbers ascends Oregon's South Sister's standard (non-technical, southeast) route, whereas far fewer tackle North Sister, slighter lower, or Three-Fingered Jack farther north.

Volcanoes, crowd magnets *and* wilderness areas, invite wilderness experience if not personal transformation. How do we reconcile these contrary traditions? A USDA interagency General Technical Report, *Keeping It Wild: An Interagency Strategy To Monitor Trends in Wilderness Character Across the NWPS System*, defines "wilderness character"—the guarantor of "wilderness experience"—as "the combination of biophysical, experiential, and symbolic ideals that distinguishes wilderness from other lands." These ideals—natural environments mostly free from human alteration; personal experiences in these environments apart from those characteristic of contemporary society; and symbolic interpretation of the concepts of humility, restraint, and interdependence in terms of our interactions with the natural world—don't match up with crowds or the status game of peak bagging. Paraphrases of twentieth-century wilderness philosophy, the ideals depend upon four criteria ("Untrammeled," "Natural," "Undeveloped," and "Solitude or Primitive and Unconfined Recreation"), each of which includes a set of "monitoring questions" and "indicators."[18]

This set is highly relevant to the Northwest volcanoes, particularly the fourth criterion. One monitoring question asks, "What are the trends in outstanding opportunities for *solitude* or *primitive and unconfined recreation* inside wilderness?" (italics original). The "indicators" (e.g., "Remoteness from sights and sounds of people inside the wilderness,") show that wilderness mandates don't exist at many of the volcanoes' base camps and standard routes, and that "wilderness character" is an ideal, not a reality.[19] *Keeping It Wild*, a fairly recent document, suggests that policy, while an accurate descriptor of many Northwest wilderness areas, is seriously out of step with the legions on volcano glaciers and snowfields.

In addition to their erosion of open access, quota systems manifest practical problems because of uncontrollable variables. And when it comes to mountains, there's a real resistance to them. One veteran Mountaineer, photographer Ira Spring—whose longtime collaboration with Harvey Manning in the Mountaineers' ongoing series of Washington hiking books has arguably increased backcountry population more than any other single factor—has ruefully noted one sad prospect: the possibility of strict systems to steeply reduce weekend use in the Alpine Lakes Wilderness Area and the Gifford Pinchot National Forest, resulting in the necessity for securing permits far in advance of current weather and trail conditions.[20] These proposals have not come to pass. Others have claimed a local bias in such systems, as urban Northwest climbers monitor local conditions more easily than those outside the region.

Quota systems have been commonplace on western whitewater rivers for decades, but mountaineers resist "their" volcanoes or peaks being treated like "Wild and Scenic" rivers, many subject to a rationed permit system. In extreme cases private parties wait many years to secure a floating permit. The volcanoes, taller and bigger than the Cascades they rise amidst, remain giant white flames drawing the most people. Some national parks like Yosemite, Sequoia, and Kings Canyon use a trailhead quota system to "regulate the number of backpackers starting each trail, each day." The quotas imitate those used on "Scenic and Wild" rivers (e.g., the Salmon River branches in Idaho, and the Colorado River through Grand Canyon). Such a system of "pulse releases" could be adopted at Northwest volcanoes, which see thousands of climbers per summer season. The Mount Adams Ranger Station, for example, issues at least 350 "Cascade Volcano Passes" on a summer weekend. Certainly quotas would lessen resource degradation and get lucky participants closer to "wilderness character."

Not only have numbers increased, but also their attitudes have changed. Doubts have arisen about the contemporary climbing community's interest in wilderness character. In the current scene some climbers act indifferent or even hostile to "wilderness experience" as a resource. One famous Northwest ski mountaineer, Lowell Skoog, has questioned "whether the younger climbers really care as much about the wilderness values as the older ones and what that might mean."[21] The history of modern mountaineering, regional and otherwise, reveals practices antithetical to the Wilderness Act and the recent *Keeping It Wild* report. Some younger climbers climb for the immediate route and little more: they ascend with blinders in place, like thoroughbreds on a track. To the extent that they narrow their vision and divorce "the technical climb" from wider "experience," they enact a reduced, atrophied version of being in the mountains. They might claim, though, that in their single-mindedness they conform to the traditional sociability of climbing wherein solitude plays little to no role. It's all about being noticed, not going unnoticed.

That's a fundamental shift from the historical reasons for climbing snowpeaks. In MRNP, for example, backpackers value the experience of solitude more than do climbers, as noted by park officials. On sections of the Wonderland Trail or side trails, there's a higher chance of walking apart than on the most popular routes above. That distinction derives, in part, from the fact that most climbers are interdependent, not alone; the solo backpacker walks and camps independently. But on Rainier's two standard routes, and in spots along the Wonderland Trail, it looks like use capacity has been exceeded.

At Rainier and Hood, wilderness experience abuts industrial-scale tourism, the concept of "recreational carrying capacity" a sliding measuring stick of conflicting agendas. On hard routes or on particular, less publicized volcanoes this isn't an issue. In the later twentieth century, public wildlands are construed as a valid natural resource not only by agency personnel and professionals, but the general public. We expect wilderness as a public right at our most exceptional mountains and elsewhere. Furthermore, thanks in part to the Wilderness Act we prize "solitude or a primitive and unconfined type of recreation" though our tolerance for that varies considerably.[22] This kind of experience occurs infrequently on volcano standard routes.

At MRNP, nearly synonymous with official wilderness for a generation, users carry particular expectations about solitude and "primitive recreation" with their backpacks once they're hours beyond parking lots or trailheads. A mid-1970s a backcountry reservation system was scrapped after one year due to flaws. This system favored long-distance backpackers (e.g., complete Wonderland Trail hikers) over more casual weekend backpackers.[23] A modified, more nuanced system reintroduced about a decade ago balances reservations with traditional, first-come, first-serve permits, and requires the applicant to appear in person to claim the reservation. The system takes a shot at fair rationing, no matter the applicant's location, even if it doesn't guarantee "ideal isolation" in the backcountry.

In the past three decades, Rainier has proven a test case of curbing development and preserving or restoring resources while maintaining open access. By the early 2000s the balancing act had turned precarious, and the Nisqually–Paradise corridor still feels congested. In the early 1970s MRNP decided to halt any additional substantial infrastructure in the park, its 1972 master plan capping development at the current road system and fifteen extant locations, most categorized as Class II, general outdoor recreation areas: fee stations, developed campgrounds, and visitor centers, most dating from MRNP's first forty years.[24] Most visitors don't step far beyond the 3 percent non-wilderness corridor, the Nisqually-Longmire-Paradise area (the oldest and most popular), with one- or two-stop shopping at the end: visitor center, souvenir shop, café.

By MRNP's centennial in 1999 the corridor was often saturated in high season. Recreational carrying capacity was defined by parking lots: since the 1990s visitors have frequently discovered "Full" signs and must drive around a loop, their visit thwarted for the time being. Full lots describe the tipping point of adverse visitor experience. Parking stalls seem a reductive definition of recreational carrying capacity, an urban (or suburban) benchmark that supports "National Parking Service" criticism. This interpretation also seems a failure of vision in its dependency upon private vehicles for the definition of quality visitor experience, however short or long. We don't think past our cars.

The full lots are an initial indicator of crowded conditions sometimes replicated just above them, along paved nature trails in the alpine parks that, however congested, try to contain the flow and reduce informal switchbacks and off-trail paths. Meadows restoration projects, conceptualized in the Paradise Meadows Plan of 1989 just beyond the Paradise Visitor Center and other buildings, blunt and minimize generations of damage caused by feet if not hatchets used in early twentieth-century camping. This detailed "Meadow Plan," which included work by a range of disciplines, turned conditions around in the meadows in the face of increasing use.[25] Despite ongoing restoration, though, Paradise still shows the impact of visitors. Keeping Muir's lower Gardens of Eden pristine is difficult, as alpine plants and grasses do not always regrow fast enough as more feet step near or on them.

The Mount Rainier National Park Wilderness Act of 1988 encompassed the ever-popular Paradise–Camp Muir trail, a longtime day hike in its own right. Camp Muir symbolizes the dilemma at Mount Rainier: legal wilderness yet prevalent conditions antithetical to wilderness experience. How can this four-thousand-foot hike-climb, site of the long-ago Silver Skis Race and used by thousands every summer, be called or managed as wilderness? John Muir proved too successful as writer and publicist, and would be appalled at what he and other early proselytizers wrought. The area named after him looked battered by the twentieth century's end. In high season Camp Muir, with two of its buildings dating from MRNP's first generation, buzzes like a hive, encampments spread out across the Muir Snowfield (like the Emmons Flats overflow on Rainier's northeast side).

The scene forces painful questions about different user groups and infrastructural problems (e.g., water, sewage). The thousands of hikers create the latter. The problems at Muir—like Mount Hood's Palmer chairlift, which tops out at 8600 feet on Mount Hood's south central side, and Silcox Hut, a rustic alpine lodge (1939; 1993) located just below the 7000-foot level on the Timberline ski hill—are exacerbated by the steady stream of day hikers: both unregulated and traditionally more careless about "Leave No Trace" impact. Maybe a more fleeting presence occasions a fleeting sense of attachment and stewardship. In addition to these two "villages" on Rainier, MRNP was monitoring (1991) eleven alpine areas that showed signs of wear in the camping spots.[26] The cumulative human trammels include more than abandoned trash or discarded gear.

Shit happens. Our poop, in alpine environments especially, proves the most personal, embarrassing trace of our passage. By the late twentieth century, human waste was the glaring detritus of mass mountaineering, particularly on standard routes, both in the Northwest and in high ranges around the world. Feces, like bodies, do not decompose in extreme cold or snow conditions, and increasing traffic leaves increasing deposits for subsequent traffic to encounter. A *Seattle Times* story in 1998 proclaimed that, according to the best guess, five tons of poop had accumulated on Mount Rainier, almost all on the two standard routes. By the 1990s, climbing registration personnel and rangers issued blue bags so that "pack it out" carried literal and absolute reference. No snow latrines, no deposits below rock outcroppings. But we don't all pack it out for many sorry reasons. In July 1994, MRNP initiated a "Mountain Cost Recovery Program": a special use fee for sum-miteers that helps cover administration, high camp staffing, and human waste removal costs. Blue bags and climber education have lessened this noxious impact but haven't eliminated it. The blue bag program begun at Rainier was subsequently employed at Mounts Baker, Adams, and Hood.[27] All climbers need to use them—like best practice, Leave No Trace behavior in any wilderness area. But best presumes less than best.

A minority will never take responsibility for their own shit (literal and otherwise). But Mike Gauthier, former chief climbing ranger at MRNP, estimated that only 1 percent of Rainier climbers violate the policy. In his instructions to staff and climbers, his two main marching orders included 1) safety and 2) poop. In his judgment, the big problem concerns pit toilets, an unresolved issue at Camp Muir despite recent renovations. Gauthier escorted Washington Senator Maria Cantwell to Camp Muir in 2007, and she complained about the foul toilets. She has a lot of company. When masses collect at higher altitudes, human waste becomes a noxious problem that solar toilets—which don't always work that well—only partially solve.

In MRNP, personnel work as high-altitude monitors and janitors but never eliminate all traces; the other volcanoes lack field crews, among others. And then there are sloppy climbers. Climbing rangers have policed Rainier's two standard routes for many years. According to the *Mount Rainier National Park, 2009* report, they maintained a constant presence at Camps Muir and Schurman in the summer season doing camp patrols; rangers spent about two hours an evening talking with climbers, reminding those in need of it about Leave No Trace requirements. They also spent over eighty hours cleaning the Camp Muir public shelter since day hikers' food scraps attracted foxes. Food scraps resulted in animals becoming accustomed to the upper mountain, far above normal altitudes for foxes. Climbing rangers also spent nearly two hundred hours cleaning five solar dehydrating toilets at Camps Muir and Schurman, including emptying and rotating the toilet paper baskets.[28] Budget restraints render this problem well outside the dictates of wilderness management.

The wear and tear along standard routes signifies a problem far beyond definitions of wilderness character or wilderness experience. These conditions imitate the maintenance or restoration challenges of city parks or greenbelts, or along roadways. Because of their position and fame, Rainier and Hood act as bellwethers broadcasting the crowd problems in volcano wilderness areas more conspicuously than the other peaks. At Rainier, the high camps focus the high-density-in-wilderness contradictions as nowhere else. After an extensive snowmelt in 2009, the Muir Snowfield revealed many problem areas due to networks of informal trails and non-regulated campsites, which ranger crews did their best to rehabilitate. The Snowfield stays busy year round.[29] The Muir Snowfield, official wilderness, neither looks nor feels like one. Those long-ago large-group climbs proved an ironic foretaste of non-wilderness in wilderness.

Adverse human impacts also occurred on the Kautz Glacier route—for a generation in the mid-twentieth century, Rainier's most popular climbing route. In 2009 climbing rangers monitored more non-regulated campsites and hauled abandoned gear down from the Kautz ice cliffs.[30] Poop is not the only trace left behind. With the spike in climbers, the carelessness of a few carries a multiplier effect. In the early twenty-first century, almost five thousand climbers tackle Mount Adams, the Cascades' third highest volcano, per year, almost all of them using the standard, South Climb route and over half of them summiting: same funnel, same non-wilderness.

The expectation of solitude or primitive recreation in wilderness depends, as much as any felt experience, upon quiet, and quiet is not the norm on standard routes. At Mount Rainier quiet is threatened from another source, one that both epitomizes and parodies wilderness consumerism. Flyovers provide a luxurious amenity for those with deep enough pockets, no matter their contemptuous disregard of most others' expectations. Here is windshield wilderness from above as "visitors," comfortably ensconced, gain the omniscient point of view. A 2010 *Seattle Times* story, "Mt. Rainier air tours are up for discussion," reviewed the current debate about limiting commercial sightseeing flights in MRNP—a controversial subject in other national parks, like the Grand Canyon. Over 1.7 million visitors entered MRNP in 2009, and the vast majority wanted natural quiet—as do the mountain goats. Staff writer Lynda V. Mapes stated that five operators were licensed to run up to 113 MRNP "sightseeing air tours" a year.

Given public preference, it seems odd that any are allowed. The air tour approximates an aerial amusement park ride and it confuses domains, imposing "sky train" expectations at a volcano or other outstanding natural feature. The invasive spread, even ubiquity, of noise pollution is a stark antagonist of wilderness experience. Yet aircraft line urban and suburban skies, so according to a common mind-set, why not allow them equal access to wilderness airspace? In an era when connectivity means wired, increasing segments of the public ignore or reject "wilderness character." Or it steadily loses relevance.

Is preservation at the snowpeaks a rearguard action in the early twenty-first century? Rainier air tours represent one risk accruing from the ongoing commitment to unchecked access. The inundation of people in MRNP occasions, according to its leading historian, a "cultural anxiety," as park personnel must define preservation in the twenty-first century.[31] The mandate is to manage all but 3 percent of MRNP as wilderness, not unlike other Northwest volcanoes, but the common corridors like Camp Muir sadly parody consensus benchmarks of wilderness character. They are problematic as wilderness thresholds. As Ranger John Madden stated, "It's that pressure, pressure, pressure."[32] How will MRNP climbing rangers or personnel in the other volcano wilderness areas better persuade all users to Leave No Trace so that hikers and climbers will continue to find clean lines, fresh powder, and pure water? It remains to be seen how we will collectively reverse the manifest signs of heavily used wilderness.

In the past half century, a growing gap exists between "wilderness experience" as a resource and management mandate and mass mountaineering. Bagging the volcanoes, high-end trophies, conflates elements of wilderness consumerism and status tourism. Limiting climbing parties to twelve represents a shaky compromise between the big group climbs of old and Wilderness Act dictates. The limit of twelve confirms the sociability of mountaineering: sociability at odds with more than one cornerstone of "wilderness character" (e.g., *Keeping It Wild*). For many, twelve would comprise far too large a climbing or backpacking party, a size that precludes experiences of solitude. Mount Hood's image as supreme winter playground has solidified since the Wilderness Act. On the peak's standard route, crowd climbing and skiing abut as nowhere else in the region, each uneasily accommodating the other. In the 1980s and 1990s, Mount Hood Meadows expanded to become the biggest ski area on the mountain. Greater Portland and MHNF have figuratively overlapped for a long time, and that creates an illusion of leisure without limits, though winter weather and mountain borders, in another sense, suggest finite limits.[33] By the early twenty-first century the myopic refusal to accept greater Mount Hood, for example, as a finite system has produced clear stresses. This economy is driven by a regional sensibility wherein people expect to have it both ways: funky, sophisticated city and easy alpine (or coast) access. "Keep Portland Weird" (and "Beered") *and* keep wilderness un-weird—and close.

A recreation economy starkly divides haves from have-nots, and plenty of studies demonstrate, for example, the proportionately low number of some minority populations within wilderness areas. That demographic tendency is of a piece with historical urban park design, which ignored racial and ethnic minority populations, for the most part, in advancing an upper- and middle-class, mostly white recreational agenda. Too, the tendency reflects the habits of wilderness consumerism, wherein those with discretionary income and leisure time use wilderness areas, and poorer city dwellers typically do not. The MHNF wilderness areas, which help make the scaffolding upon which metro Portland's recreation economy rests, show signs of degradation. An "urban national forest" obviously implies urban problems including upkeep.

On Mount Hood, differing versions of the recreation economy exist cheek by jowl. These competing interests carry different assumptions and expectations, and often clash. The two main ski hills border the Mount Hood Wilderness Area and include a thin slice

(Timberline) or wedge (Mount Hood Meadows) of the volcano. The slice and the wedge show higher numbers than anywhere else in the area, particularly between November and April.

Nothing is more urban than the monumental hotel, symbol of an early, twentieth-century rustic luxury, that rises at Hood's southern base. More people visited Timberline Lodge than all of MRNP in 2009. The lodge, a famous cultural artifact, represents a supreme extant example of a Matherian destination resort. CCC crews (Company 928, from Zigzag, OR) and WPA crews, along with USFS personnel, created a monument of 1930s rustic architecture with its exposed beams, pegged oak floors, and huge hexagonal stone fireplace. These craftsmen recycled materials and built infrastructure: old, cut power poles were carved into stairwell newel posts, old railroad tracks were forged and hammered into andirons, and old CCC uniform scraps were woven into rugs.[34] The CCC crews also built the road and water system. A massive, symmetric edifice, the Lodge signifies a manmade marvel to complement the peak above—an icon poised near the edge of wilderness like the Prince of Wales Hotel in Waterton Lakes National Park (Alberta).

Timberline Lodge has been a mecca since it first opened its doors. When the Roosevelts visited the Lodge for its dedication on September 28, 1937, FDR's balcony speech was broadcast live. Hotel and ski hill were immediately national news. The lodge's reputation explains, at least partially, the popularity of climbing Mount Hood, though that tradition long precedes the lodge. Forty-three years after Roosevelt's national broadcast, film director Stanley Kubrick employed a crew to take exterior shots of the lodge for his horror film, *The Shining* (1980). As movie prop the lodge became famous again, but divorced from its volcano.

The fact that lodge, ski hill, and circumambulating trail share a name poses an irony. The Timberline Trail, which wends through the Mount Hood Wilderness Area, signifies uses antithetical to those symbolized by hotel and chairlift. Backpackers on the Timberline Trail or climbers on a route other than the south side or

Cooper Spur routes have a chance to discover "wilderness experience": an irrelevant concept at Timberline or Mount Hood Meadows, where fresh powder matters most. For most "Timberline" means lodge or ski hill, not a trail through a wilderness area that skirts above and below the upper edge of trees.

The recent history of Mount Hood's south side route reveals similar management problems found on Mount Rainier's Paradise–Camp Muir corridor, and ongoing adjustments by MHNF personnel: adjustments that again reveal the gap between wilderness experience management and high density use. As at Rainier, "wilderness threshold" remains a vexed concept since the clusters of climbers above Palmer chairlift within the wilderness area, while not as large as those below, step along a well-trodden path. Even the rule of twelve or less in a party appears arbitrary and bears unfortunate consequences. Groups who worked hardest on cleanup and trail restoration were excluded because of the size rule. In his years of study, Mount Hood's most famous historian, Jack Grauer, has noted a pattern of small groups' sloppy camping habits that features slashed branches and piles of cans and bottles in campfire rings.[35] Nowadays small groups are much less likely to trash campsites, though some still do. These inconsistencies suggest that the size rule fails as a compromise, ignores the histories of mountain or environmental clubs, and does not promote the Leave No Trace ethic. The rule poses another example of a number that sometimes neglects social realities and works against preservation.

Mount Hood evidences the lag between changing scales of use, wilderness policies and subsequent implementation problems, and new bids for agency-public cooperation. Perhaps most climbers in the line prefer the line to something untrammeled or solitary, believing the more, the better and safer. Enforcing the group size rule—that effort to redistribute the crowds into smaller clumps—led to occasionally absurd outcomes, with rangers waiting like cops in a speed trap. In 1998 a ranger positioned near Crater Rock (more than halfway up the route) to issue citations for infractions assumed friends greeting friends (in different parties) meant too large a group.[36] A common scenario in an urban district becomes an occasion for citation in mandated wilderness. Arguably, this rule alienated those very preservationist lobbies most dedicated to helping the agency manage wilderness experience as a resource. Something is way off base in this scene, with enforcement tied to an overly rigid, anachronistic policy. Given the thousands opposing the 1999 quota system, this proposed rationing had no chance, but as elsewhere in the region, the problem of recreational carrying capacity being exceeded won't go away. Further, safety in numbers is an illusion because numbers easily compound problems, as on any road.

Yet in the early twenty-first century the MHNF has reached out as never before to both occasional visitors and local environmental organizations, actively soliciting their cooperation and help. Rallying the forces potentially if not actually lessens seemingly endless litigation. Sustained outreach raises visibility and builds both the constituency and advocacy. An *Oregonian* editorial from December 11, 2000, "One Last Chance on Mount Hood," complimented the USFS for its more active outreach even as it stressed shared responsibility with wilderness area users. The editorial's title recognized, among other things, the sorry consequences of heavily used wilderness on and below the mountain. The only way to get it right entails ongoing public education, lobbying, and policing—peer pressure as a prod for compliance.

As an urban national forest MHNF seeks public buy-in and visible support in a number of ways like savvy PR recruiting campaigns. The executive summary of the MHNF Strategic Stewardship Plan (2006) stresses collaboration with various public stakeholders. The plan points out that in a five-year period alone (2000–2004), the Vancouver-Portland metro area's population increased 5 percent. That demographic pressure underlines its five challenges, among them to "Work together with public, private, and civic interests for sustainable regional recreation, which is essential to our spirits and our economy." In keeping with wilderness philosophy, the matrix of recreational and spiritual values exists above and before financial values. The question of ecological sustainability is crucial to the stability of the regional recreation economy. Sustainability suggests a new access-preservation matrix, one in which preservation is less compromised. Sustainability means, primarily, resource stability, yet the most elusive resource on popular routes above and below tree line is wilderness experience. Something has to give.

A national forest needs its advocates, especially if hundreds of thousands live next door. The recent shift in definition and strategy points up its dependency on the contiguous metro area, where most of its visitors live. MHNF relies on Portlanders and vice versa—in some respects, a symbiosis.

On Mount Hood's south side, recreational activities, especially climbing and skiing, are prioritized. Unsurprisingly, numbers run the game. Among the nine "On the climb" recommendations, in the current MHNF "Climbing Mt. Hood" regulations, the final one addresses historic and contemporary conflicting uses near Palmer chairlift: "Avoid climbing on the groomed ski runs of the Palmer Snowfield" and the "Snowboard terrain features" including parks and jumps.[37] For a generation, Mount Hood has been a leader in the sport of snowboarding, hosting competitions and developing innovative terrain parks. The camp hosted by famed snowboarder Tim Windell recruits approximately 1400 snowboarders per summer and almost 5600 (including mountain bikers) the rest of the year.[38] That's about two thirds of the number of climbers tackling Hood every year.

Mount Hood's current standard route (south climb) regulations reflect its iconic status as a mass climb, at least half of which falls within official wilderness. The regulations make no pretense of sustaining mandated wilderness experience, accepting the reality of traffic jam above Crater Rock, a formation just east of the route and not much more than a thousand feet below the summit.

FIG. 10. Mount Hood, south climb (standard) route in late summer, with Crater Rock left of center and Steel Cliffs, center background. Wikimedia Commons.

MHNF asks climbers to strictly adhere to established climber paths or, in the absence of paths, disperse parties to reduce impact. The request sends mixed signals, as approach paths have a way of endlessly braiding and widening. Recognizing the common bottleneck higher up, from the Hogsback through the Pearly Gates, MHNF advises climbers to communicate with nearby parties if a traffic jam occurs, climb during weekdays, or climb early in order to descend to the Hogsback before the day's main traffic. Common sense alternatives depend, of course, on schedule flexibility and the sacrosanct criterion of personal convenience.

On the problem of poop, MHNF reminds climbers of the blue bag policy—optional—and of a waste barrel in the Salmon River parking lot. Yet some don't summit carrying their shit, as though their waste degrades their aspiration. The MHNF website notes that climbers sometimes leave a blue bag to pack out on the descent, whereupon ravens pick them apart. The website reminds climbers to secure poop bags in gear and pack all food scraps out because of animal habits, like those foxes at Camp Muir on Rainier.[39] The association creates unwanted animal behaviors. Field mice, packrats, coyotes, bears, ravens, and "alpine" foxes follow people and their droppings. You must take it with you. But not everyone does.

How can shared stewardship, a form of peer pressure, prevent that noncompliant fraction from growing, let alone change the behavior of careless day hikers or climbers? Clearly a new matrix favoring greater preservation needs to be realized. In the Northwest, designating wilderness has proven enormously successful over the past half century: the fact that almost half (42%) of Washington's Mount Baker–Snoqualmie National Forest is designated as wilderness areas marks the achievement of the preservationist lobbies and the greening of Washington's population. Most of this mountainscape remains pretty empty. But sustaining "wilderness character" in popular spots has been harder. If a volcano wilderness area resembles a commons, more users equals more evidence of use. These arctic island corridors enact the contradiction noted by one mountain historian over three decades ago: "To make wilderness more available is, paradoxically, to make it less so."[40] More boot prints mean that wilderness experience keeps receding into the distance as though it were a vanishing condition.

Further, the volcanoes are not immune to satellite communications technologies, and while no cellphone towers exist on glaciers, many pack their networked expectations with them. Too often we carry our wired worlds in our rucksacks or heads as the virtual environment enters these arctic wildernesses. It's a mixed blessing at best. Not all volcanoes require climber registration though website and print information makes it clear that registration facilitates search and rescue operations in the event of emergencies. Satellite communications greatly aid not only backcountry skiers and climbers but also search and rescue personnel. But the ubiquity of cell and smartphones and related electronic devices demonstrates an urban sensibility imported into high altitudes.

Like transistor radios at Glacier Peak's Image Lake forty years ago, these communications technologies on mountains vitiate wilderness experience, sharply reminding listeners both what they have and do not have. For most, such devices increase noise pollution as nothing else does. Climbers mimic the general population. According to a recent (February 9, 2013) *Chicago Tribune* editorial, some don't accept any difference between national park and theme park. As the writer argues, such folks don't belong in a national park or on a volcano, as "they're the very demographic the rest of us go to Yellowstone [or name your comparable park or wilderness] to escape. . . . The call of the wild doesn't need a ring tone." A theme park exists as antithetical space to a wilderness area, and to the extent that the former represents a pop cultural norm, many people unsurprisingly and inappropriately export theme park expectations into contrary domains. Wilderness areas confuse or scare folks accustomed to crowds. In the Cascades, many unhesitatingly bring their wired world with them.

Growing numbers of news stories in recent years chronicle climbers, some un- or under-prepared, making rescue calls and placing large (including financial) demands upon search and rescue personnel and equipment. The idea and practice of rescue is not in dispute; the fact that some, perhaps after a few weeks of practice on a climbing wall, end up on routes well beyond their ability suggests an overreliance upon professional help (as well as the yawning gap between fake and real rock). In some cases distressed climbers call loved ones far away, who in turn contact search and rescue groups closest to that volcano or peak for help. At Rainier and Hood the numbers include novices who assume that help, if needed, is on the way. Rescue costs have developed into a robust debate, with most believing that costs should be borne by the victims, not absorbed by local or regional rescue groups or taxpayers.

A fundamental contradiction exists between climbing and wilderness area mandates. The tableau atop peaks of summiteers with cellphones symbolizes the current condition of mass mountaineering as fundamentally non-wilderness. This spectacle updates the Mazamas' inaugural scene. The contemporary version is a motley collection of transitory small groups, who presume and expect instant connectivity, as though craters are high-priced extensions of their regular settings. Management practices need to be modified to accommodate and control the urban realities of standard routes and approaches.

Maybe Leave No Trace needs to be amended for particular application to the volcanoes, which as wilderness areas pose a special case of fragility. Maybe the "wilderness character" criterion, "Solitude or Primitive and Unconfined Recreation," should be abandoned so the appropriate agency may develop a flexible set of guidelines particular to one volcano: guidelines that reflect the ebb and flow of climbers and treat the route in urban terms. Most climbing routes whose difficulty exceeds the capacity of novice or occasional climbers illustrate Wilderness Act philosophy; standard routes, however, violate it. The numbers on Northwest volcanoes erode the intent of the Wilderness Act. Those numbers, which increase on our most exceptional mountains, require new education and new enforcement guidelines to minimize and offset adverse impacts.

Perhaps a Northwest volcano resembles a Congressionally-designated "Wild and Scenic River," which affords a series of protections and restrictions. Should Mount Jefferson, Mount Washington, or Glacier Peak be managed like Idaho's famous Middle Fork of the Salmon River—perhaps the premiere whitewater river in the Northwest? The permit system on the region's (and the West's) whitewater rivers is strict, with only a finite number of trips released per day, like pulses into the river canyon. Commercial operators acquire more permits than private parties. This difference—guided trips versus private parties—doesn't occur on the volcanoes, nor do restrictions for private parties except in their size. But do we need to adopt a quota system of releases per day so that climbers enjoy some approximation of wilderness experience? Maybe the time has come to match the quota system governing many "Wild and

Scenic" rivers. A permit system clarifies the reality of backcountry (or high altitude) consumerism, since a coveted permit signifies a consensus high price, like a moose hunting tag in Montana.

Meanwhile, the graphs documenting the increasing popularity of volcano standard routes show rising lines, a steady flow of climbers for whom the notion of finding your own pace and place rarely happens. The extreme example of crowds on a volcano, Japan's Mount Fuji in high season (particularly *Obon* in mid-August), shows tens of thousands of climbers staying in huts and walking between cables on a clearly marked, zigzagging route. Small bobcats and bulldozers are deployed at various elevations to continually "upgrade" the track; a post office and noodle shops await the climber on top. There is a "passing lane" but one stays inside the cables: deviating off-route is not acceptable.

Northwest volcanoes will not develop comparable infrastructure, of course, but other signs and habits of mass tourism exist. Maybe we need a system wherein local environmental organization volunteers, working under the auspices of agency personnel, man summits and other key points to minimize impacts. This occurs on various Northeast peaks, for example Vermont's Mount Mansfield, which hosts approximately fifty thousand visitors per year. Or the vast majority of Colorado's fifty-three mountains that rise above fourteen thousand feet that because of their height draw hikers and climbers from afar, and are monitored by the Colorado Fourteeners Initiative.[41] There are many forms of fragility, after all, and it's past time for all interested parties to accept them in the greater interest of preserving—or restoring—pristine conditions on our snowpeaks.

EPILOGUE

I summited Washington's five volcanoes and two of Oregon's many more in the 1990s. Those climbs became crucial markers in my life and identity. I climbed the Washington Five one per summer from highest to lowest, though I had not planned that order. Three friends from southwest Montana and I climbed Rainier a few days after the summer solstice in 1993 on the Emmons-Winthrop route: the second, standard route on Rainier's northeast side, which sees less than one fifth of the annual traffic.[1] Our quartet formed part of a packed tent community at Camp Schurman (9400 feet), though parties were dispersed before dawn. On the midday descent down Rainier's small Inter Glacier the following day, we passed a veritable stream of climbers fanned across the glacier, in all colors and group sizes, chunking upwards. It was a migration, a small village on the move. A few solo climbers—alpha males—stood out because of their Day-Glo colors and quicker pace. One loud guy, a stud who stomped big steps and blew forcefully, left an impression.

The transitory scene epitomizes mass climbing, and the image of that soloist has endured: an image defining one version of current mountaineer. A year later, on the summit of Mount Baker, he sprung back to mind as I contemplated the meaning of that black Labrador retreating with his owner. Both man and dog attest to the contemporary relationship between Northwest volcanoes and people. Part of that relationship has volcanoes serving as park playgrounds and sites for competition. Such behavior presumes a dominance and familiarity in the mental maps of some residents and visitors.

The prominent place of the Northwest's two most prominent volcanoes has been confirmed anew, in recent years, by a novel and a U.S. Mint quarter.

In the climax of Jim Lynch's third novel, *Truth Like the Sun* (2012), hard-hitting journalist Helen Gulanos, a recent arrival from Ohio, has come to terms with her new city and region. She has fallen in love with Seattle: "She took lunch breaks at the Pike Place Market and heard herself asking strangers, 'Have you seen the mountain today?' It was creeping into her, this cheery notion that something exceptional was going on here" (251). Lynch captures the regional ethos and flattering rhetoric.[2] Gulanos's appropriation of one regional mantra—and it's not just Rainier—marks her conversion as an insider and aligns her with elder statesman Dan Evans and myriad other residents. To voice the question is not only to claim residency. The question signifies the relation between the volcanoes and regional chauvinism, at least for some. To ask it is to accept Rainier's—and other volcanoes'—special place in regional, municipal, or individual identity.

The influence of the Northwest's most exceptional mountains in the national imaginary was confirmed in 2010 by the U.S. Mint, when the "Mount Hood National Forest Quarter" was chosen as the fifth and final quarter in the mint's "America the Beautiful" series. This quarter is the only one in the series featuring a volcano, and the design chosen by Treasury Secretary Tim Geithner closely resembles the iconic view from Lost Lake long painted, sketched, and photographed. It is also the only National Forest Quarter (three of the earlier four celebrating National Parks unsurprisingly featuring the biggies, Yellowstone, Yosemite, and Grand Canyon). Stamped on a new quarter, this quintessential Northwest scene underlines the big role played by the volcanoes in monumental American landscapes—and identity. This foreshortened view—volcano, sloping conifer forest, rippling lake, bereft of human presence—

excludes Portland and vicinity but the eyes of Oregon, especially Portland, claim it.

The view can center on Mount McLoughlin or Mount Washington or Mount Jefferson or Glacier Peak from any number of perspectives, west slope or east, not just Rainier or Hood. "Something exceptional" has been unfolding for generations according to this preferred narrative. In myriad forms many residents and visitors, in increasing masses, have imaginatively or literally crossed the sightlines in making various claims upon the snowpeaks: objects of love, obsession, and cultural ownership. The ongoing habit of taking their measure bears a range of consequences, some of them unfortunate.

Insofar as the national imaginary remains a westering one, the Northwest has come to occupy a privileged position. In fact, the association of the volcanoes with this growing self-esteem threads through the region's history. From his Rainier communion Theodore Winthrop (1862) claimed that this "new and grander New England of the West" would nurture a "fuller growth of the American Idea": that a "strong race" would "achieve a destiny" here. Maybe Winthrop, a Boston Brahmin, would have climbed Rainier or Hood if presented the opportunity, but his vision for the Northwest described citizens at a contemplative distance, not on the glaciers. One kindred spirit, Swedish-American violinist Olof O. Bull, climbed with his violin on July 28, 1896 and on Rainier's summit played several tunes including "Nearer My God, To Thee."[3] Bull's offering defined volcano climbing as an act of pilgrimage and captured the deepest spiritual impulse behind summiting.

In John R. Williams's two early mountain books, he described the Northwest as the final act in the great drama of nation building: a drama symbolized by *The Mountain That Was "God"* (1910: Rainier) and the three *Guardians of the Columbia* (1912: St. Helens, Adams, Hood). In this script, northwesterners can't look better and the closer they come, the better they look. In the early twenty-first century, poet Gary Snyder likened the snowpeaks to the Himalayas, with images from Tibetan Buddhism of high stone shrines and prayer wheels, which broadens the appeal by association with the world's highest range—ultimate lodestar of mountaineering status. This Eastern appeal only firms up the Rainier-Himalayas linkage present since the 1960s.

Habits of veneration come, in specific locations, at an increasing cost. What's next for the volcanoes?

Human activities on the volcanoes reveal both consistent patterns and new variations. The volcanoes' lure is stronger now than a century ago. Occasionally a community (e.g., Sisters OR, 1888) takes its name and identity directly from nearly volcanoes. Snow-peaks have long served as marketing brands and extensions of a given city's parks or open spaces. In the late-nineteenth century, volcanoes (e.g., Mount Hood) sometimes figured as backdrops in larger-than-life theatrical spectacles.[4] Painters, poets, composers, and others have used volcanoes in their work without setting foot on them.

Volcanoes also figure as geothermal energy sources. An AP story by Jeff Barnard, "Project to pour water into volcano to make power," describes a huge pilot project at Oregon's Newberry Volcano for the summer of 2012. At least $43 million is being invested in the project to pump twenty-four million gallons of water via enhanced geothermal systems and hydroshearing into its side, down a well over one mile long. In theory the dispersed, heated water is captured and pumped to the surface as steam, where it will generate electricity through turbines.[5] In practical and philosophical ways, volcanoes play across the arcs of many lives, urban or rural, those vaunted sightlines bonding the viewer to their shape and mass. Residents and occasionally visitors feel as though they belong to one or several snowpeaks.

Unsurprisingly, the human footprint near or on the volcanoes has changed dramatically in the past century and a half, standard routes in summer season imitating in miniature the west slope's urban centers. Folks from all walks of life come to the volcanoes to hike, ski, or climb. They seek to script an active role in the preferred narrative of exceptionality: the flattering story they tell about themselves. The opportunity for adventure and potential for personal transformation, in the ostensibly more secular present, remain as high as that recorded in the testimony of first generation of climbers.

Yet the goals of volcano climbing have diversified, particularly as mountaineering has morphed into a mass sport. In the past generation, as baby boomers reached their maximum income-earning years, the surging ecotourism trade and widening acceptance of "risk recreation" both boosted the status of climbing. The snow-peaks still promise a chance for self-transcendence but have also become a site for management training. Or charity fundraising: since 1986 the American Lung Association has sponsored a "Climb For Clean Air Program," and in 2011, for example, their "Reach The Summit" fundraiser included Mounts Hood, Adams, and Rainier climbs requiring individual "fundraising commitments" of $3000 or more.[6] In this vein, volcano climbs have joined common cause with distance bike races or marathons.

With typical macho flourish, Ernest Hemingway once quipped that only three true sports exist—auto racing, bull fighting, and mountain climbing—because only these flirt with possible death; all other sports are only games. His boast, however inaccurate, helps explain the industrial scale of mountaineering in the Northwest and other regions in the past two generations. Of course, many other activities (e.g., skiing, hiking, backpacking, mountain biking) take place on or just below the volcanoes, but climbing holds a special status, a shining lure. In the sociology of mountaineering, self-styled pros often hold little patience with amateurs. And there are far more amateurs, many of them guided. The number of guides and guiding services has sharply increased in the past two generations, in keeping with the sport's huge growth. Most guides, male and female, tend to be in their twenties and thirties and are exceptionally fit and smart about that volcano's particular routes and risks. They're also good at assessing clients' fitness levels and personalities. Guiding provides many with full-time if seasonal work.

Given mountaineering's narrowed focus, its relentless pushing the envelope through ever-harder routes and faster speeds, a wide gap exists between climbing rationales and styles. That gap is measured by a telltale comment from British climber-writer Chris Jones, author of *Climbing in North America*. On a 1972 visit to Tacoma with longtime climber-guide-artist-writer Dee Molenaar, he considered the definition of mountaineers as those who, seeing Rainier, are so "bugged by the peak" that "they had to go for it."[7] Jones was both right and wrong. He does not understand the myriad dependencies implicit in the more common, physically distant relation of many residents to volcanoes. And by the time he published his definition, his claim about the (small) number of "modern-day counterparts" was anachronistic, as the tide was ineluctably changing.

Particularly since the 1960s, interacting with the snowpeaks from a distance has proven insufficient to increasing numbers. Instead of background, the snowpeaks loom in the foreground for the "bugged" masses who, like Lewis Carroll's Alice, step through the looking glass. They follow in the footsteps of the proselytizing early climbers (not exactly "unknown") and club enthusiasts who have always proclaimed the John Muir gospel: "Go for it!" And when they go for it, they bring increasing amounts of fancy gear they like to be noticed. Increasing numbers expect instant communications (and potentially quick rescue) at all altitudes, as though mountain camps or "bivi" sites imitate Wi-Fi Internet cafes. In sheer numbers and shifting expectations, the fundamental differences between volcanoes and the rest of their lives lessen—or seem to lessen. That dangerous illusion sometimes leads to injury or death.

By the twentieth century's final two decades, the culture of climbing had changed as dramatically as the scale of the mountain gear industry. By the 1970s the majority of the American population increasingly embraced the tenets of mainstream environmentalism even as increasing hordes, "bugged by the [snow]peaks," decided to "go for it." Agency personnel were and are charged with protecting wildlife and habitat resources, above all the human-driven resource of wilderness experience.

By the 1980s and 1990s, these divergent streams and contrary agendas collided with increasing frequency. Crowds of skiers (e.g., at Mounts Baker and Hood, and at Bachelor Butte above Bend) adjacent to wilderness boundaries are one thing; crowds of hikers or climbers above them are another. People want their cars and Internet. They uphold equal opportunity and access yet also want—well, some want—"wilderness experience." In particular on-the-ground conditions in particular locations, resource degradation exists and "wilderness experience" appears a pipedream, an invalid and unattainable category. For the vast majority on most volcanoes, it just isn't happening.

The restoration and ongoing validation of wilderness experience on the volcanoes' most popular routes seems to be the primary management challenge of the near future. How can the legal mandates of approximately the past half century best be revised and modified to accommodate ground realities while preserving natural resources? The concept of "recreational carrying capacity" seems endlessly researched and crudely applied—if applied at all. Answers to the question of how many is too many prove annoyingly variable and elusive.

It's not that the volcanoes are being loved to death. Most who love them do so from a distance. But more and more insist on stepping up. Almost all of a given volcano's mass remains untrammeled, but over three quarters of those climbing it follow the same approaches and routes and in those thin corridors, it's no wilderness experience. Because of their level of ability or experience, and for other reasons, hikers and climbers stay on the beaten path, as they should.

Wilderness area legal mandates and management practices can be modified such that the aesthetic dimensions of "recreational carrying capacity" are not badly compromised or lost. If everyone accepted wilderness education, packed everything (including feces) out, and worked harder to minimize visual impacts, those climbing on these exceptional mountains would likely have experiences closer to those envisioned by the Bob Marshalls and Howard Zahnisers. Given human nature, this expectation is too high. To realign standard routes with some measure of wilderness experience, permit systems should be adopted as they're used in the backcountry of certain California national parks and on Wild and Scenic Rivers. That is, on any given day—weekend day—during high season, the number and flow of climbing parties should be restricted and regulated. Such a system creates greater risk for applicants who cannot predict weather or climbing conditions months in advance. Similarly variable conditions govern rivers (e.g., the Smith River in Montana) when applicants put in for a launch date many months earlier.

A system of modified access would lessen and distribute crowds. Certainly climbers should not face the lines visible on Mount Adams and South Sister. Human activities at the volcanoes will only increase in number and mass during the twenty-first century.

Five years after Mount Rainier, I climbed Mount St. Helens in early August. The campground (3600 feet) was crowded but I started early and reached the yawning crater rim by 8:30. Solo, I savored the quiet and sun. On my descent, I greeted the occasional other parties. Maybe I was just lucky, but I felt as though I had wilderness experience on St. Helens' crowded Monitor Ridge, the standard route. My quiet climb contrasted with the village-on-the-move on Rainier's Inter Glacier. Plenty of others climbed St. Helens that day but I felt part of a wilderness, not a crowd. That is what I wish for others.

Many go to the snowpeaks and other peaks to sense, in composer Alan Hovhaness's words about Mount St. Helens, "the volcanic energy, renewing the vitality of our peaceful planet, the living earth, the life-giving force building the majestic Cascade Mountains rising, piercing the clouds of heaven."[8] For all our human longings and for all our "traces," though, the snowpeaks loom far above and beyond human traffic past and present. Human desires are never reciprocated and visitation, even at today's industrial scale, remains only fleeting. As beacons they forever lure and enhance visitors but while footprints fade away, leavings—trash—remains.

NOTES

INTRODUCTION

1. Keeble, *Yellowfish*, 114.
2. Rothman, *Devil's Bargains*, 15.
3. Snyder, *Danger on Peaks*, 7.

1. THE LEGACY OF EXCEPTIONALISM

1. Barcott titles his study of Rainier and the Northwest imagination *The Measure of a Mountain*.
2. Wolfe, *Western Journal*, 68.
3. Bell, *On Mount Hood*, x.
4. Proctor and Berry coin this term as a descriptor of Pacific Northwest identity in "Ecotopian Exceptionalism."
5. The title of Nicholas O'Connell's study of Northwest literature, *On Sacred Ground*, reflects his thesis and this sensibility.
6. Abbott, *Greater Portland*, 17.
7. McNulty and O'Hara, *Washington's Mount Rainier National Park*, 12.
8. The phrases come from Rothman's *Devil's Bargains*, 15.
9. Carpenter, *Where The Waters Begin*, 21, 24–25.
10. Nicolson's thesis in her pioneering study, *Mountain Gloom and Mountain Glory*.
11. O'Connell, *On Sacred Ground*, 37.
12. Scholars Proctor and Berry remind us, "Exceptionalism is always predicated on a utopian yearning." "Ecotopian Exceptionalism," 150.
13. Molenaar, *Challenge of Rainier*, 30–32.
14. In his "Ascent of Mount Tahoma," (*Overland Quarterly*, September 1886), Bayley extols the Cascades as "the wildest and most inaccessible region within the boundaries of the United States." Schullery, *Island in the Sky*, 100, 80.

15. Fobes, "To The Summit of Tacoma," West Shore, 1885; Schullery, *Island in the Sky*, 265–69.
16. Muir, *Our National Parks*, 471.
17. Reprinted in Schullery, *Island in the Sky*, 123.
18. Longtime Rainier climber, guide, and artist Dee Molenaar titled his history *The Challenge of Rainier*.
19. Muir, "Ascent of Mount Rainier," and Albright and Schenck, *Creating the National Park Service*, 234.
20. Schullery, *Island in the Sky*, 140.
21. Van Trump, "Mount Tahoma."
22. Catton, *National Park, City Playground*, 10.
23. Proctor and Berry, "Ecotopian Exceptionalism,"161.
24. Robbins, *Great Northwest*, 177–78.
25. Snyder, *Danger on Peaks*, 7.
26. The term comes from Rothman Jr.'s *Devil's Bargains*, and represents Rothman's contemporary mode of tourism.

2. STANDARD ROUTES, STANDARD HIGHWAYS

1. *Rainier: The Mountain*.
2. Robbins and Barber, *Nature's Northwest*, 231–32. Italics mine.
3. Oregon's oldest mountaineering conservation club, a spinoff of California's Sierra Club (1892), itself only two years old.
4. According to MRNP Annual Visitor Statistics, in 1978 over 2.5 million visited that year, and though the number has fallen below two million a year since the mid-1990s, over 1.5 million visit every year. In 1992, MRNP recorded over eight hundred thousand vehicles; since then, consistently over half a million vehicles have entered the park each year. Lah, "Wilderness Encounters in MRNP."
5. Washington's venerable mountaineering conservation club, based in Seattle and founded in 1906.
6. August Kautz, quoted in Schullery, *Island in the Sky*, 47–48.
7. Schullery, *Island in the Sky*, 128.
8. George Dickson, "Narrative" published in the *Tacomian*, January 7, 1893; Schullery, *Island in the Sky*, 147.
9. Catton, *National Park, City Playground*, 98–99.
10. Kirk, *Sunrise to Paradise*, 69–71.
11. Kirk, *Sunrise to Paradise*, 20.
12. This paradox forms the basis of David Louter's scholarly study, *Windshield Wilderness*. He defines his title as the everyday tourist

condition wherein "it is possible for machines and nature to coexist without the same industrial transformation that was affecting other parts of the nation," Louter, *Windshield Wilderness*, 4.

13. Louter, *Windshield Wilderness*, 15, 17.
14. Grauer, *Mount Hood*, 32
15. Guggenheim, *Spirit Lake People*, 9–10, 29–44.
16. Albright and Schenck, *Creating The National Park Service*, 89.
17. Albright and Schenck, *Creating the National Park Service*, 90. Italics original.
18. Albright and Schenck, *Creating the National Park Service*, 292.
19. Manning, *Wilderness Alps*, 57.
20. Grauer, *Mount Hood*, 304; Manning, *Wilderness Alps*, 77.
21. Albright and Schenck, *Creating the National Park Service*, 88.
22. Albright and Schenck, *Creating the National Park Service*, 87–88.
23. Catton, *National Park, City Playground*, 46.
24. Wolfe, *A Western Journal*, 4–5.
25. U.S. Department of Agriculture, "Mount Hood National Forest Strategic Stewardship Plan."
26. Kirk, *Sunrise to Paradise*, 70.
27. Kirk, *Sunrise to Paradise*, 70.
28. Catton, *National Park, City Playground*, 63–64.
29. Catton, *National Park, City Playground*, 81–82, 127–38.
30. Kirk, *Sunrise to Paradise*, 119–20.
31. Catton, *National Park, City Playground*, 104, 106.
32. Mount Hood historian Jack Grauer writes, "By the 1980s Mount Hood Meadows was planning a city in an area the USFS had previously considered a scenic, wild area. . . . The Sierra Club and Mazamas stepped up their attention to the problem, and other conservation groups arose to deal with the destruction of Mount Hood environs." Grauer, *Mount Hood*, 314.
33. Grauer, *Mount Hood*, 45, 48, 105–9, 122–23, 241.
34. U.S. Department of Agriculture, "Mount Hood National Forest Strategic Stewardship Plan."
35. Manning, *REI*, 96, 168.
36. Price, *Mountains & Men*, 430.
37. Some of these figures come from Dee Molenaar's *The Challenge of Rainier*, 228–30, Addendum.
38. Gauthier, "Mount Rainier National Park, 2006"; Lofgren et al, "Mount Rainier National Park, 2009."

39. It describes "an increased number of displaced blue bags and piles of human waste," "Climbing rangers also carried down more trash from high camps than ever before, almost 700 lbs." Gauthier, "Mount Rainier National Park, 2006," 122.
40. Gauthier, "Mount Rainier National Park, 2006."
41. Nicholas et al., *Imagining The Big Open*, 107.
42. McNulty and O'Hara, Foreword to *Washington's Mount Rainier National Park*.

3. CITIES AND THEIR VOLCANOES

1. Quoted in Schwantes, *Pacific Northwest*, 5.
2. Abbott, *Greater Portland*, 17.
3. Bell, *On Mount Hood*, 5.
4. Schwantes, *Pacific Northwest*, 5.
5. Two historians clarify the case of the economically privileged, often highly paid newer arrivals working for Microsoft, Google, and related corporations. Carlos Schwantes argues, "The juxtaposition of metropolitan trendsetter and hinterland is, in fact, the defining quality of life in the modern Northwest. The accessibility of the hinterland from metropolitan centers remains the *key* feature of what residents regard as a desirable life style." Schwantes, *Pacific Northwest*, 508.
   Matthew Klingle specifies this sensibility in *Emerald City*: "Hiking alpine trails in the morning, kayaking in the shadow of gleaming new skyscrapers, grilling fresh salmon for dinner, and attending opera at night—Seattle was an ideal blend of the urbane and the wild" (251).
6. The phrase comes from Tim Egan's description to legendary climber Fred Beckey. Egan, *Good Rain*, 84.
7. Lynch, *Truth Like The Sun*, 13–14.
8. *Rainier: The Mountain.*
9. Lynch, *Truth Like The Sun*, 29.
10. Catton's study (2006, print), a lengthy revision of his earlier *An Administrative Guide to Mount Rainier National Park*.
11. Catton, *National Park, City Playground*, 4.
12. Catton, *National Park, City Playground*, 6.
13. Louter, *Windshield Wilderness*, 28.
14. Klingle, *Emerald City*, 155.
15. The pattern has been thoroughly documented in many scholarly studies including David Mark Spence's *Dispossessing The Wilderness*.

16. Catton, *National Park, City Playground*, 38–42.
17. Catton, *National Park, City Playground*, 69–72; Klingle, *Emerald City*, 65–79.
18. Environmental historian Matthew Klingle calls "Seattle's charmed lands," which by extension include M R N P, "geographies of arrested development": "What the more prosperous votaries of the backpack and fly rod would not recognize was how their passion for all things wild and natural could be just as self-interested and greedy as that of the most rapacious capitalist or even the most well-meaning reformer. Their ethic of place did not include any awareness of others unlike them." Klingle, *Emerald City*, 179.
19. Louter, *Windshield Wilderness*, 27.
20. Whatcom Co., Washington, "Ski to Sea Race."
21. A similar, 195-mile "Hood to Coast Relay," an annual event for over three decades, solidifies the link between volcano and ocean, with Portland in the middle. Abbott, *Greater Portland*, 55.
22. Beckey, *Range of Glaciers*, 414.
23. Manning, *Wilderness Alps*, 14.
24. Manning, *Wilderness Alps*, 72.
25. Beckey, *Range of Glaciers*, 415.
26. Skoog, *Alpenglow Ski Mountaineering History Project*.
27. Peattie, *The Cascades*, 11–12.
28. Goble and Hirt, *"Setting the Pacific Northwest Stage,"* 8.
29. *Rainier: The Mountain*.
30. Grauer, *Mount Hood*, Chapter 16 devoted to "Illumination and Heliography at Mount Hood."
31. *Rainier: The Mountain*.

4. GREEN CONSUMERISM AND THE VOLCANOES

1. Industrial-scale tourism has been defined as "the packaging and marketing of experience as commodity within the boundaries of the accepted level of convenience to the public." Rothman, *Devil's Bargains*, 13.
2. Nicholas et al., *Imagining The Big Open*, 98.
3. Nicholas et al., *Imagining The Big Open*, 94.
4. Frykman, *Seattle's Historian and Promoter*, 195.
5. Scott, *We Climb High*, 1.
6. Grauer, *Mount Hood*, 192.
7. Scott, *We Climb High*, 8, 18.

8. Scott, *We Climb High*, 64–65.
9. Kjeldsen, *The Mountaineers*, 37.
10. Weiselberg, "The Early Mazamas," 20–21.
11. Frykman, *Seattle's Historian and Promoter*, 133, 195, 198.
12. Frykman, *Seattle's Historian and Promoter*, 199.
13. Kjeldsen, *The Mountaineers*, 44–45.
14. Bates, *Cascade Voices*, 4.
15. Bates, *Cascade Voices*, 27.
16. Bates, *Cascade Voices*, 25; Manning, REI, 11.
17. Kjeldsen, *The Mountaineers*, 50, 54, 108.
18. Kjeldsen, *The Mountaineers*, 102–5.
19. Kjeldsen, *The Mountaineers*, 62, 65.
20. Bates, *Cascade Voices*, 80.
21. Bates, *Cascade Voices*, 96.
22. Kjeldsen, *The Mountaineers*, 118.
23. As Jim Kjeldsen notes in *The Mountaineers*, "By 1928, the Eddie Bauer store in downtown Seattle was stocking a full line of skis imported from Europe. And by 1933, Eddie Bauer Inc. had embarked on some light manufacturing of skis, as had other Northwest firms." Kjeldsen, *The Mountaineers,* 81.
24. By Chris Jones, in his ambitious *Climbing in North America.*
25. Kjeldsen, *The Mountaineers*, 139.
26. Manning, REI, 109.
27. As Manning noted, "The provincial Co-op had evolved into the national-international REI." REI, 81.
28. Manning, REI, 84.
29. Bates, *Cascade Voices*, 28, 69.
30. Bates, *Cascade Voices*, 103.
31. Bates, *Cascade Voices*, 105.
32. Manning, REI, 65.
33. Bates, *Cascade Voices*, 99–100.
34. Bates, *Cascade Voices*, 103.
35. Bates, *Cascade Voices*, 138–39.
36. Eskenazi, "Call to Mountaineering."
37. "Climbing the Pinnacle at Seattle REI," March 8, 2010, http://rei.com/stores/seattle/climb-class.html.
38. Brooks, *Bobos in Paradise*, 211, 213.
39. Brooks, *Bobos in Paradise*, 213–15.
40. Nicholas et al., *Imagining The Big Open*, 73–91.

41. Miller, *Cities and Nature in the American West*, 249.

42. "REI Story: History and Today." May 23, 2008, http://www.rei.com /jobs/story.jsp.

43. Egan, "Secretary to Match the Setting."

44. Venema, "Mount Rainier, 100 Years Later."

5. WILDERNESS AND VOLCANOES

1. Muhn, "Forest Reserve Act."

2. The phrase is David Louter's, in *Windshield Wilderness*, 27.

3. As USFS historian Gerald Williams comments, "This unique Forest Service monument is much more like a national park than a national forest." It is one of six national monuments managed by the USFS. Williams, "National Monuments and the Forest Service."

4. Miller, *Cities and Nature in the American West*, 150–51.

5. Miller, *Cities and Nature in the American West*, 149–50.

6. Vale, *The American Wilderness*, 139.

7. Harvey, *Wilderness Forever*, 119; Louter, *Windshield Wilderness*, 133; Marsh, *Drawing Lines in the Forest*, 63.

8. Louter, *Windshield Wilderness*, 133; Marsh, *Drawing Lines in the Forest*, 63.

9. Curtis, "A Mount Rainier Centennial."

10. Lipin, *Workers in the Wild*, 113.

11. *New York Times*, "A Chicken for Every Pot," https://research.archives .gov/id/187095.

12. Kjeldsen, *The Mountaineers*, 129.

13. Manning, *Wilderness Alps*, 72.

14. Catton, *National Park, City Playground*, 86–89.

15. Sutter, *Driven Wild*, 15–16, 242–43.

16. Sutter, *Driven Wild*, 209, 237.

17. Miller, *Cities and Nature in the American West*, 155.

18. Alfred Runte, *Trains of Discovery*, 78. Runte points out that in their guidebooks (1885ff.), the Northern Pacific called St. Helens "'the great SugarLoaf' of the Pacific Northwest." (5)

19. Schlepfer, *Nature's Altars*, 211.

20. Marsh, *Drawing Lines in the Forest*, 15, 64–65.

21. Lipin, *Workers and the Wild*, 160.

22. Schlepfer, *Nature's Altars*, 211.

23. Dietrich, *The Final Forest*, 174.

24. Schlepfer, *Nature's Altars*, 222.

25. Schlepfer, *Nature's Altars*, 203.

26. Schlepfer, *Nature's Altars*, 212.

27. Manning, *Wilderness Alps*, 162.

28. In "National Monuments and The Forest Service," Gerald Williams reviews a 1970s proposal for a Cascades Volcanic National Park that precisely echoed David Simon's earlier proposal—and with similar results. Williams, "National Monuments and the Forest Service."

29. Schlepfer, *Nature's Altars*, 213.

30. Douglas, *My Wilderness*, 121.

31. Douglas, *My Wilderness*, 131.

32. Douglas, *My Wilderness*, 76.

33. Douglas, *My Wilderness*, 80.

34. Harvey, *Wilderness Forever*, 110, 119.

35. Schlepfer, *Nature's Altars*, 226.

36. Miller, *Cities and Nature in the American West*, 149.

37. Manning, *Wilderness Alps*, 208.

38. Manning, *Wilderness Alps*, 208, 212, 424.

39. Vale, *The American Wilderness*, 125.

40. Schlepfer, *Nature's Altars*, 225.

41. McPhee, *Encounters*, 7.

42. McPhee, *Encounters*, 10, 20–21.

43. McPhee, *Encounters*, 52–53.

44. McPhee, *Encounters*, 55.

45. McPhee, *Encounters*, 74–75.

46. McPhee, *Encounters*, 49.

47. Catton, *National Parks, City Playgrounds*, 148.

48. Catton, *National Parks, City Playgrounds*, 149.

49. Grauer, *Mount Hood*, 314–15.

50. Guggenheim, *Spirit Lake People*, 117, 123.

51. Manning, *Wilderness Alps*, 223.

52. Marsh, *Drawing Lines in the Forest*, 140.

53. Louter, *Windshield Wilderness*, 133, 135.

54. Marsh, *Drawing Lines in the Forest*, 53.

55. Dietrich, *The Final Forest*, 159.

56. Dietrich, *The Final Forest*, 165.

57. Dietrich, *The Final Forest*, 288.

58. Bell, *On Mount Hood*, 54.

59. Harvey, *Wilderness Forever*, 203.

6. VOLCANOES AND CROWDS

1. Price, *Mountains & Man*, 430.
2. "Current Wilderness Management Issues."
3. For interesting sociological data derived from MRNP's Paradise Meadows one generation ago, see Catton, *National Park, City Playground*, 171.
4. Sax, *Mountains Without Handrails*, 76.
5. McPhee, *Encounters*, 58–59.
6. McPhee, *Encounters*, 59.
7. Bell, *On Mount Hood*, 125.
8. Vale, *The American Wilderness*, 113.
9. Grauer, *Mount Hood*, 314.
10. "Conservation" and "Mazamas Position on Cooper Spur Expansion."
11. Bell, *On Mount Hood*, 189.
12. Sax, *Mountains Without Handrails*, 14–15, 104.
13. Discover Your Northwest, "About Us." March 1, 2011, http://discover nw.org/aboutus/htm#vision
14. Runte, *Trains of Discovery*, 7, 84.
15. Villwock-Witte, "Intelligent Transportation System."
16. Frome, *The Battle for Wilderness*, 98–99.
17. Kjeldsen, *The Mountaineers*, 178.
18. "Keeping It Wild," 6–7.
19. "Keeping It Wild," ii.
20. Kjeldsen, *The Mountaineers*, 179.
21. Bates, *Cascade Voices*, 182.
22. Vale, *The American Wilderness*, 4, 175.
23. Catton, *National Park, City Playground*, 152.
24. Catton, *National Park, City Playground*, 155.
25. Catton, *National Park, City Playground*, 172.
26. Catton, *National Park, City Playground*, 162–64.
27. Gauthier, telephone conversation with author, January 25, 2010.
28. Lofgren, Gottlieb, and Payne, *Mount Rainier National Park, 2009*.
29. Lofgren, Gottlieb, and Payne, *Mount Rainier National Park, 2009*.
30. Lofgren, Gottlieb, and Payne, *Mount Rainier National Park, 2009*.
31. Catton, *National Park, City Playground*, 176.
32. *Rainier: The Mountain.*

33. Abbott, *Greater Portland*, 13.
34. Hill, *In The Shadow of the Mountain*, 132–33.
35. Grauer, *Mount Hood*, 312.
36. Grauer, *Mount Hood*, 312.
37. "Climbing Mount Hood."
38. Bell, *On Mount Hood*, 99–102.
39. "Climbing Mount Hood."
40. Price, *Mountains & Men*, xxi.
41. Colorado Fourteeners Initiative, www.14ers.org. As their website reveals, the population of Colorado more than doubled between 1990 and 2007. The CFI was founded by many environmental organizations (1994) to protect the peaks in their highest elevation zones, due to mass use.

EPILOGUE

1. Lofgren, Gottlieb, and Payne, "Mount Rainier National Park, 2009."
2. The Seattle-Rainier symbiosis was memorably expressed two generations ago in another Washington novel, Tom Robbins's *Another Roadside Attraction* (1971). Robbins's character, Marx Marvelous, fancies a fatal attraction ending in apocalyptic destruction, but not from Rainier erupting: "*I imagined Mt. Rainier to be an iceberg toward which the crowded city was sailing full speed ahead. At any moment there would be a heavens-splitting crunch. Seattle would go down like the Titanic.*" (italics original, 133).
3. Blecha, "Bull plays his fiddle."
4. Grauer, *Mount Hood*, 279–86.
5. Barnard, "Project to pour water."
6. American Lung Association, "2011 Reach The Summit."
7. Jones, *Climbing in North America*, 12.
8. Hovhaness, "Original Unedited Draft of Program Notes."

BIBLIOGRAPHY

Abbott, Carl. *Greater Portland: Urban Life and Landscape in the Pacific Northwest.* Philadelphia: University of Pennsylvania Press, 2001.

Albright, Horace M., and Marian Albright Schenck. *Creating the National Park Service: The Missing Years.* Norman: University of Oklahoma Press, 1999.

Allen, Chester. "Push to Remake Mount St. Helens as National Park." *Great Falls Tribune,* December 11, 2007.

American Lung Association in Oregon. "2011 Reach The Summit." Pamphlet.

Anderson, Ross. "Anything But Lonely At The Top." *Seattle Times,* August 7, 1994.

Archbold, Mike. "Longmire's Lasting Style." *Eastside Reporter,* June 13, 1999.

———. "Many Climbers Have Lost Their Lives." *Eastside Reporter,* July 11, 1999.

———. "Planning Paradise." *Eastside Reporter,* June 13, 1999.

Aspland, Patricia L., and Katharine A. Pawelko. "Carrying Capacity: Evolution of Management Concepts for the National Parks." *Trends* 20, no. 3 (1983): 22–26.

Barcott, Bruce. *The Measure of a Mountain: Beauty and Terror on Mount Rainier.* Seattle: Sasquatch Books, 1997.

Barnard, Jeff. "Project to Pour Water into Volcano to Make Power." *Great Falls Tribune,* January 15, 2012.

Bates, Malcolm. *Cascade Voices: Conversations with Washington Mountaineers.* Seattle: Cloudcap Books, dist. by Snohomish: Alpenbooks, 1993.

Bayers, Peter. *Imperial Ascent: Mountaineering, Masculinity, and Empire.* Boulder: University Press of Colorado, 2003.

Beckey, Fred. *Range of Glaciers: The Exploration and Survey of the Northern Cascade Range*. Portland: Oregon Historical Society Press, 2003.

Bell, Jon. *On Mount Hood: A Biography of Oregon's Perilous Peak*. Seattle: Sasquatch Books, 2011.

Blecha, Peter. "Tacoma's Olof Bull Plays his Fiddle on the Summit of Mount Rainier on July 28, 1896," December 26, 2009, http://www .historylink.org.

Brooks, David. *Bobos in Paradise*. New York: Simon & Schuster, 2000.

Calderazzo, John. *Rising Fire: Volcanoes and Our Inner Lives*. Guilford: The Lyons Press, 2004.

Carpenter, Cecelia Svinth. *Where The Waters Begin: The Traditional Nisqually Indian History of Mount Rainier*. Seattle: Northwest Interpretive Association, 1994.

Catton, Theodore. *Mount Rainier National Park: Wonderland: An Administrative History* (NPS, 1996), February 20, 2008, http://www .nps.gov/parkhistory/online_books/mora/adhi/.

————. *National Park, City Playground: Mount Rainier in the Twentieth Century*. Seattle: University of Washington Press, 2006.

Cornwall, Warren. "After the Deluge," in "The Rough Road Ahead," *Seattle Times Pacific Northwest*, June 24, 2007.

Curtis, Asahel. "A Mount Rainier Centennial." *Pacific Northwest Quarterly* 21, no. 1 (1930): 18–22.

Dietrich, William. *The Final Forest: The Battle for the Last Great Trees of the Pacific Northwest*. New York: Simon & Schuster, 1992.

Doughton, Sandi. "Debris Chokes Rivers as Glaciers in Washington's Mount Rainier Shrink." *Seattle Times,* January 13, 2010.

————. "The Next Big Eruption: Will We Have Warning?" *Seattle Times*, May 17, 2010.

————. "Paradise Rediscovered." *Seattle Times*, October 8, 2008.

————. "Rainier's Rocks Filling Rivers." *Seattle Times*, January 4, 2010.

Douglas, William O. *My Wilderness: The Pacific West*. New York: Pyramid Books, 1960.

Duncan, Dayton, and Ken Burns. *The National Parks: America's Best Idea*. New York: Alfred A. Knopf, 2009.

Eastside Reporter. "Trying to Reach Mount Rainier's Peak." July 11, 1999.

Egan, Timothy. *The Good Rain: Across Time and Terrain in the Pacific Northwest*. New York: Vintage, 1991.

———. "A Natural Identity: Cradled in Hill and High Water, Our Urban Life Thrives." *Seattle Times*, November 21, 2004.

———. "A Secretary to Match the Setting." *New York Times*, February 10, 2013.

Eskenazi, Stuart. "Call To Mountaineering: New Headquarters Gives Club Chance to Invite Other to Join the Adventure." *Seattle Times*, October 14, 2008.

"Friends of Mount Hood," March 1, 2011, http://friendsofmounthood .org/fmh.thm.

Frome, Michael. *Battle for the Wilderness*. 1974. Reprint, Salt Lake City: University of Utah Press, 1997.

Frykman, George A. *Seattle's Historian and Promoter: The Life of Edmond Stephen Meany*. Pullman: Washington State University Press, 1998.

Gallagher, Leo. "That Old Hotel in Paradise." *National Parks Magazine* 38 no. 198 (January 1964): 4–7.

Gauthier, Mike. *Mount Rainier: A Climbing Guide*. Seattle: The Mountaineers Books, 2005, 4th ed. 2009.

———. "Mount Rainier National Park, 2006." *Northwest Mountaineering Journal* 4, http://www.mountaineers.org/nwmj/07/071_mrnp _Report.html.

———. Phone conversation with author, January 25, 2010.

Gifford Pinchot National Forest: Recreation, "Climbing Mt. Adams," October 15, 2007, http://www.fs.fed.us/gpnf/recreation/mount -adams/index.shtml.

Goble, Dale D., and Paul W. Hirt, eds., "Setting the Pacific Northwest Stage: The Influence of the Natural Environment." In *Northwest Lands, Northwest Peoples*. Seattle: University of Washington Press, 1999.

Grauer, Jack. *Mount Hood: A Complete History*. 3rd ed. Vancouver: Jack Grauer, 2005.

Guggenheim, Alan. *Spirit Lake People: Memories of Mount St. Helens*, ed. James Mortland. Gresham: Salem Press, 1986.

Haberman, Margaret. "Rebirth of Mount St. Helens." *American Profile Weekly* (May 6, 2010): 8–11, http://www.americanprofile.com/articles /category/travel-destinations/page9.

Harmon, Kitty, ed., *The Pacific Northwest Landscape: A Painted History*. Seattle: Sasquatch Books, 2001.

Harris, Stephen. *Fire and Ice: The Cascade Volcanoes*. Seattle: The Mountaineers, Pacific Search Books, 1976.

Harvey, Mark. *Wilderness Forever: Howard Zahniser and the Path to the Wilderness Act*. Seattle: University of Washington Press, 2005.

Hill, Edwin G. *In the Shadow of the Mountain*. Pullman: Washington State University Press, 1990.

Hovhaness, Alan. "Original Unedited Draft of Program Notes," *Alan Hovhaness: Mysterious Mountain*, with the Royal Liverpool Philharmonic Orchestra, conducted by Gerard Schwarz, recorded 2003, Telarc, SACD-60604, Super Audio CD.

Johnson, Darryll R. "A Study of Visitor Attitudes Toward Initiation of a Visitor Transportation System at MRNP." NPS, Cooperative Park Studies Unit, University of Washington College of Forest Resources, 1990.

Johnson, Darryll R., Karen P. Foster, and Katherine I. Kerr. *Mount Rainier National Park 1990 Visitor Survey*. NPS, Cooperative Park Studies Unit, University of Washington College of Forest Resources.

Jones, Chris. *Climbing in North America*. Berkeley: University of California Press for the American Alpine Club, 1976.

Keeble, John. *Yellowfish*. 1980. Reprint, Seattle: University of Washington Press, 2008.

Kirk, Ruth. *Sunrise to Paradise: The Story of Mount Rainier National Park*. Seattle: University of Washington Press, 1999.

Kjeldsen, Jim. *The Mountaineers: A History*. Seattle: The Mountaineers Books, 1998.

Klingle, Matthew. *Emerald City: An Environmental History of Seattle*. Seattle: University of Washington Press, 2007.

Lah, Kristopher J, "Developing Social Standards for Wilderness Encounters in MRNP: Manager-Defined Versus Visitor-Defined Standards," 2000, http://www.academia.edu/6131970.

Levertov, Denise. "Settling," "Against Intrusion," "Open Secret," In *Evening Train*. New York: New Directions, 1992.

Lindholdt, Paul. "From Sublimnity to Ecopornography: Assessing the Bureau of Reclamation Art Collection." *Journal of Ecocriticism* 1 (January 2009): 1–25.

———. "West of Winthrop." *American Transcendental Quarterly* 18 no. 3 (September 2004): 155–77

Lipin, Lawrence. *Workers and the Wild: Conservation, Consumerism, and Labor in Oregon, 1910–1930*. Urbana: University of Illinois Press, 2007.

Lofgren, Stephen, David Gottlieb, and Tom Payne, "Mount Rainier National Park, 2009." *Northwest Mountaineering Journal 7*, September
11, 2013, http://www.mountaineers.org/nwmj/10/101_mrnp_Report
.html.

———. Correspondence with author. (5 climbing graphs, Mount
Rainier, 4 of them 2002–8 data), January 25, 2010.

Louter, David. *Windshield Wilderness*. Seattle: University of Washington Press, 2006.

Lynch, Jim. *Truth Like the Sun*. New York: Knopf, 2012.

Manning, Harvey. *Mountaineering: The Freedom of the Hills*. Seattle:
The Mountaineers Books, 1960, 8th ed. 2010.

———. *REI: Fifty Years of Climbing Together*. Seattle: REI, Inc., 1988.

———. *Washington Wilderness: The Unfinished Work*. Seattle: The
Mountaineers Books, 1984.

———. *Wilderness Alps: Conservation and Conflict in Washington's
North Cascades*, Ken Wilcox ed. Bellingham: Northwest Wild
Books, 2007.

Mapes, Lynda V. "Mt. Rainier Air Tours are Up for Discussion." *Seattle
Times*, May 10, 2010.

Marsh, Kevin R. *Drawing Lines in the Forest: Creating Wilderness Areas in
the Pacific Northwest*. Seattle: University of Washington Press, 2007.

Mazamas. "Conservation," "About Us," May 24, 2008, http://www
.mazamas.org/."Mazamas Position on Cooper Spur Expansion,"
March 1, 2011, http://mazamas.org/about-us/cooper-spur-develop
ment/.

McNulty, Tim, and Pat O'Hara, *Washington's Mount Rainier National
Park: A Centennial Celebration*. Seattle: The Mountaineers Books,
1998.

McPhee, John. *Encounters With The Archdruid*. New York: Farrar,
Straus & Giroux, 1971.

McQuade, Mike. "A Quick Altitude Adjustment." *Seattle Times*, August
28, 2008.

Miller, Char, ed., *Cities and Nature in the American West*. Reno: University of Nevada Press, 2010.

Molenaar, Dee. *The Challenge of Rainier*. Seattle: The Mountaineers
Books, 1971. Revised 1987.

———. "A Neophyte Guide on Mount Rainier, Part 2." *Northwest
Mountaineering Journal 3*, http://www.mountaineers.org.nwmj/06
/061_Molenaar.html.

Monroe, Robert D., review of *The Asahel Curtis Sampler: Photographs of Puget Sound Past, Pacific Northwest Quarterly* 66 no. 1 (1975): 40–41.

Morgan, Murray. *Puget's Sound: A Narrative of Early Tacoma and the Southern Sound.* Seattle: University of Washington Press, 1979.

"Mount Adams Wilderness." Gifford Pinchot National Forest, USFS, Pacific Northwest Region, U.S. Government Printing Office, 1991.

"Mount Rainier National Park—Climbing (U. S. National Park Service)," May 22, 2008, http://www.nps.gov/mora/planyourvisit /climbing.htm.

"Mount Rainier: Official Map and Guide." NPS, Reprint, 1995.

"Mount. St. Helens Climbing Information." Gifford Pinchot National Forest, USFS, Pacific Northwest Region, undated.

Mount St. Helens National Volcanic Monument, "Climbing Mount St. Helens," October 15, 2007, http://www.fs.fed.us/gpnf/recreation /mount-st-helens/permit-syster.shtml.

"Mount St. Helens National Volcanic Monument." Gifford Pinchot National Forest, USFS, Pacific Northwest Region, U. S. Government Printing Office, 1993.

Mt. Baker–Snoqualmie National Forest, "Current Wilderness Management Issues," October 15, 2007, http://www.fs.fed.us/r6/mbs/rec reation/special/wilderness/mgmt_issues.shtml.

"Mt. Baker Wilderness Area," "Mt. Baker–Snoqualmie National Forest Recreational Activities," October 15, 2007, http://www.fs.fed.us/r6 /mbs/recreation/special/wilderness/mtbaker.shtml.

Mt. Hood National Forest—Recreational Activities, "Climbing Mount Hood," September 9, 2010, http://www.fs.fed.us/r6/mthood/rec reation/climbing/background.shtml.

Muhn, James, BLM, "Early Administration of the Forest Reserve Act: Interior Department and General Land Office Politics, 1891–1897," in *The Origins of the National Forests: A Centennial Symposium*, ed. Harold K. Steen (Durham: Forest History Society 1992), http://www.foresthistory .org/Publications/Books/Origins_National_Forests/sec17.htm.

Muir, John. "The Ascent of Mount Rainier." *The Pacific Monthly* 8 (1902): 197–204; Reprint, *Steep Trails*. Boston: Houghton Mifflin, 1918; Reprint, *John Muir: The Eight Wilderness-Discovery Books*. Seattle: The Mountaineers Books, 1992, Reprint, 1995: 967–70.

———. *Our National Parks.* Boston: Houghton Mifflin, 1901, Reprint, *John Muir: The Eight Wilderness-Discovery Books*. Seattle: The Mountaineers Books, 1992, Reprint, 1995.

New York Times. "A Chicken for Every Pot" political ad and rebuttal, October 30, 1928. The National Archives Catalog online, National Archives Identifier 187095, https://research.archives.gov/id/187095.

Nicholas, Liza, Elaine M. Bapis, and Thomas J. Harvey, eds. *Imagining The Big Open: Nature, Identity, and Play in the New West.* Salt Lake City: University of Utah Press, 2003.

Nicolson, Marjorie. *Mountain Gloom and Mountain Glory: The Development of the Aesthetics of the Infinite.* 1959, Reprint. Seattle: University of Washington Press, 1997.

Novak, Barbara. *Nature and Culture: American Landscape and Painting.* London: Oxford University Press, 1980, 3rd ed. 2007.

O'Connell, Nicholas. *On Sacred Ground: The Spirit of Place in Pacific Northwest Literature.* Seattle: University of Washington Press, 2003.

Peattie, Roderick. *The Cascades: Mountains of the Pacific Northwest.* New York: Vanguard Press, 1949.

Price, Larry. *Mountains & Man: A Study of Process and Environment.* Berkeley: University of California Press, 1981.

Proctor, James D., and Evan Berry. "Ecotopian Exceptionalism." *Journal for the Study of Religion, Nature, and Culture* 5 no. 2 (2011): 145–63.

Raban, Jonathan, and William L. Lang, *Here There Nowhere.* Portland: Nobius Projects, 2007; dist. Oregon State University Press, 2007.

Rainier: The Mountain. Directed by Jean Walkinshaw. Kinonation, 1999; (ASIN B00212P13M, 2009), Blu-Ray DVD.

Rainier: A National Park at 100: Through Your Eyes, Eastside Journal "Special Section," February 27, 1999.

Reiner, Cathy. "Cool Caves & Wildlife Walks: Mount St. Helens Offers Many Moods, Destinations." *Seattle Times,* June 29, 1996.

Robbins, Tom. *Another Roadside Attraction.* 1971. Reprint, New York: Bantam, 1990.

Robbins, William G., ed., *The Great Northwest: The Search for Regional Identity.* Corvallis: Oregon State University Press, 2001.

Robbins, William, and Katrine Barber. *Nature's Northwest: The North Pacific Slope in the Twentieth Century.* Tucson: University of Arizona Press, 2011.

Rothman, Hal K., Jr. *Devil's Bargains: Tourism in the Twentieth-Century American West.* Lawrence: University Press of Kansas, 1998.

Ryke, Nancy. Mt. Adams District Ranger, Gifford Pinchot National Forest, correspondence (incl. 2 graphs), file code 2300, October 2, 2008.

Runte, Alfred. *Trains of Discovery*. 1984, 4th ed. Lanham: Roberts Rinehart, 1998.

Sax, Joseph. *Mountains Without Handrails*. Ann Arbor: University of Michigan Press, 1980.

Sayre, Gordon, "Urban Climbers in the Wilderness." In *Imagining the Big Open: Nature, Identity, and Play in the New West*, edited by Liza Nicholas, Elaine M. Bapis, and Thomas J. Harvey, 92–110. Salt Lake City: University of Utah Press, 2003.

Schmoe, Floyd. *A Year in Paradise*. Rutland: Charles E. Tuttle Co., Revised ed. 1968.

Schlepfer, Susan R. *Nature's Altars: Mountains, Gender, and American Environmentalism*. Lawrence: University Press of Kansas, 2005.

Schullery, Paul, ed. *Island in the Sky: Pioneering Accounts of Mount Rainier 1833–1894*. Seattle: The Mountaineers Books, 1987.

Schwantes, Carlos. *The Pacific Northwest: An Interpretive History*. Lincoln: University of Nebraska Press, 1989, 3rd ed. 2000.

Scott, John D. *We Climb High: A Chronology of the Mazamas, 1894–1964*. Portland: The Mazamas, 1969.

Seelye, Katharine Q. "This Summer Winter Never Left Rainier." *Seattle Times*, August 14, 2011.

Skoog, Lowell, ed., *The Alpenglow Ski Mountaineering History Project*. http://www.alpenglow.org/ski-history.htm.

———. "Wolf Bauer: Eighty Years on the Sharp End," *Northwest Mountaineering Journal* 2, http://www.mountaineers.org/nwmj/05/051 _Bauer3.html.

Snyder, Gary. *Danger on Peaks*. Washington D C: Shoemaker Hoard, 2004.

Spence, David Mark. *Dispossessing the Wilderness*. London: Oxford University Press, 2000.

Stadler, Matthew. "Council Crest Park," *Wikipedia*, November 2, 2011, http://www.wikipedia.org/wiki/Council_Crest_Park.

Suman, Josh. "Climbing Crossroads: Stone Gardens Brings Over 21,000 Square Feet of Rock Climbing Terrain Indoors." *Bellevue Reporter*, October 28, 2011.

Sutter, Paul S. *Driven Wild: How the Fight Against Automobiles Launched the Modern Wilderness Movement*. Seattle: University of Washington Press, 2002.

Trainor, Tim. "Climbers Ascend Mount Hood in Memory of Woman." *The Montana Standard*, March 9, 2010.

Uhler, John William. "Mount Rainier National Park Hiking Page,"
1995–2007, January 7, 2010, http://www.mount.rainier.national-park
.com/hike.htm.

U.S. Department of Agriculture, "Mount Hood National Forest Strategic Stewardship Plan: Weaving Together the Environment, People
and the Economy," (Forest Service, Pacific Northwest region, 2006),
http://www.fs.usda.gov/Internet/fse_documents/fsbdev3_036319
.pdf.

———. "Keeping It Wild: An Interagency Strategy to Monitor Trends
in Wilderness Character Across the National Wilderness Preservation System," General Technical Report #212. Rocky Mountain
Research Station, July 2009.

Vale, Thomas. *The American Wilderness: Reflections on Nature Protection in the United States.* Charlottesville: University of Virginia
Press, 2005.

Van Trump, Philemon Beecher. "Mount Tahoma." *Sierra Club Bulletin*
1 (1894): 109–32, Reprint, Paul Schullery, ed. *Island in the Sky: Pioneering Accounts on Mount Rainier 1833–1894.* Seattle: The Mountaineers Books, 1987.

Venema, Don. "Mount Rainier, 100 Years Later," *Northwest Mountaineering Journal* 5, http://www.mountaineers.org/nwmj/08/081_Rainier
100.html.

Villwock-Witte, Natalie, "(ROMO) Pilot Intelligent Transportation
System," (Rocky Mountain National Park: Western Transportation
Institute, Montana State University College of Engineering), http://
www.recpro.org/assets/Conference_Proceedings/2011_managing
_congestion_through_alt_transportation_villwock-witte.pdf.

Weiselberg, Eric. "The Early Mazamas: Modern Climbers on Top During the Golden Age of Mountaineering in the Pacific Northwest."
Mazama 1999: 20–21.

Welch, Craig. "The Battle to be King of the Mountain." *Seattle Times,*
December 29, 2002.

———. "Careful Isn't Always Enough." *Seattle Times,* June 2, 2014.

Weltzien, O. Alan. "Fathers and Sons, Trails and Mountains." In *Eco-
Man: New Perspectives in Masculinity and Nature,* ed. Mark Allister.
Charlottesville: University of Virginia Press, 2004.

———. "On Tahoma." *The Climbing Art* 27 (1994): 53–62.

Whatcom Co., WA, "Ski to Sea Race," (1973-present), http://www.skito
sea.com.

"Whittaker's Secret for Adventure: Luck." *Seattle Times* "chat online," print, April 11, 2013.

"Wi-Fi and Wildlife Don't Mix." editorial, *Chicago Tribune*, February 9, 2013.

Williams, Gerald, "National Monuments and the Forest Service," (Washington DC: USDA, November 18, 2003), http://www.sequoia forestkeeper.org.

Williams, John H. *The Guardians of the Columbia*. Tacoma: John H. Williams, 1912. New York Public Library, Google Scholar, www .google.docs.

———. *The Mountain That Was "God."* 1910. Reprint, New York: G. P. Putnam's Sons, 1911.

Winthrop, Theodore. *The Canoe and The Saddle*, Paul Lindholdt, ed. Lincoln: University of Nebraska Press, 2006.

Wolfe, Thomas. *A Western Journal: A Daily Log of the Great Parks Trip, June 20-July 2, 1938*. Pittsburgh: University of Pittsburgh Press, 1951.

Wood, Terry. "First Conquered, Then Triumphant, Writer Summits Rainier," *Seattle Times*, August 18, 2010.

———. "Is This Your Year to Summit Rainier?" *Seattle Times*, February 4, 2010.

INDEX

Page numbers in italic indicate illustrations.

Abbey, Edward, 69

Abbott, Carl, 12, 73

accessibility: and appropriation of volcanoes, 76–77; and auto tourism, 44–45, 51–52, 55–56, 82, 93; and challenges of overuse, 41–42; and development, 46–53, 60–62; and human connection, 32; impact on scale of tourism, 56–59; impact on wilderness areas, 136–37, 149, 171, 211–12; and permit systems, 59–60, 178, 183, 185–86, 202–3; and socioeconomic divides, 113, 152, 194, 218n5; tension between preservation and, 1–2, 111–12, 176, 179–80, 188–90; tradeoff dilemma, 181–83. *See also* roads

Adams, Mount: images of, *11*; impact of increased access on, 148–49; increasing numbers on, 55–56, 57, 192; mass climbs on, 55, 110–11; national park lobby efforts, 89; native origin stories, 134; remoteness of, 132; tribal claims at, 159–60; in the Wilderness Act,

152; wilderness areas surrounding, 132, 142, 159

"Against Intrusion" (poem), 32

air tours, 192–93

Alaska-Yukon-Pacific Exposition (1909), 79–80

Albright, Horace, 49, 53–55, 89

Allen, Edward, 137

Alpine Ascents International, 68

Alpine Lakes Wilderness Area, 76, 166

Anderson, Lloyd, 65, 107, 109, 112, 114

Anderson, Mary, 106–7

Another Roadside Attraction (Robbins), 224n2

army (U.S.), 108

Atlantic Monthly, 22, 45

auto tourism: and accessibility, 44–45, 51–52, 55–56, 82, 93; adverse impacts of, 56–59, 139; shifts toward, 50–52; in wilderness areas, 136–37, 141, 216n12

Baker, Mount: images of, *74*, *102*; management challenges at, 175; national park lobbying efforts,

Baker, Mount (*continued*)
88–89, 153; resort at, 89; road
access to, 55; skiing at, 62–63, 89–
90; urban appropriation of, 1, 3,
88–90, 205; in the Wilderness Act,
152; wilderness areas surrounding,
132, 164
Barcott, Bruce, 97, 101, 123
Barnard, Jeff, 208
Bates, Malcolm, 116
Battle for the Wilderness (Frome),
183
Bauer, Wolf, 107
Bayley, George, 22
Beckey, Fred, 108–9
Bell, Jon, 10–11, 169–70, 178
Bellingham (WA), 72, 88–90, 95–96
Bend (OR), 72, 94
Berry, Evan, 215n12
Bialowieza National Park (Poland),
171–72
Bierstadt, Albert, 84
Bishop, Barry, 67
blue bag program, 69, 190, 199–200
Brooks, David, 123
Brower, David, 142, 146, 155–58, 177
Bull, Olof O., 207

Caesar, George Vanderbilt, 137
The Call of the Wild (film), 90
Camp Muir, 68, 189, 191
Camp of the Clouds (tent city),
49–50
Camp Schurman, 191
The Canoe and the Saddle (Win-
throp), 16–17, 18–21
Cantwell, Maria, 191
carrying capacity, 59–60, 160–61,
178, 182–83

"The Cascade Range" (McConnell), 29
The Cascades (Peattie), 90
CFI (Colorado Fourteeners Initiative), 203, 224n41
Chicago Tribune (newspaper), 201
Choinard, Yvon, 123
"The Climb" (Snyder), 6, 36
climbing. *See* mountaineering
climbing clubs. *See* mountaineering
clubs
climbing courses, 65, 107–8
climbing walls, 120–22
CLNP (Crater Lake National Park),
40, 54–55
clothing industry, 100–101, 111, 122–
26, 177–78
clubs (mountaineering), 91, 99–100,
110, 119–20, 135, 144, 146. *See also*
Mazamas (climbing club); Mountaineers (climbing club)
Cody, Robin, 73
coins, commemorative, 206
Colorado Fourteeners Initiative
(CFI), 203, 224n41
communication technology, 176–
78, 200–201
Congress (U.S.), 84, 89, 164, 165, 166
conservation. *See* preservation
Cooperative Campers movement,
86
Cooper Spur (Mount Hood), 42,
43, 64
Cooper Spur Inn, 180–81
Council Crest Park, 73, 81
Crater Lake Lodge, 52
Crater Lake National Park, 40,
54–55
Curtis, Asahel, 60–61, 85, 103

de facto wilderness, 160, 166–67
degradation. *See* human impacts
Diamond Peak Wilderness Area, 132, 143, 152, 164
dirtbag climbers, 109, 115–16, 124
Discover Your Northwest (organization), 181–82
Douglas, William O., 145, 147–49
Dyer, Polly, 135, 151

ecosystem management, 163–64
Eddie Bauer, Inc., 112, 220n23
Encounters with the Archdruid (McPhee), 155–58
environmental consumerism, 100–101, 111–12, 117–18, 122–26, 129, 133
environmentalism: and consumerism, 124–25, 129; of the gear industry, 117–18, 124–26; growth of, 111, 155–56; of mountaineering clubs, 135–36, 180–82. *See also* preservation
equipment. *See* gear industry
Evans, Dan, 70, 118
Everest, Mount, 67
exceptionalism: basis for, 215n12; defined, 9; depicted in regional literature, 12–15; due to volcano proximity, 78–79; fostered by climbers' narratives, 21–25; and privilege, 11–12, 206, 209; through appropriation, 14–15, 27–30, 206. *See also* regional identity

Fire and Ice (Harris), 30
flyovers, 192–93
Forest Reserve Act (1891), 131
Frome, Michael, 183
Fuji, Mount, 203

Fuller, Fay, 24–25

Gable, Clark, 90
Gauthier, Mike, 94–95, 190–91
gear industry, 66, 100–101, 111, 113–15, 122–26, 177–78
Geithner, Tim, 206
geothermal energy systems, 208
Gifford, Sanford, 84
Glacier National Park, 59, 60
Glacier Peak: accessibility of, 56; contrary agendas in, 154–58; images of, *157*; northern spotted owls in, 167; and the NPS, 153; remoteness of, 131–32; in the Wilderness Act, 152; wilderness area of, 132, 140, 145–48, 165
Goat Rocks Wilderness Area, *11*, 132, 152
Grauer, Jack, 161, 178, 196, 217n32
Greater Portland (Abbott), 12
The Great Northwest (Robbins), 33
The Great Parks Trip (Wolfe), 10
group climbing, *43*, 99–100, 101–5, 110–11
Guardians of the Columbia (Williams), 207
guiding services, 68, 209–10
Gulanos, Helen, 206

Harris, Stephen L., 30
Harrison, Benjamin, 131
Harvey, Mark, 150
Hemingway, Ernest, 209
Henry Jackson Wilderness Area, 165
highways. *See* roads
Hood, Mount: attempts at permit systems, 178, 197; and carrying

Hood, Mount (*continued*)
capacity, 187; contrary agendas at, 194–99; development on, 52–53, 143, 179–81, 194–96; downhill skiing at, 62–65, 161, 180, 194–96, 198; as forest reserve, 131; images of, *11, 34, 43, 199*; impact on identity, 10–11, 12–13; increased congestion on, 41–42, 64–65, 66; national park lobbying efforts, 54; native origin stories, 134; Portland's appropriation of, 72–73; as proving grounds, 107–8; quarter commemorating, 206; risks of, 40–41; road access to, 44–45; standard routes on, 45–46, 66, 198–99; and the Wilderness Act, 152; wilderness areas surrounding, 132, 161–62, 179–80. *See also* Mount Hood National Forest (MHNF)
Hood to Coast Relay race, 219n21
Hornbein, Tom, 67
Hovhaness, Alan, 12, 29, 130, 212–13
human impacts: and auto tourism, 139; human waste issues, 69, 190–91, 199–200; on Mount Rainier, 58, 218n39; related to increased access, 69–71, 189–93; symbiosis of, 117–18; and wilderness experience management, 173–76

Ickes, Harold, 54
identity. *See* individual identity; municipal identity; regional identity
Indian Henry (Yakama guide), 15
individual identity: and consumerism, 114–15; link to national identity, 145; and personal transfor-

mation, 16–18, 23–25, 67, 77; role of volcanoes in defining, 10–12, 14–15, 27–28, 30–31; and status tourism, 27, 97–99, 100
indoor climbing walls, 120–22
industrial-scale tourism, 69; accessibility's impact on, 56; adverse impacts of, 41; commodification of, 115, 120; contemporary pressures of, 101; defined, 219n1; impact of climbers' narratives on, 22; in Japan, 203; and mountaineering, 98–99, 120, 128
Ingraham, Edward, 27
Island in the Sky (Schullery), 21

Jackson, Henry, 62, 153, 165
Jefferson, Mount, 131, 132, 152, 159–60
Jerstad, Lute, 67
Jewell, Sally, 126
Jones, Chris, 210

Kautz, August V., 9, 21–22
Kautz Glacier route, 192
Keeble, John, 3
Keeping It Wild (report), 185
Kennecott Copper Corporation, 154–58
Kennedy, Robert, 115
Kjeldsen, Jim, 220n23
Klingle, Matthew, 219n18
Kubrick, Stanley, 195

labor unions, 143–44
Landes, Henry, 111
landscape composition, 23, 33–35, 74, 84, 131
Lang, Otto, 64

Lassen, Mount, 53–54
Leave No Trace policy, 173–77, 190–93, 202
Leopold, Aldo, 139
Levertov, Denise, 31–32
literature. *See* regional literature
logging industry, 142–47, 152–53, 162–64, 166, 167–68
London, Jack, 90
Lundblad, Michael, 124
Lynch, Jim, 206

Madden, John, 173, 193
Magnuson, Warren, 62
Mahre, Dave, 110–11
Manning, Harvey, 54, 107, 108, 112, 115, 143, 153, 164–65
Mapes, Lynda V., 192
Marshall, Robert, 130, 139–40, 147
Mather, Stephen T., 49, 53–55, 86, 89, 138, 181
Mazamas (climbing club): advocacy work of, 135, 146, 181, 217n32; changing focuses of, 99–100; climbing course, 65; contrary agendas of, 179; early focus of, 101–3, 104–5; expedition climbs, *43*, 45, *102*, *104*; founding of, 42; growth of, 91; images of, *43*, *102*, *104*; mission statement of, 111
Mazama, Mount, 40
McConnell, Grant, 29
McNamara, Robert, 115
McNulty, Tim, 13
McPhee, John, 155–58, 176
Meany, Edmond S., 105–6
The Measure of the Mountain (Barcott), 97
Meeds, Lloyd, 158

military training, 108
mining industry, 154–59, 166
Mission 66 program, 57
Molenaar, Dee, 210
Moore, Marianne, 31
Mount Adams Wilderness Area, 132, 142, 159. *See also* Adams, Mount
mountaineering: adverse impacts of, 69–70, 174–76, 190–92; antiestablishment figures in, 108–9; commodification of, 99, 100, 112, 113–15, 120, 121, 129; conflicting with wilderness experience, 193; diverse reasons for, 6–7, 19–20, 94–95, 170, 209–10; environmental activism in, 144; funnel effect in, 45–46; generational conflicts in, 118; impact of technology on, 66, 116, 176–78, 200–201; increasing popularity of, 65–68, 110, 116–17, 210–11; and indoor climbing walls, 120–22; and industrial tourism, 70; linked to gear industry, 100–101, 109–10; narratives and identity formation, 21–25; permit systems for, 178, 185–86, 202–3, 212; personal transformation through, 17–18, 23–25; regional history of, 99–101; risks of, 23–24, 178; sociability of, 77, 127–28, 140, 184, 186–87, 193–94, 205; speed climbing, 116, 118–19, 128; spiritual aspects of, 13, 19–20, 24–25, 35–36; status through, 27, 37, 97–99, 100, 115, 119, 128; and wilderness mandates, 201–3. *See also* standard climbing routes; technical climbing routes

Mountaineering (Manning), 108
mountaineering clubs, 91, 99–100,
110, 119–20, 135, 144, 146. *See also*
Mazamas (climbing club); Mountaineers (climbing club)
Mountaineers (climbing club):
advocacy work of, 137, 138, 146;
changing focus of, 99–100; climbing courses, 107–8; climbing walls,
121; connection to REI, 109–10;
generational conflict in, 65, 106–7;
growth of, 91; market niches,
119–20; mass climbs, 45, 103, 106;
under Edmond Meany, 105–6;
mission statement of, 111
The Mountaineers (Kjeldsen),
183–84
Mountain Rescue Association
(MRA), 108
The Mountain That Was "God"
(Williams), 207
Mount Baker Wilderness Area, 132,
164. *See also* Baker, Mount
Mount Hood (Grauer), 178
Mount Hood (painting), 33–35
Mount Hood Meadows, 161–62,
180–81, 194–95, 217n32
Mount Hood National Forest
(MHNF): attempts at permit systems, 178; competing interests at,
169–70, 194–96; development at,
52; quarter commemorating, 206;
in relation to Portland, 44, 58, 198;
Strategic Stewardship Plan, 58,
70–71, 169–70; wilderness areas
within, 132, 161–62, 179–80. *See
also* Hood, Mount

Mount Hood Wilderness Area, 132,
161–62, 179–80. *See also* Hood,
Mount
Mount Rainier National Park
(MRNP): accessibility of, 44, 49–
51; carrying capacity in, 187–88;
changing tourism modes in, 50–
51, 61–62; creation of, 21; development in, 48–51, 60–61; human
waste issues in, 69, 190–91; images
of, 59; increased congestion in, 57–
58, 179, 188–89, 216n4; management challenges, 58–59, 188–91;
riparian zones in, 168–69; role of
volcanoes in, 39; urban appropriation of, 62–63, 80–81, 85–86;
wilderness areas within, 137–38,
160–61. *See also* Rainier, Mount
Mount St. Helens Limited Area,
142–43. *See also* St. Helens, Mount
Mount St. Helens National Monument, 132, 154, 162–63, 221n3
MRNP (Mount Rainier National
Park). *See* Mount Rainier National Park (MRNP)
Muir, Camp, 68, 189, 191
Muir, John, 21, 23–24, 45, 72–73, 134
Multnomah tribe, 134
municipal identity: adverse impacts
from, 42–44, 58–59, 90–91; appropriation of volcanoes in, 72–75,
87–90; due to volcano proximity,
76, 78–83; limits to appropriation,
94–95; and urban expectations,
91–93; volcanoes as playgrounds
in, 82–83, 86–87
My Wilderness (Douglas), 148–49

N3C (North Cascades Conservation Council), 147

National Forest Management Act, 163–64

national identity, 20, 22, 40, 57, 141–42, 145, 206–8

National Park, City Playground (Catton), 80

national parks: forced tribal removal from, 83; funnel effect at, 39; lobbying efforts for, 53–54, 88–89, 153; role of volcanoes in, 39–40; scenic infrastructure in, 166

National Park Service (NPS): and city-volcano juxtaposition, 85–86; and the Coop Campers, 86; costs of accessibility, 59; creation of, 48; criticism of, 179; interagency rivalries, 135, 152; management challenges, 173–76, 190–92; under Stephen Mather, 49, 53–54, 89; Mission 66 program, 57; role of nostalgia in policy, 141–42

National Parks Magazine, 162

National Ski Association, 63

National Wilderness Preservation System (NWPS), 133, 152, 153–54

Native Americans, 15, 83–84, 134, 141, 149, 159–60

NCNP (North Cascades National Park), 153, 165, 166

Newberry Volcano, 208

New York Times (newspaper), 126

Nicandri, David, 39

Nisqually tribe, 15, 24, 83–84

Noble, John, 131

North Cascades Conservation Council (N3C), 147

North Cascades National Park (NCNP), 153, 165, 166

Northern Pacific Railroad, 21, 25–26, 46, 50, 142–43, 221n18

northern spotted owls, 167

The Northwest Coast (Swan), 131

NPS (National Park Service). *See* National Park Service (NPS)

NWPS (National Wilderness Preservation System), 133, 152, 153–54

"An Octopus" (poem), 31

O'Hara, Pat, 164

Olmsted, Frederic Law, 86

Olmsted Plan, 86

Olympia (WA), 42, 79

On Mount Hood (Bell), 10–11

"Open Secret" (poem), 32

Oregonian, 197

Oregon Trail, 44–45

Oregon Wilderness Act (1984), 164

Overland Quarterly, 9, 45

Owen, Reginald, 90

Pacific Monthly, 72

paintings, 23, 33–35, 74, 84, 131

Palmer chairlift (Timberline), 64, 161

Paradise (Mount Rainier): creation of, 24; development at, 48–50; human impacts at, 189; images of, 59; increased congestion in, 55, 57–58; John Muir's praise for, 23, 24; skiing at, 62–63

Paradise Inn, 48

Park, Charles, 155
parking lots, 57, 59, 176–77, 188–89
Parrott, William Samuel, 33–35
Patagonia, Inc., 123–25
Peattie, Roderick, 90
permit systems, 178, 183, 185–86, 188, 197, 202–3, 212
personal identity. *See* individual identity
photography, 74, 81, 110, 131, 147
Poland, 171–72
Portland (OR), 44, 72–73, 75, 81, 92, 198
The Practice of the Wild (Snyder), 150
preservation: and de facto wilderness, 166; endorsed by organized labor, 143–44; and permit systems, 59–60, 178, 183, 185–86, 202–3; tensions between access and, 1–2, 111–12, 176, 179–80, 188–90; trade-off dilemma, 181–83; of wilderness experience, 211–12. *See also* environmentalism
Price, Montelius, 103
Proctor, James D., 215n12
public transportation systems, 59–60, 182

quarters (coins), 206
quota systems, 178, 183, 185–86, 188, 197, 202–3, 212

races, 63, 88, 219n21
railroads, 21, 25–26, 46, 49–50, 60, 142–43, 182, 221n18
Rainier, Mount: accessibility of, 44, 45; adverse human impacts on, 189–93, 218n39; auto tourism in,

50–52; challenges in writing, 14; commodification of, 82–83, 85; depicted by pioneering climbers, 21–25; development at, 46–49, 57, 188; downhill skiing at, 62–63; as forest reserve area, 131; as gateway mountain, 115–16; gospel of sublimity portrayals, 16–20; images of, *11, 102, 104*; increasing numbers at, 41–42, 58, 66, 67–68, 175, 188–89; management challenges, 61, 188–91; military training on, 108; and Native Americans, 15, 83–84; risks of, 40; role in identity formation, 9–10, 12–13, 30, 39, 79; standard routes on, 45–46; in status tourism, 98, 107–8; urban appropriation of, 2–3, 30, 79–81, 82–83, 84–86, 205, 224n2; wilderness areas surrounding, 132. *See also* Mount Rainier National Park (MRNP)
Rainier Mountaineering, Inc. (RMI), 68, 115–16
Rainier National Park Company (RNPC), 48, 49, 86, 138
Range of Glaciers (Beckey), 109
RARE II (Roadless Area Review and Evaluation II), 162–63
recreational carrying capacity, 59–60, 160–61, 178, 182–83
recreational tourism, 61–62, 91, 104. *See also* tourism
regional identity: appropriation of volcanoes in, 27–29, 90–91; and the gospel of sublimity, 16–18, 20–21; in nineteenth-century writing, 15–16; and privilege, 11–12, 33, 37–38, 206; role of volcanoes in

forming, 1–7, 9–12, 39–40; shifts in, 14–15; spiritual connections in, 12–13, 75–76; and volcanoes' risks, 30–31; and volcano proximity, 30, 78–79

regional literature: gospel of sublimity, 16–21; nineteenth-century writings, 15–16; pioneering climbers' narratives, 21–25, 45; rhetoric of exceptionalism in, 9, 12–13, 14

REI (Manning), 112

REI, Inc.: commodifying status, 122–23; environmental advocacy of, 117–18; environmental consumerism of, 101, 112–15, 125; and the federal government, 126; relationship with mountaineering, 109, 112–13; Seattle climbing wall, 122

rescue operations, 108, 200, 201

resorts, 48, 52–53, 89–90, 138, 161–62, 180–81, 194–96, 217n32

resource extraction, 142–47, 152–53, 162–64, 166, 167–68

Ricksecker, Eugene, 51

Ricochet River (Cody), 73

riparian zones, 168

RNPC (Rainier National Park Company), 48, 49, 86, 138

Roadless Area Review and Evaluation II (RARE II), 162–63

roads: appropriation of volcanoes through, 51–52, 76–77, 86; as scenic narratives, 51–52, 54–56, 166; and traffic flow, 44–45; tree tunnel designs, 47–48; and wilderness areas, 136–37, 149, 171. *See also* accessibility; auto tourism

Robbins, Tom, 224n2

Robbins, William G., 33

Rocky Mountain National Park, 59

Roosevelt, Franklin D., 195

Sayre, Gordon, 120

Schlepfer, Susan, 145

Schullery, Paul, 14, 21

Schurman, Camp, 191

Schwantes, Carlos, 75, 218n5

search and rescue, 108, 200, 201

Seattle (WA), 72, 79–81, 82–83, 84–86, 92–93, 122, 224n2

Seattle Times (newspaper), 58, 98, 190

self identity. *See* individual identity

"Settling" (poem), 31

Sherpas (mountaineering club), 110–11

The Shining (film), 195

Sierra Club, 26, 134, 144, 146, 147, 217n32

Sierra Club Bulletin, 25, 26, 146

Silver Skis races, 63

Simon, David, 146

skiing: funnel effect in, 39, 62–65; and the gear industry, 112; and industrial tourism, 70; at Mount Baker, 62–63, 89–90; at Mount Hood, 62–65, 161, 180, 194–96, 198; at Mount Rainier, 62–63

ski mountaineering course, 108

Ski to Sea Race, 88

Skoog, Lowell, 186

Sluiskin (Klickitat guide), 15

Snoqualmie National Forest, 164, 175. *See also* Baker, Mount

snowboarding, 64, 198

Snyder, Gary, 6, 14, 35–36, 123–24, 150, 207–8

speed climbing, 116, 118–19, 128
spiritual experience, 12–13, 16–20, 24–25, 33, 35–36, 75–76
spotted owls, 167
Spring, Bob, 81, 110
Spring, Ira, 81, 110, 185–86
standard climbing routes: congestion on, 42, 65, 66, 69–70; human impacts on, 174–76, 191–92; increasing popularity of, 67, 203; permit systems for, 183, 212; reasons for use, 45–46, 69; regulations for, 198–99, 202
"starfish proposal," 146–47
status tourism: and crowds, 91; defined, 37, 70; and the gear industry, 113–15, 122–26; and identity, 27, 36–38; and mountaineering, 46, 65, 67, 97–99, 100, 119, 128; socioeconomic divides in, 113, 152, 218n5
Steel, William G., 43, 55
Stephen Mather Wilderness, 166–67
Stevens, Hazard, 22
St. Helens, Mount: corporate use of, 159, 162–63; eruption of, 15, 40, 163; images of, 11; as a national monument, 132, 154, 162–63, 221n3; native origin stories, 134; road access to, 44, 52, 55; wilderness areas surrounding, 132, 142–43
Strong, Anna Louise, 86
Sun Fair climb, 110–11
Sunrise to Paradise (Nicandri), 39
Sutter, Paul, 140–41
Swan, James G., 131, 145–46

Tacoma (wa), 72, 79, 80, 82–85

Tacoma Eastern Railroad, 50, 60
technical climbing routes, 45; human impacts on, 70; impact of technology on, 66, 116; increased traffic on, 42, 66, 68; proposed guidelines for, 202; reasons for use, 67, 108; wilderness experience on, 175
Thielsen, Mount, 132
Three Sisters Primitive Area, 145–46
Three Sisters Wilderness Area, 94, 132, 143–44, 152
"Three Ways of Looking" (Levertov), 31–32
Tiegen, Carolyn, 40
timber industry, 142–47, 152–53, 162–64, 166, 167–68
Timberline Lodge, 53, 81, 161, 195–96
Timberline ski hill, 62–63, 64, 161, 195–96
Timberline Trail, 195–96
Tolmie, William Fraser, 16
tourism: adverse impacts of, 4–5, 173–76; conflicting with preservation, 138–41; contrary values in, 46–53, 60–62; funnel effect in, 39, 41; growth of, 16, 22; impact of access on scale of, 56–59; railroads' impact on, 21; and regional identity, 2; shifting styles of, 13–14, 37; in wilderness areas, 166, 169–70, 216n12. See also auto tourism; industrial-scale tourism; mountaineering; status tourism
Truth Like the Sun (Lynch), 206

United States Forest Service (usfs): ecosystem management phi-

losophy, 163–64, 167; employee advocacy, 168; infrastructure construction, 55–56; interagency rivalries, 135, 152; management challenges, 173–76, 178; at Mount Baker, 89; outreach programs of, 197; preservation work of, 54; wilderness area designations, 138, 140–41, 162–63
University of Washington, 79–80
Unsoeld, Willi, 67
U.S. Army, 108
U.S. Congress, 84, 89, 164, 165, 166
USFS (United States Forest Service). *See* United States Forest Service (USFS)
U.S. Mint quarter, 206

Vale, Thomas R., 134, 154
Vancouver, George, 15–16
Van Trump, Philemon B., 22, 25
Venema, Donn, 127–28
Venema, Harry, 127
volcanoes: commodification of, 81–83, 99, 100, 111–12, 125; cultural value of, 35–36, 37–38; depicted in regional literature, 9, 12–13, 15–25; funnel effect at, 39; geological reality of, 94–96; human connections to, 30–35; language about, 36–37; minimizing impacts on, 202–3; remoteness of, 130–32, 141, 145, 146, 148; risks of, 40–41; role in national identity, 22, 206–8; role in regional identity, 1–7, 39–40; spiritual connections through, 12–13, 16–20, 24–25, 35–36, 75–76; technology creep on, 116, 176–78, 200–201; urban appropriation of,

72, 74–75, 81–83, 93–95, 176–78; urban threats to, 42–44

Warm Springs reservation, 159–60
Warner, Arthur C., 45
Washington (state), 5–6, 10, 28, 132
Washington, Mount, 132, 143, 152
Washington Wilderness (Manning), 164–65
Washington Wilderness Act (1984), 164
Watson, Emmett, 93
We Climb High (Scott), 101–3
Western Journal (Wolfe), 56
Weyerhaeuser, 142, 162
Whatcom County (WA), 87–88
whitewater rivers, 202–3
Whittaker, Jim, 67, 114–15, 117–18, 135, 181
Whittaker, Lou, 68, 79, 115–16
Wilderness Act (1964), 133, 140, 147, 150–52, 154–57, 173, 202
Wilderness Act (1984), 164
wilderness areas: advocacy for, 135–37, 139–40, 142–50, 152–53, 161–62, 164–65; commodification of experience in, 133–34, 139, 151–52; conflicting values in, 138–39, 143, 149–51, 152–58, 162–63; forced tribal removal from, 83; juxtaposed to urban areas, 76; management challenges in, 160–61, 163–64, 165–68, 201–3; opponents to creation of, 170–71; role of volcanoes in, 130–32, 134–35; urban scenes in, 200–201. *See also* wilderness experience
"The Wilderness as Minority Right" (Marshall), 140

wilderness consumerism: adverse impacts of, 173–74; air tours as, 192–93; increasing demand, 177; and permit systems, 203; and socioeconomic divides, 152, 194, 218n5

wilderness experience: conflicting with climbing, 193, 211; contradictions in defining, 185; and the crowd mind-set, 184; elusiveness of, 70, 175; management challenges, 70–71, 173–74, 196–200, 211–12; as a resource, 174; and use capacity, 183, 187–88

wilderness thresholds, 165–67, 180–81, 196

Wild Sky Wilderness Area, 165

Williams, Gerald, 221n3

Williams, John R., 207

Windell, Tim, 198

Winthrop, Theodore, 14, 16–17, 18–21, 75, 87, 207

Wolfe, Thomas, 10, 56

Wonderland guide series, 25, 46

World War II, 108

Yakama Nation, 15, 24, 83, 149, 159–60

Yakima (wa), 89, 110–11

Yellowfish (Keeble), 3

Young, Loretta, 90

Zahniser, Howard, 135, 142, 150, 151, 170, 171

Zalesky, Phil, 158

CPSIA information can be obtained at www.ICGtesting.com
Printed in the USA
BVOW08*0757030616

450399BV00002B/3/P